Routledge Revivals

Industrial Fatigue and Efficiency

First published in 1921, *Industrial Fatigue and Efficiency* aims to provide a fairly complete overview of industrial fatigue and its influence on efficiency. It brings crucial themes like fatigue and its measurement; output in relation to weekly hours of work; output and hours of work in various industries; the six-hours day and multiple shifts; work spells and rest periods; limitation of output; lost time and its causation; sickness and mortality; industrial accidents and their causation; the prevention of industrial accidents; and adoption of healthy factory conditions, to showcase the importance of adequate lighting, heating and ventilation, washing facilities, cloak rooms, ambulance room and a well found canteen as basic requirements in factories. This book is an important historical document for scholars and researchers of labour studies, labour economics, industrial studies, and political economy.

CW00821762

Industrial Fatigue and Efficiency

H. M. Vernon

Routledge
Taylor & Francis Group

First published in 1921
by George Routledge & Sons

This edition first published in 2022 by Routledge
4 Park Square, Milton Park, Abingdon, Oxon, OX14 4RN

and by Routledge
605 Third Avenue, New York, NY 10017

Routledge is an imprint of the Taylor & Francis Group, an informa business

Publisher's Note
The publisher has gone to great lengths to ensure the quality of this reprint but points out that some imperfections in the original copies may be apparent.

Disclaimer
The publisher has made every effort to trace copyright holders and welcomes correspondence from those they have been unable to contact.

A Library of Congress record exists under LCCN: 22006734

ISBN: 978-1-032-27034-0 (hbk)
ISBN: 978-1-003-29104-6 (ebk)
ISBN: 978-1-032-27036-4 (pbk)

Book DOI 10.4324/9781003291046

INDUSTRIAL FATIGUE AND EFFICIENCY

BY

H. M. VERNON, M.A., M.D.

*Investigator for the Industrial Fatigue
Research Board ;
Late Fellow of Magdalen College, Oxford.*

LONDON :
GEORGE ROUTLEDGE & SONS, LTD.
NEW YORK: E. P. DUTTON & CO.
1921

PREFACE

The object of this book is to give a fairly complete account of our present-day knowledge concerning Industrial Fatigue and its influence on Efficiency. The information adduced relates only to workshop practice, as laboratory investigations on fatigue, though holding out promise of useful results in the future, have hitherto not afforded much evidence of direct and practical value. I have not attempted to discuss Scientific Management, for I have very little first-hand knowledge of it, and, moreover, the subject is so large a one that it needs independent treatment. For similar reasons I have not attempted to deal with Vocational Selection in industry.

I wish to take this opportunity of expressing my indebtedness to Professor E. L. Collis for his kindness in reading through my manuscript, and for making many useful suggestions.

H. M. VERNON

OXFORD

CONTENTS

CONTENTS

CHAPTER I

FATIGUE AND ITS MEASUREMENT

CONTENTS

INTRODUCTION

Fatigue is defined by the Health of Munition Workers Committee[1] as " the sum of the results of activity which show themselves in a diminished capacity for doing work." The British Association Committee on ' Fatigue from the Economic Standpoint '[2] defined fatigue as a ' diminution of the capacity for work which follows excess of work or lack of rest, and which is recognised on the subjective side by a characteristic malaise.' The latter half of this definition, though true in many instances, is not so invariably. To make still another quotation, Dr. Rivers points out[3] that "A distinction must be made between the sense of fatigue—the sensations which supervene during the performance of work, and the lowered capacity for work executed. These conditions, which may be spoken of as subjective and objective fatigue respectively, do not always run parallel courses. In the performance of mental work especially, decided sensations of fatigue may be experienced when the objective record shows that increasing and not decreasing amounts of work are being done; and there may be complete absence of any sensations of fatigue when the objective record shows that the work is falling off in quantity, or quality, or in both."

In the study of Industrial Fatigue it is natural for us to pay special attention to the objective side of the phenomenon, the capacity for work, though sooner or later we are inevitably driven to study the subjective side as well, and in no less degree. Though a worker suffering from fatigue sufficient to diminish his working capacity may not at first experience subjective sensations of

[1] Memo. No. 7, 1916.
[2] British Association Reports, 1915, p. 283.
[3] Quoted from British Association Report, 1915, p. 284.

A

fatigue, he is bound to do so sooner or later. Subjective fatigue tends to be cumulative, and to react on the health of the worker, and if his health gives way he may perforce lose his productive capacity entirely until his health is regained.

The Objects of Fatigue Study

It follows that one of the most important objects of fatigue study is to determine whether the fatigue induced by an industrial occupation has an unfavourable influence on the health of the worker. Supposing it be found that health is not adversely affected, then the fatigue incurred, even though it may have been considerable at the time, and have produced severe subjective sensations in the worker, could not be described as abnormal. It was physiological, not pathological, and serious objection could not be taken to it on the ground of the sensations produced. At the same time it must be borne in mind that effects on health do not necessarily show themselves at once. Their appearance may be delayed for weeks, months, or even for years. Again, it is usually very difficult to determine whether a diminution of health, especially if its onset be long delayed, is due to the direct fatigue induced by the occupation, or to the adverse conditions under which the work is performed. It is evident, therefore, that the problem of determining the influence of Industrial Fatigue on the health of the worker is no easy one. Its solution can be effected only very gradually, and as the result of much observation and experiment.

Next to the primary object of avoiding injurious fatigue, comes the avoidance of *unnecessary* fatigue in industry. Every healthy industrial worker begins each day with a certain stock of physical energy, the whole of which he can, if he so desires, expend upon his daily round of labour.   But if he has adequate food and a good night's rest, he recuperates completely and starts next day with the same stock of available energy.   It is not to be expected that, under ordinary conditions, the worker should expend the whole of his energy upon his industrial labour.   It is only reasonable that he should retain some of it for his own purposes, whether they lie in the direction of useful work in his house and garden, or in the direction of physical recreation and amusement. Or again, he may prefer to retain a certain store of his physical energy in hand, and not work up to his physiological limit of strength.   In any case, the healthy worker has each day a certain supply of energy which he puts into his daily task, and it is evident that the more of this energy he expends in wasteful and unnecessary directions, the less he has for application to useful ends.   Every time he expends energy unnecessarily he diminishes his efficiency.   It is not to be imagined for a moment that the industrial worker ought to expect to escape from doing a good day's work, and from expending a reasonable amount of energy over his labour, however much the character of his work is lightened in some directions by the adoption of labour-saving methods and devices. Such devices leave him a greater stock of energy to expend in other directions, and he is thereby enabled to exert himself more vigorously, and to increase his productivity.

FATIGUE AND EFFICIENCY

It follows that in most respects fatigue is the antithesis to efficiency. By so much as fatigue is avoided or eliminated in industrial operations, the efficiency of the worker is increased. The study of Industrial Fatigue and its elimination is therefore an investigation of some of the methods necessary for the attainment of increased efficiency, though it does not follow that all methods adopted for the increase of efficiency necessarily imply a diminution in the fatigue of the worker. Sometimes they tend in the reverse direction, though this is the exception.

The object of industrial efficiency is to obtain a maximum production with a minimum of effort, for thereby the material prosperity of the whole community will be most signally increased. Supposing that by some miracle of industrial organization every worker were able to double his previous output without increased expenditure of labour, then it would follow that in course of time the amount of housing accommodation in the country would be doubled, the amount of clothing and of home-grown food would be doubled likewise. Or supposing that there were no need for the increased output of certain articles, the worker could neutralise the greater productivity by working a shorter day. It is true that thereby he would be relieved of a part of his physical labour, but there is no reason why he should not expend some of his extra leisure in education and other intellectual pursuits. It must be admitted that manual work, taken as a whole, is much more monotonous and uninteresting than mental work, so the more the latter can be substituted for the former, the greater should be the happiness of the community.

THE MEASUREMENT OF FATIGUE

Numerous attempts have been made to measure fatigue experimentally by laboratory methods, and these investigations have thrown much light on the nature of fatigue, and its localisation. They have shown that fatigue is frequently bound up with the production of various chemical products, some of which, such as sarco-lactic acid, are well defined chemical substances, whilst others, the so-called 'fatigue toxins,' are very indefinite and uncertain. Experiment has likewise shown that as a rule the chief seat of fatigue is not in the muscles themselves, as subjective sensations would lead us to infer, or even in the nerves supplying the muscles, but in the central nervous system. Here again fatigue is localised, not so much in the nerve cells, as in the junctions between nerve processes and cells, the so-called *synapses*.

It is not my intention, however, to describe fatigue from what may be termed its laboratory side, but to keep as far as possible to its relations to workshop practice. For this reason no reference will be made to the various laboratory methods which have been adopted for investigating fatigue. Suffice it to say that, though some of them have thrown a great deal of light upon the conditions of production and avoidance of fatigue, none of them afford a satisfactory measure of fatigue under industrial conditions. The ideal to be aimed at is a test which can be easily applied, in the course of a few minutes, to any industrial worker at any time in the course of his working day, and afford a quantitative measure of his state of fatigue.

It is highly improbable that any single test will ever be found sufficient for all industrial workers, for the character and localisation of fatigue is so different in different occupations. In the watch-maker engaged in cleaning watches and putting them together, the fatigue would be chiefly in the muscles of the forearm and hands, and in the eyes and brain. The muscles of the lower limbs would be scarcely fatigued at all, and at the end of his day's work the watch-maker would probably be capable of strenuous physical labour in his garden. On the other hand a gardener, at the end of his day's labour, would be tired in his muscles, but would be capable of mental work, whilst an over-head crane man, sitting all day in his cabin, and on the alert to move his crane just when and where it was wanted, would be suffering mostly from mental fatigue. He would, like the watch-maker, be ready for strenuous physical labour when his day's work was over.

It is true that very heavy work, whether physical or mental, greatly reduces a man's powers of doing work of an opposite kind. The manual worker, tired out by his day's labour, is in no condition to attend educational classes in the evening, and the business man, tired out by his office work, does not feel much inclination for strenuous physical exercise after it. Nevertheless the fact remains that in most kinds of industrial work there is localisation in the seat of fatigue, and that a method suitable for testing the fatigue experienced in one industrial operation would not be suitable for testing it in another. The only satisfactory test at present available is off distinctly owing to the effects of fatigue or of monotony. In the last full hour of work it rose 8 per cent. owing to end-spurt.

The output of six other sections at the fuse factory besides that of the women turning fuse bodies was determined for six days by the indirect method. The average values obtained[1] show that in the sections of women engaged in turning brass fuses and fuse rings, and in the section of girls drilling fuse rings, the hourly output variations resembled those just described. The sections of men engaged in tool-making, of men controlling automatic machines, and of men and women turning 2 lb. shells, showed a rise of output (due to practice-efficiency) during the first three or four hours of the morning spell, but in the afternoon the output fell away fairly steadily throughout, and it was 7 to 10 per cent. less in the last full hour of the spell than in the first full hour. That is to say, there was a well-marked fatigue effect, but no trace of an end-spurt.

Taking hourly output records as a whole, it may be said that end-spurt is shown comparatively seldom. In fact, I have never found unequivocal signs of its presence except in workers engaged upon munitions, and its presence in their case may be the genuine result of a patriotic effort which would not exist in other industrial workers. In addition to the results already referred to, a well marked end-spurt was shown by a group of women employed in inspecting small shells.[2] During the morning spell of work these women achieved their maximum output in the fourth hour, and fell off considerably in the fifth hour, but in the after-dinner spell their output improved throughout the afternoon. In the last hour it was 19 per cent. bigger than in the first hour, and it was, moreover, 4 per cent. bigger than the maximum observed in the morning.

COMPARISON OF AFTERNOON AND MORNING OUTPUT

It will be gathered that in most hourly output records the genuine fatigue effects are so overlaid by practice-efficiency and end-spurt effects that they are largely hidden. That is to say, the records do not afford at all a reliable index of fatigue. Another method of estimating fatigue, which ignores the factors of practice-efficiency and end-spurt, is to compare the average hourly output during the afternoon spell of work with that observed in the morning spell. If the manual labour performed in the morning spell causes a substantial amount of fatigue in the worker, we should expect that his average capacity for work in the afternoon would be appreciably lessened.

[1] Cf. *Op. cit.*
[2] Cf. H. C. Link. Journal of Industrial Hygiene, I., p. 233. 1919.

In order to test this hypothesis, I have recorded in the Table the ratio observed between average hourly output in the afternoon and that in the morning, or in the second and first spells of night work, in every instance where suitable data were available. The operations labelled (B.A.), are quoted from the British Association Reports (1915 and 1916), and those labelled (Lee), are from Prof. Lee's Book on the Human Machine in Industry. That labelled (Osborne) represents the hourly output, observed by Mrs. E. A. Osborne,[1] of women engaged in the operation of ' ripping ' six-inch shells, and it represents the mean of the outputs observed in the morning, afternoon, and night shifts. The other data in the Table are recorded by myself, either in the memorandum already cited, or in Reports Nos. 1 and 5 of the Industrial Fatigue Research Board.

The data are arranged in order according to the duration of the shift worked, and they have been averaged in four groups. In the first and second groups the shifts had an average duration of 7.5 and 8.8 hours respectively, and the ratio of afternoon output to morning output came exactly to 1.00 in each case. It is true that in individual operations the ratio varied from .96 to 1.10, but this latter ratio occurred only once, and in no other instance did it rise above 1.04.

---

[1] Report No. 2 of Industrial Fatigue Research Board. 1919.

COMPARISON OF MORNING AND AFTERNOON OUTPUT

Operation.	Length of working day in hours.	Ratio of hourly output in afternoon to that in morning.
8 tinplate millmen for 2 days	6	1.03
8 ,, ,, ,, ...	8	.98
23 women shell making for 6 days (Osborne)	7	.97
20 women chocolate-covering by machine for 10 days (B.A.)	7½	.97
4 women choc'l'e-covering by hand for 10 days (B.A.)	7½	1.10
12 women stencilling biscuits for 6 days (B.A.) ...	7½ {7.5	.99 } 1.00
12 men filling blast furnace for 82 days (afternoons)	7½	1.01
12 men filling blast furnace for 81 days (nights) ...	7½	.97
4 men type-setting by machine for 10 days (B.A.)...	8	1.02
4 women labelling tin boxes for 5 days (B.A.) ...	8	.98
3 men and 2 women type-setting by hand for 10 days (B.A.)	8	.97
7 women making flannel belts for 8 days (B.A.) ...	8½	.96
6 women straightening tins for 6 days (B.A.) ...	8½	1.00
6 women labelling tins for 6 days (B.A.)	8½ {8.8	.96 } 1.00
10 women soldering boxes for 10 days (B.A.)	9	1.04
6 women soldering tins for 6 days (B.A.)	9	1.00
23 women working stamping presses for 4 days (B.A.)	9	1.02
4 men hand-tapping fuse sockets for 2 days	9¾	1.04
16 men sizing fuse bodies for 1 day each	10	.97
43 women turning aluminium fuse bodies for 1 day each	10	1.00
160 women turning aluminium fuse bodies for 6 days	10	1.01
300 women turning brass fuse rings and bodies for 6 days	10	1.01
170 women turning brass time fuses & primers for 6 days	10 {10.0	.96 } .98
500 girls drilling and finishing fuse rings for 6 days ...	10	.96
160 men and women turning 2lb. shells for 6 days ...	10	.97
150 men controlling automatic machines for 6 days ...	10	.96
130 men tool-making for 6 days	10	.96
Women painting fuse holes with lacquer (Lee)...	10	.94
Men polishing metal by hand (Lee)	10 {12.0	.91 } .90
Men drilling and reaming holes in fuse (Lee) ...	12	.84
12 men filling blast furnace for 10 Sundays	16	.91

In the third group the shifts lasted 10.0 hours, and the ratio averaged .98. In the fourth group, when the shifts lasted 12.0 hours, the ratio averaged .90. Hence it may be said that only in this last group was there a definite and substantial reduction of output in the afternoon spell of work as compared with that in the morning spell. The data included in this group are to some extent selected, as two of them relate to workers on 10 hour shifts, and only the remaining two to workers on longer shifts than 10 hours.

In addition to the information recorded in this Table, we have a large body of hourly output data recently published by the U.S. Public Service.[1] Part of the data were collected at a motor car factory, where the 36,000 workers employed were on an 8 hour day, and the other part at a fuse factory, where most of the 13,000 workers employed were on a 10 hour day. The 37 day shift operations studied were split up into four categories, of which (a) was designated dexterous handwork, and included such operations as working a rivet press and assembling fuses. Group (b) related to muscular handwork, and included such operations as assembling motors and "retapping top caps." Group (c) comprised lathe machine work, and group (d) included miscellaneous machine work, such as working drop forges and punch presses.

The ratios of output observed in the four-hour afternoon and morning spells of the motor car factory, and in the five-hour spells of the fuse factory, are shown in the Table, and it will be seen that on an average the afternoon output was 1 per cent. less than the morning output at the 8-hour plant, whilst it was 3 per cent. less at the 10-hour plant. Passing to the various categories of work, we see that whilst the machine work output showed no falling off in the afternoon spell, the hand work showed a very distinct deterioration. The muscular work was 10 per cent. less at the 10-hour plant than in the morning, and it was 5 per cent. less at the 8-hour plant, whilst the dexterous handwork showed smaller degrees of deterioration.

Character of Work.	Number of Operations Studied.	Ratio of Afternoon Output to Morning Output taken as 100.	
		Individual Operations.	Mean.
8-hr. plant (a) Dexterous hand work	4	97, 96. 99, 97	97
(b) Muscular hand work	4	100, 100, 89, 97, 90	95
(c) Lathe machine work	5	104, 107, 98, 99, 102, 102	102 ⎰ 99
(d) Miscellaneous machine work	8	101. 100. 101, 100, 108, 104, 95, 102	101
10-hr. plant (a) Dexterous hand work	7	95, 92, 93, 92, 93, 95, 95	94
(b) Muscular hand work	4	92, 84, 94, 90	90
(c) Lathe machine work	2	105, 99	102 ⎰ 97
(d) Miscellaneous machine work	3	99, 100, 101	100

Taking these latter results in conjunction with the former series, it may be said that with few exceptions the hourly output in the afternoon spell is as great as that in the morning spell, provided that the hours of work do not exceed 10 per

[1] Bulletin No. 106. 1920.

day. We must not conclude, however, that such a result indicates no fatigue in the workers. We saw that in the morning spell the workers generally failed to produce their full output owing to lack of practice-efficiency, and they very seldom improved their output by an end-spurt. In the afternoon spell, on the other hand, they benefited by much of the practice-efficiency acquired in the morning, and they sometimes showed an end-spurt. Hence it follows that there was a sufficient fatigue effect in the afternoon to neutralise the access of productivity produced by the operation of these two factors.

The comparatively slight effect even of considerable fatigue in reducing hourly output is shown by some observations on

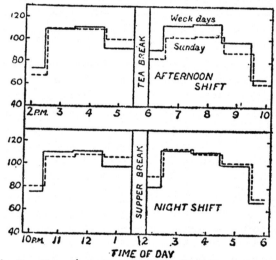

Fig. 8 — Hourly rate of charging blast furnace.

blast furnace men.[1] The men were employed in charging a furnace, and they had to shovel up iron ore, limestone, or coke into heavy iron barrows, which, when loaded, weighed about a ton. The barrows had to be wheeled 20 to 30 yards to the hoist of the furnace, so the work was very heavy. Each of the three shifts of 12 men usually worked for 8 hours, with half-an-hour meal break, but on Sundays one of the shifts worked for 16 hours on end, viz., from 6 a.m. till 10 p.m. The rate of charging the blast furnace was investigated over a five month period, and averages were taken. In Fig. 8 is shown the relative output (rate of charging) of the men in the afternoon

[1] Report No. 5 of the Industrial Fatigue Research Board. 1920.

shift (2 to 10 p.m.) and night shift (10 p.m. to 6 a.m.), and it will be seen that in each spell of each shift the output showed a practice-efficiency effect followed by a fatigue effect. The dotted lines show the output on Sundays, and it will be seen that between 2 and 5.30 p.m. the men maintained practically as good an output as they did on week days, though they had already done 8 hours of the heavy work between 6 a.m. and 2 p.m. Only after the tea interval did their output show a substantial falling off, and it averaged 9 per cent. less per hour than on week days, but the total output for the whole shift was only 4.7 per cent. less.

The night work on Sundays was undertaken by a fresh shift of men, and their output was slightly greater than that observed on week nights. Hence the smaller output observed on Sunday afternoons was not in any way dependent on the work being done on a Sunday, but it must have been a genuine fatigue effect.

The astonishingly steady output maintained by almost all the industrial workers referred to in the Table, and even by the considerably fatigued blast furnace men on Sunday afternoon, is due, I believe, to the habit which most manual labourers get into of working at as steady a rate as possible under all circumstances. This steady rate is adopted unconsciously, and it is dependent on a principle which is so important and so widely observed that I venture to term it *the law of maximum production with minimum effort.* We shall see that in respect of their weekly output, their choice of rest pauses and in other ways, the workers unconsciously adopt habits which tend towards the greatest possible output with the least possible exertion on their part. Their unconscious efforts are frequently not so successful in attaining their object as organised and conscious efforts would be, but they are nevertheless of great value to them.

Consider how the adoption of a steady rate of hourly production tends towards the fulfilment of the law, or consider rather how the adoption of an irregular rate would tend towards its negation. It is well known that work done at high pressure is relatively more exhausting than work done at low pressure. For instance, if a man walks at the rate of five miles per hour he needs to employ twice as much extra energy, per mile of ground covered, as when he walks two miles an hour.[1] Hence if the worker over-exerted himself in the first few hours of his working day, so as to increase his output, he would get so over-fatigued that his output in the last part of the day would fall off by a more than proportionate amount, and the total output

[1] Cf. Chap. III., p. 49.

for the day would be less than if he had worked at a steady rate all through.   Again, supposing he puts on such a spurt in the last hour or two of his working day that he over-fatigues himself, he will find that next morning he does not start on his day's work in his usual condition of vigour, and his day's output is below normal.

The blast furnace men above mentioned worked a 16-hour shift only once in three weeks, and I imagine that in consequence of this infrequency they had settled down into such a steady rate of work, adapted to the length of their usual 8-hour shift, that they unconsciously strove to maintain this rate throughout the 16 hours.   In consequence they would over-fatigue themselves, and for the next day or two after their long shift they would be below their normal condition of vigour.

The principle of economy of effort has been discussed by several independent investigators.   Imbert[1] maintained that the human body is constructed upon a general plan and presents such harmony of action that all useless expenditure of energy is, or at least may be, avoided. Mdlle. Ioteyko, in her comments on the subject,[2] points out that " effort and fatigue are correlated sensations, for a great effort invariably leads to fatigue, and when a young apprentice, in the course of time, acquires the best movements, it is because he is convinced by experience that they lead to the minimum of fatigue."   On the other hand, she agrees with Le Chatelier in protesting against the supposition that skilled workmen understand quite well how to make the best use of their forces in order to obtain a given result with the minimum amount of fatigue.

The law may be stated in the following terms—*Experienced industrial workers unconsciously adopt habits of work which tend to the production of a maximum output with the minimum of effort.*

DAILY OUTPUT VARIATIONS

Daily output variations show all the same features that are observed in hourly output variations.   They are due to precisely the same causes, only these causes are operating over a longer interval of time, viz., the week instead of the day.   The cessation of work between Saturday afternoon and Monday morning naturally causes a greater loss of neuro-muscular co-ordination than that observed between each week day, and consequently the output on Monday morning tends to be lower

[1] A. Imbert. ' Mode de functionnement économique de l'organisme,' 1902. Quoted from J. Ioteyko. ' The Science of Labour and its Organisation,' 1919, p. 13.

[2] *Op. cit.*, p. 20.

than that observed on any other morning of the week.   The loss of practice-efficiency owing to the week-end rest is so considerable that the remainder of the week may be needed for recovery, but as a rule the fatigue induced by the daily round of labour gradually accumulates in sufficient degree, first to neutralise the improvement due to practice-efficiency, and then to overpower it.   That is to say, most daily output records show a rise during the first part of the week, followed by a fall in the latter part.   The point of culmination of output is usually in the middle of the week, but it may be on any day but the first.   The disinclination to work on a Monday owing to the week-end rest must be familiar to everyone, whether he works with his hands or his brain.   In industry it is almost invariably accompanied by a low output, which Kent[1] has termed ' the Monday effect.'

The recorded information on daily output is very small, as it is usually troublesome to collect.[2] Of the data here adduced, (a) relates to the relative daily output of the button-sawing department of an American Button Company over a six weeks interval;[3] whilst (b) relates to the output of the men (both day and night shifts) engaged in charging a blast furnace over a 50 week period.[4] It will be seen that in each instance the output was at a minimum on Monday, and gradually improved to a maximum on Wednesday.   Then it gradually fell away again and reached a minimum on the last day of the working week.   The output of the blast furnace men on Sunday is of a composite character, as half of the men were working the normal 8-hour shift, whilst the other half were working a 16-hour shift.

DAILY OUTPUT VARIATIONS

	Mon.	Tues.	Wed.	Th.	Fri.	Sat.	Sun.
(a) Button sawers ...	98.1	100.6	**101.6**	101.1	98.6	—	—
(b) Blast furnace men...	96	100	**105**	103	101	101	94
(c) Weavers ...	96.0	98.9	**102.6**	99.3	101.2	102.1	—
(d) Bobbin winders ...	94.6	96.7	97.6	105.4	96.3	**109.4**	—

The data (c) relate to the output of a group of Westphalian weavers, some of whom were minding one loom, and some two.[5] The output reached a maximum on Wednesday, and then fell away, but it reached a second maximum on the Saturday.

[1] A. F. S. Kent. Second Interim Report on Industrial Fatigue. London, 1916. Also Journ. Physiol. Proc. lv., 1916.
[2] For recent observations in the Boot and Shoe Industry see Report No. 10 of the Industrial Fatigue Research Board. 1920.
[3] Cf. British Association Report, 1915, p. 323.
[4] Report No. 5 of Industrial Fatigue Research Board, p. 12, 1920.
[5] Cf. British Association Report, 1915, p. 323.

Presumably this was an end-spurt, comparable to that sometimes met with in hourly output.   The data (d) show a still
bigger end-spurt, as the output on Saturday was the maximum
for the week, and was 9.4 per cent. above the average.   It
relates to four bobbin winders who were on a 12-hour day, but
with 8 hours' work on Saturday.[1]   The shortened hours have
been allowed for in calculating output, and probably some of
the spurt was directly due to the shortened hours.   Of the five
12-hour days worked by the winders, Thursday showed the
biggest output.

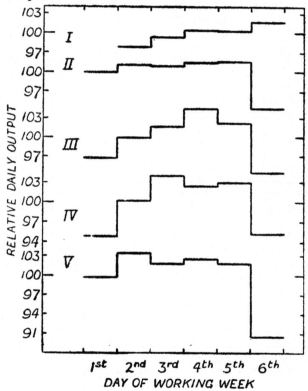

Fig. 9. Diurnal variations of output

The play of forces between practice-efficiency on the one
hand and fatigue on the other is well shown by some of the
data which I collected at three large munition works.[2] Curve I.

[1] Deduced from data quoted by Kent. Interim Report, p. 29.
[2] Memo. No. 18 of Health of Munition Workers Committee. 1917.

shows the output of a group of 73 men working 52.5 hours a week on night shift for a five week period. The men were engaged in turning and boring 3-inch shells, and it will be seen that their output improved right through the working week, and reached its maximum on the last night. Another group of men, working 53 hours per week for four weeks on similar operations, but by day instead of by night, reached their maximum output on the last day but one of the working week. (Curve II.) The considerable fall of output observed on the last day (Saturday), was probably due in part to the fact that wages were paid on Friday afternoon, and they were sometimes spent injudiciously in the evening, and in part to the fact that only a half day was being worked, during which it was difficult to settle down. It may have been also due in part to fatigue.

Curve III shows the output of about 1,000 women, who were working 58½ hours a week (day shift) at various lathe and drilling operations on fuse parts, and in stamping out fuse parts with electrically controlled stamps. Their output was determined indirectly by reading the watt-meters registering the power supplied every day for a week. As it was not possible to determine and allow for the fraction of power used for driving the shafting, which would be required almost equally whether all the machines were running or not, the data quoted afford only a relative measure of the output variations. They show that output steadily rose to a maximum on the Thursday, or the last day but two of the working week, and then fell off considerably.

Curves IV. and V. relate to the output of 116 to 140 women who were engaged on various (rifle) cartridge operations for periods of 4 to 20 weeks. The women worked alternately a 57.4 hour day shift, and a 63.0 hour night shift. When on day shift their output reached its maximum on the third day of the working week, and then gradually declined (Curve IV.) When they were on the longer and more tiring night shift, it reached its maximum on the second night of the working week. Then it declined, gradually at first, but so rapidly between the last two nights that its final value was 13 per cent. lower than the maximum observed on the second night (Curve V). This rapid fall was not in any way due to the injudicious spending of wages, as they were not paid till the last night.

It will be noted that in women working 57.4 hours a week on cartridge operations, the fatigue effect overpowered the practice-efficiency effect a day earlier than it did in women working the slightly longer 58.5 hours a week on fuse operations. As a matter of fact the cartridge women kept so much better time than the fuse women that they put in rather longer hours of actual work. Also their work was much more monotonous in character, and was on the whole more laborious. Hence it may be said that the particular day of the working week when the depression of output due to fatigue overpowers the access of output due to practice-efficiency, depends closely on the length of the hours worked, and the heaviness of the work performed.

In view of the fact that the night shift men employed in turning and boring shells improved their output throughout the working week, it might be suggested that if they had worked continuously at this operation, without any week-end break whatever, they would have permanently maintained their output at, or above, the level reached on the last night. Experimental results described in a subsequent chapter prove decisively, however, that Sunday work does not pay, and that a week-end rest is imperative if a good output is to be maintained over a long period of time. It is true that a week-end rest causes a temporary diminution in the ease and accuracy with which the complex neuro-muscular mechanisms concerned in manual labour accomplish their appointed tasks, but by enabling the system to recover from the clogging effects of cumulative fatigue, it raises the whole level of efficiency above anything of which a continuously working, but fatigue-depressed system, is capable.

CHAPTER III

OUTPUT IN RELATION TO WEEKLY HOURS OF WORK

CONTENTS

Introduction—The Attainment of Steady Output—The slow Attainment of Equilibrium between Output and reduced Hours of Work—The Relationship between Output and Hours of Work in various Fuse Operations—The Factors concerned in the Improvement of Output—How can Total Output be increased by shortening Hours of Work?—The Optimum Hours of Work in Fuse Operations—The Evils of Overtime—Fatigue, Practice-Efficiency, and End-Spurt in Weekly Output.

INTRODUCTION

A much more important performance test than hourly output or daily output, is the weekly output of the manual labourer. The successful maintenance of an industry depends on the worker achieving a good output, not for a few hours or days, but for periods of weeks, months and years. That is to say, the conditions of production must be such that they do not lead to any cumulative fatigue. There is no harm in the worker being rather more tired at the end of his week's work than at the beginning, provided that his week-end rest enables him to recuperate completely. If it does not do so, his output will steadily fall owing to the effects of fatigue, until he learns by experience to work so far as possible within his physical powers.

We shall see that it is comparatively seldom that the industrial worker allows himself to lapse into a condition of over-fatigue, but it does not by any means follow that, provided he falls short of this condition, it is desirable to impose the longest possible hours of labour upon him when a maximum output is required. The biggest output may accrue when the hours of work are comparatively short. It is of great importance for us to know what weekly hours of work will yield a maximum output in various occupations and industries, though not in order that we may habitually impose these hours on the workers. We want to know the maximum achievement of which the worker is capable in times of prolonged stress, such as occurred during the late war, and in briefer periods such as may occasionally occur in times of industrial pressure. Having fixed as accurately as possible the hours of maximum production, when the workers are near their limit, we shall be in a better position to decide on the hours which may reasonably be expected under normal conditions of industry. Such hours ought to be very distinctly shorter than those required for maximum production, in order that the workers may have each day a period of leisure at their disposal, and retain a surplus of energy which they can devote to other pursuits such as household work and gardening, to games and other forms of relaxation, or to education.

The relation of output to hours of work in various industries has been investigated and measured from time to time for a hundred years or more, and a good deal of the information obtained is described in the next chapter. The usual method has been to ascertain the total production of a factory over a definite period, generally two months to a year, before and after some change in the hours of work. This method has yielded very valuable information, but it labours under the disability that it is seldom, if ever, that all the conditions of production remain absolutely unchanged for several months on end. Slight alterations and improvements in the plant are made from time to time, the personnel of the management and of the manual workers is to some ,extent changed, whilst the articles produced are generally subject to such considerable alterations in their quality and quantity that it is the custom to estimate output, not in terms of the articles produced, but of the total earnings calculated at standard rates. Supposing that the scale of pay for the various articles is fixed incorrectly, the output estimation must likewise be incorrect.

It is true that these various sources of error are often small and insignificant, but there are no means of measuring their importance, so that there is always a suspicion that the results obtained by studying the total output of a factory may be to some extent at fault. In order to get accurate and reliable information it is better to study the output of individual groups of workers who are making exactly the same articles under exactly the same conditions for a long period of time. If, during this time, there is a definite change in the hours of work, one is as a rule justified in concluding that any alteration of output is due to the alteration of hours. I say advisedly, as a rule, because it is possible that even when all the material

C

conditions of production are unchanged, save the hours of work, the output may be influenced by the psychology of the workers. Some real or imaginary grievance may cause them to reduce their output, or some wave of enthusiasm to increase it. Hence one must always bear in mind that the industrial worker is not a machine, wholly dependent on material conditions. He is a reasoning, and occasionally an unreasonable, human being.

The great war offered an unrivalled opportunity of obtaining the kind of information required, for vast numbers of men and women were engaged for week after week, month after month, and even year after year, in making munitions of certain standardised patterns. Often the character of the articles produced, and the conditions of their production, remained absolutely unchanged over long periods except in one particular, viz., the hours of work. In the first eighteen months of the war it was the general custom to impose very long hours upon the workers in order to obtain the biggest possible output, but it was gradually discovered that these long hours did not pay. Owing to the over-fatigue induced output fell off, and progressive reductions of hours were instituted. Hence it was possible to study the output of groups of munition workers under several systems of hours of work.

THE ATTAINMENT OF STEADY OUTPUT

In order to obtain valid information concerning the effect of alteration in hours of work on output, we must be sure that the workers have sufficient experience at their job to settle down to a steady rate of production. The great majority of munition workers during the war migrated from other pursuits and took up war work for the first time. Hence their output was necessarily smaller at first than it became later on as experience was gained. Since most of their work was of a comparatively simple repetition character, they soon attained a steady output, but it was impossible to predict how long would be required for this purpose, and each operation had to be studied independently. It was the custom to pay the workers at a day rate when they first came on, but after a short time, generally a few days, they were put on to a piece rate, and it was possible to estimate their output accurately. In the Table are recorded the average outputs of several groups of women engaged on fuse and cartridge operations.[1] Their average output during the last four weeks (or two weeks in the reamering process), is taken as 100, and it will be seen that the women engaged in turning fuse bodies nearly attained their full output in the third

[1] Cf. Interim Report of Health of Munition Workers Committee, 1917, p. 73.

week. Those on cartridge operations took longer, the girls engaged on mouth reamering, an operation involving considerable quickness and dexterity, taking eight weeks. I found that men engaged in other fuse operations (sizing fuse bodies and boring top caps) took only about three weeks to attain steady output, but men engaged in operations upon 3 inch shells, such as ' boring the powder chamber,' and ' finishing, turning, and forming,' took three or four months. Women engaged in boring 9.2 inch shells took four weeks, but those employed on the skilled operation of 'recess and thread' improved their output steadily throughout the year for which they were under observation.[1]

NEWLY ENGAGED WORKERS

Process.	Number of operatives.	Relative hourly output during								
		1st week.	2nd week.	3rd week.	4th week.	5th week.	6th week.	7th week.	8th week.	9th week.
Turning fuse bodies. ...	16 women	67	91	96	96	96	100	99	101	100
Making cartridge cases—										
Second draw	12 women	70	81	91	96	97	99	99	100	102
Second cut-off	14 women	71	79	87	89	94	99	100	98	102
Mouth reamering ...	16 girls	48	64	67	79	78	89	89	99	101

After the workers have attained a nearly steady output they may, in some operations, continue to improve at a very slow rate for many months.[2] For instance, the average figures here recorded show that in a 22 week period a large group of experienced women on various cartridge operations improved their output 4.0 per cent., whilst another group of less experienced women improved it 9.6 per cent. Again, a group

WORKERS OF SOME EXPERIENCE

Process.	Number of operatives.	Relative hourly output during			
		Six weeks.	Next five weeks.	Next six weeks.	Next five weeks.
Various cartridge case operations {	112 experienced women ...	98.5	99.4	99.8	102.4
	146 less experienced women	95.4	97.2	103.1	104.6

[1] Report No. 6 of the Industrial Fatigue Research Board, 1920.
[2] Cf. Interim Report of Health of Munition Workers Committee, 1917, p. 73.

of experienced men engaged on a fuse operation (sizing fuse bodies) showed a relative hourly output of 137, 139, 140, and 141 in consecutive three-month periods.[1] Hence the possibility of a small and steady improvement, irrespective of any alteration in hours of work, must always be borne in mind. The only way of recognising this source of error, and of making allowance for it when present, is to ascertain the output of groups of workers over a very considerable number of consecutive weeks.

THE SLOW ATTAINMENT OF EQUILIBRIUM BETWEEN OUTPUT AND REDUCED HOURS OF WORK

When the hours of work are reduced, the speed of production does not as a rule show any change for the first week or two. Then it begins to mount up very gradually, but it may be several months before it attains a steady level, in equilibrium with the shortened hours.   A striking instance of this slow

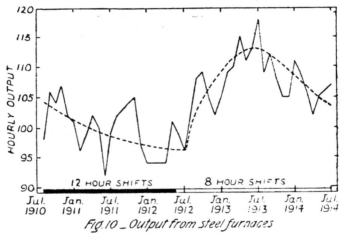

Fig. 10 _ Output from steel furnaces

response to reduced hours is indicated in Fig. 10. It relates to the output of the steel melters employed on ten 40 ton open-hearth steel furnaces.[2] For the first two years of the statistical period the men were on 12 hour shifts, and for the last two, on 8 hour shifts.   The output of the furnaces was averaged over monthly periods, and the relative monthly values, in the form of output per hour, are recorded in the Figure.[3] They are rather irregular, and the dotted line, which represents a

[1] Report No. 6 of the Industrial Fatigue Research Board, 1920.
[2] Cf. Report No. 5 of the Industrial Fatigue Research Board, 1920, p. 35.
[3] Cf. Report No. 6 of the Industrial Fatigue Research Board, 1920, p. 6.

rough average, shows that for some unknown reason the output fell gradually throughout the 12 hour shift period. When the hours were reduced there was no definite improvement of output for two months, but then it began to mount up slowly, and it attained its maximum 13 months after the shortening of hours. Another gradual fall of output then ensued (perhaps due to a deterioration of plant), so steady production was never attained, but the fact remains that the full response of improved output to shortened hours took over a year for its attainment. It amounted to an 18 per cent. increase.

In the fuse operations to be described shortly, speed of production began to improve one to four weeks after the hours of work were reduced, and equilibrium of speed was attained two to four months after. (Cf. Figs. 11, 12, and 13). Tinplate millmen engaged in rolling red-hot tinplate bars into thin sheets of steel took seven weeks to attain equilibrium when their hours were reduced from 8 to 6 per shift. (Cf. Fig. 15). The length of time necessary cannot be predicted, but it appears that the simpler the character of the operation the shorter the time. As a rule the speeding up of production on the part of the workers is adopted quite unconsciously. Owing to the shortened hours of labour they possess a surplus of available physical energy, and without knowing it they put a little more vigour than usual into their work. As they suffer no over-fatigue in consequence, they get into the habit of working at a higher speed, and they continue the process until they arrive at an approximate equilibrium of speed in relation to their hours of work. It is probable that they then tire themselves out about as much as they had previously done when working the longer hours : i.e., short hours of quick work cause as much drain on physical energy as long hours of slow work.

A striking proof that an increased speed of production is attained unconsciously is furnished by the fact that it applies to workers on a time rate no less than to those on a piece rate. In 1893 Messrs. Mather and Platt[1] reduced the length of the working week from 53 hours to 48 hours at the Salford Iron Works, a factory engaged in general engineering work. As the result of a very careful and accurate comparison of output in the year before and the year after the change, it was found that production was slightly increased, though the amount of increase is not stated. The output of the piece workers, however, was .5 per cent. less than in the preceding year, so it follows that the output of the time workers must have improved to a greater extent than that of the piece workers. On splitting up the trial year into three approximately equal

[1] W. Mather. "The Forty-eight Hours Week." Manchester, 1894.

periods, it was found that in the first period the output of the piece workers was .9 per cent. less than before : in the second period it was .7 per cent. less, and in the third period it was .1 per cent. more.   Hence in this engineering works the time required to attain equilibrium between output and reduced hours of work was at least eight months.

Supposing the workers are told that an improved output is expected of them when their hours are reduced, they may by voluntary effort increase their output immediately, but even then it takes them some weeks to get into equilibrium with the altered conditions.   When the daily hours of work at the Zeiss Optical Works, Jena, were reduced from 9 to 8, the workers made a vigorous effort to improve output, and in the first week after the change the speed of production (as estimated by electric power observations) was found by Abbé[1] to have increased 19.5 per cent.   The men had overshot the mark so much that they were over-fatigued, and in the next week the improvement fell to 5.5 per cent.   In the next two weeks it rose to 10.2 per cent. and 12.9 per cent. respectively, and then settled down to a fairly steady level.

THE RELATIONSHIP BETWEEN OUTPUT AND HOURS OF WORK IN VARIOUS FUSE OPERATIONS

In order to ascertain the relationship between output and hours of work, I collected statistical information extending over a two year period at a large fuse factory.[2]   During this time there were no changes whatever in the conditions of production of the articles, such as the character of the machinery and its speed, and in the nature and quality of the articles produced. There were, however, very extensive reductions in the hours of work.   At first the majority of the workers were on a 12-hour day, with somewhat shorter hours on Saturdays and Sundays, so that the total hours of work usually came to $77\frac{1}{4}$ per week.   As there was a Sunday holiday once a month, the hours averaged $74\frac{1}{2}$ per week.   After a time the workers were put on to a 10-hour day, though they still did Sunday labour, and their hours averaged about $63\frac{1}{2}$ per week, but when Sunday labour was abolished the hours fell to $55\frac{1}{2}$ a week.   Hence there were three clear cut systems of hours during which output could be ascertained.

[1] Abbé. Gesammelte Abhandlungen, Vol. 3, p. 223. 1906.
[2] Report No. 6 of Industrial Fatigue Research Board; also Memos. Nos. 12 and 18, and Final Report, of Health of Munitions Workers Committee.

WOMEN TURNING FUSE BODIES

In the operation of turning aluminium fuse bodies on capstan lathes the output of a large number of women was studied for 93 consecutive weeks. Owing to the heavy nature of the work there was a considerable wastage of labour, so my method was to study the output of a group of experienced women for several months, and at the end of that time to replenish the reduced numbers by the addition of a block of comparatively fresh workers. For instance, a group of 100 women was studied from Nov. 7, 1915, onwards. By April 24, 1916, the numbers had fallen to 66, so 29 fresh workers were added, and the total brought back to 95. It was found that the fresh workers (provided they had had a month's experience), achieved as great an output as experienced workers of five months' service, so that the introduction of the fresh blood did not appreciably alter output.

I have given elsewhere[1] full details of the numbers of women whose output was investigated, and their hours of work and

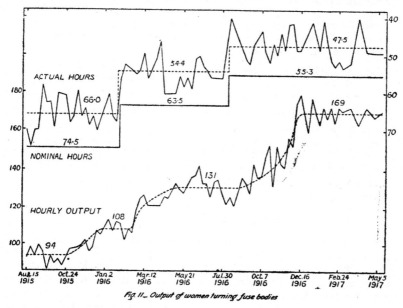

Fig. 11.— Output of women turning fuse bodies

hourly output for each of the 93 weeks. Most of these results are reproduced graphically in Fig. 11, from which it can be gathered that the $74\frac{1}{2}$ hour week was worked for 24 weeks, the

[1] Op. cit.

$63\frac{1}{2}$ hour week for 28 weeks, and the 55.3 hour week for 41 weeks. The time keeping was not good, and the women averaged only 66.0, 54.4, and 47.5 hours of actual work in the three periods (holiday weeks not being reckoned in the averages). In the first 12 weeks of the $74\frac{1}{2}$ hour period the relative output averaged 94 per hour, and then it rose gradually to 108, although the nominal hours of work were not altered. I believe this improvement to be due to the fact that in the first few weeks of the statistical period the women kept such good time (they averaged 71.2 hours per week of actual work), that they were too fatigued to attain the hourly output of which they were capable later on when they gave themselves more rests from work by keeping worse time. Hence I think that the relative hourly output of 108 may be regarded as being roughly in equilibrium with the 66 hour week of actual work.

When the 10-hour day was adopted there was no improvement of hourly output for four weeks, and then it rose gradually, and 14 weeks after the reduction of hours it became fairly steady at the average value of 131. When Sunday labour was abolished there was no improvement of hourly output for a fortnight, and it was 17 weeks before a steady value was attained. It then averaged 169, so that the main results of the observations may be expressed thus :

In the 74.5 hour week total output was $66.0 \times 108 = 7128 \,(= 100)$
  ,,   63.5   ,,   ,,   ,, $54.4 \times 131 = 7126 \,(= 100)$
  ,,   55.3   ,,   ,,   ,, $47.5 \times 169 = 8028 \,(= 113)$

These figures show that the *total* output was the same during the 10-hour day as it was in the 12-hour day, but that when Sunday labour was abolished it improved 13 per cent. Though the women averaged $18\frac{1}{2}$ hours less of work per week under the shortest system of hours than under the longest system, or three hours less per day, they could nevertheless achieve a greater output.

MEN SIZING FUSE BODIES

In this operation the output of groups of men, 27 to 90 in number, was studied for 22 consecutive months. The operation is a distinctly heavy one, as the men always worked in their shirt sleeves, and perspired freely. They never worked such long hours as the women above mentioned, but at first they put in 12 hours on some days, and 10 hours on others, with intermittent Sunday labour. Then they went on to a regular 10-hour day, but with very intermittent Sunday labour, and then Sunday labour was completely abolished, and the average length of working week was the same as with the women.

The hourly output and hours of work of these men are indicated in Fig. 12. In the first period the nominal hours of work averaged 66.7 a week and the actual hours 58.2 a week, and the output was observed over a six week period. This is

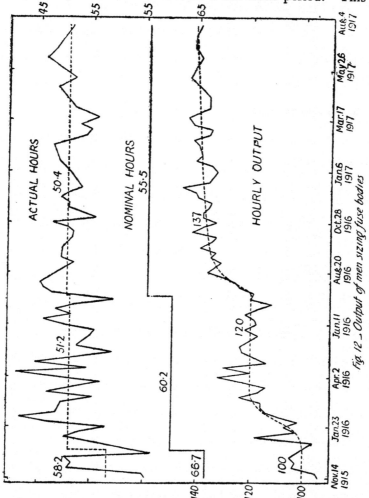

Fig. 12.—Output of men sizing fuse bodies

too short a time to render it certain that equilibrium between output and hours of work had been attained, so the relative hourly value, viz., 100, must be accepted as provisional. When the men went on to the regular 10-hour day, their hourly output began to rise after a fortnight, and it attained a fairly steady

value of 120 in 10 weeks.   After Sunday labour was completely abolished, output began to rise almost at once, and it
attained a nearly steady value of 137 nine weeks after the
change.   However, it continued to rise very slightly, and at
the end of the period recorded it averaged 141.

In the Sunday-free period, the nominal hours of work were
4.7 less per week than in the intermittent Sunday period, but
the men kept so much better time that they put in nearly as
much actual work per week as before, viz., 50.4 hours as
against 51.2 hours.   Hence the total output works out as
follows :

In the 66.7 hour week total output was 58.2 × 100 = 5820 (=100)
   „   60·2   „   „   „   51.0 × 120 = 6120 (=105)
   „   55.5   „   „   „   50.4 × 187 = 6905 (=119)

It may seem astonishing that a reduction in the nominal
hours of work amounting to 11.2 hours a week, and a reduction
in actual hours of only 7.8 a week, could have led to such a
considerable improvement of total output as 19 per cent. There
are two main reasons for this result.   In the first place, each
reduction of hours produced more *uniformity* of working conditions.   When the men were working some days for 12 hours
and some days for 10 hours, it is probable that they permanently
adopted a speed of work appropriate to the longer hours rather
than to the shorter ones.   Again, when, during the 10-hour
period, they had Sunday labour imposed on them intermittently, and they were unable to rely on getting a regular
week-end rest, they would tend to adopt a speed of work appropriate to a regular Sunday labour week, rather than a Sunday-
free week.[1]

The other reason arises from the character of the work done
by the men.   They had to fasten each fuse body to a handle,
and screw it round rapidly by hand into a steel tap, so as to
cut (or enlarge) screw threads on it.   They were quite free
from machinery, and they could quicken up their speed as
much as they liked.   On the other hand the women turning
fuse bodies were to some extent limited by machinery, as they
could not quicken up the speed with which their lathes were
running, though they could quicken the rate at which they
changed and applied the various cutting and boring tools (seven
in number) to the fuse body.   Presumably it was largely in
consequence of the mechanical limitation that they did not
improve their total output so much as the men did when their
hours of work were reduced.

[1] Cf. p. 55 of this Chapter.

In another fuse operation, known as milling a screw thread, the women engaged were still more limited by machinery, as they had to put each fuse body into a semi-automatic machine revolving at a fixed speed, and it was only when they were changing the fuse bodies, which occupied about a fifth of the total time taken, that they could quicken up at all. The output of groups of 21 to 40 women was studied for a year, and the output observed under the various systems of nominal and actual hours was as follows :

In the 71.8 hour week total output was 64.9 × 100 = 6490 (=100)
„   64.6   „   „   „   54.8 × 121 = 6631 (=102)
„   57.8   „   „   „   48.1 × 133 = 6897 (=99)

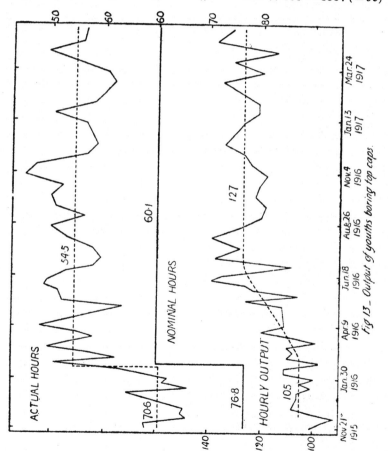

Fig 13 _ Output of youths boring top caps.

These results show that though the women managed to maintain their total output when their hours of work were reduced, they could not definitely improve on it, as in the two operations above discussed.

In a fourth fuse operation, known as *boring top caps,* the youths employed were absolutely limited by the machine. About four times a minute they unclamped one top cap from a semi-automatic machine and clamped in another, these two clampings together occupying less than two seconds. For the rest of the time they stood at their machines doing nothing. I studied their output for 79 consecutive weeks, during the first 13 weeks of which they were on a 12¼ hour day, with some Sunday labour. Time keeping was so good that they averaged 70.6 hours of actual work per week. Then the youths went on to a 10-hour day, sometimes with Sunday labour and sometimes without, and they often worked alternate fortnights of day and night shift. Taking the whole 66 weeks together, the nominal hours of work averaged 60.1 per week, and the actual hours 54.5 per week. It will be seen from Fig. 13 that when the 12¼ hour day was abolished it took about four months before the hourly output attained rough equilibrium with the shortened hours, and it then averaged 127, as compared with the value of 105 observed during the longer hours. Hence the total output works out as follows :

In the 76.8 hour week total output was $70.6 \times 105 = 7413 (=100)$

,, 60.1 ,, ,, ,, $54.5 \times 127 = 6922 (=93)$

Thus the youths were unable to improve their hourly output sufficiently to make up for the reduction of hours, and their total output showed a distinct fall.

The main results obtained in the various fuse operations may be summarised thus :

Operation.	Speeding up of operation possible.	Reduction in weekly hours of actual work.	Alteration of total output effected.
1. Men sizing ...	Throughout, and without limit	58.2 to 50.4 = 7.8	+ 19 %
2. Women turning fuse bodies	Throughout, to a limited extent	66.0 to 47.5 = 18.5	+ 13
3. Women milling screw thread	For a fifth of the total time taken	64.9 to 48.1 = 16.8	− 1
4. Youths boring top caps	Not at all	70.6 to 54.5 = 16.1	− 7

It is possible that the total output alterations indicated in the last column are slightly too favourable, as no allowance has been made for the small degree of improvement of output which might have occurred even if no reduction whatever had been made in the hours of work.   The allowance would in any case be small, and it would not disprove the two main conclusions deduced from these figures, to the effect that (a) when the hours of work are very long, a reduction of hours may lead to a distinct increase of total output ; (b) the effect produced depends on the character of the operation, being greatest in those which are chiefly dependent on the human element, and least in those which are chiefly dependent on the mechanical element.

THE FACTORS CONCERNED IN THE IMPROVEMENT OF OUTPUT

The improvement of the output per hour induced by shortening the hours of work in the first two of the four operations recorded in the above Table was doubtless due in large part to

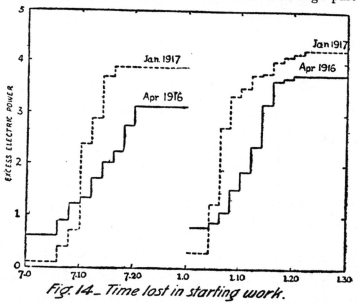

Fig. 14— Time lost in starting work.

the increased speed with which the manual work was performed, but this is not true of the last two operations.   A casual observer of the youths engaged in boring top caps would say that by no possibility could they increase their speed of production, however short their hours of work.   And yet it was found by statistical examination that they increased it by 21 per cent. or more when their hours were reduced. The improvement must have been due entirely to the greater persistency with which they applied themselves to their work. No observations were made on these particular workers, but the women engaged in turning fuse bodies were tested a number of times.

By the method of reading the watt-meters at two-minute intervals at the beginning and end of the work spells, it was possible to ascertain approximately the amount of time lost in starting work, and in stopping before the whistle blew. Fig. 14 shows the mean of three sets of power records taken in April-May, 1916. They indicate that when the women came on to work at 7.0 a.m., no appreciable number of them started till 7.6 a.m., whilst all of them had started by 7.20 a.m. The average amount of time lost was 14.0 minutes, but in January, 1917, or nine months later, it had fallen to 10.0 minutes. The figures recorded in the Table show that altogether 37 minutes were lost in April-May, 1916, in each 10-hour day shift by starting late and stopping early, but six weeks later this time had fallen to 33 minutes, and seven months later, to 26.5 minutes.

TIME LOST IN STARTING AND STOPPING WORK

Time of year at which power records were taken.	Average number of minutes lost when—				Total number minutes lost.	Relative hourly output.
	Starting work in morning.	Finishing work in morning.	Starting work in afternoon.	Finishing work in afternoon.		
Apr. 13-May 1, 1916	14.0	1.5	12.3	9.3	37.1	126
June 6-7, 1916	12.5	2.5	10.0	8.0	33.0	137
January 10-18, 1917	10.0	0.5	7.0	9.0	26.5	166

In that the relative hourly output of fuse bodies in the three periods mentioned was 126, 137, and 166 respectively, it follows that only a small portion of the improvement can have been due to the extra time saved in the way mentioned. However, a good deal more time could be saved during the course of the working day by taking shorter rests from work. Prof. W. Neilson Jones, who was working in conjunction with me, observed all the rest pauses taken by small groups of the women on five days in April-May, 1916. Altogether 27 women were observed, and, ignoring all rest pauses of less than three minutes duration, he found that in each 10-hour shift the women rested on an average no less than 125 minutes. That is to say, they were actually at work only for $7\frac{3}{4}$ to 8 hours per day. Of the total resting time, 62 minutes were involuntary, as they were needed by the tool setters for attending to the lathes, but the remaining 65 minutes (37 of which were due to late starting and early stopping) were taken voluntarily.

I myself observed the fuse body women for two days when they were on 12-hour shifts, and I found that they lost 90 minutes per shift by voluntary rests. Eight women were kept under observation, but two of them stopped work altogether at 5.45 p.m., and did not work their short 6.15 to 8.30 p.m. evening shift, so I did not include them. Such stoppage of work was by no means uncommon, and if it had been reckoned in with the other voluntary rests it would have raised the average considerably. In any case the women took a good deal more voluntary rest during the 12-hour day than during the 10-hour day, and there can be little doubt that if further 10-hour day observations had been made in 1917, it would have been found that the increased speed of production was partly due to a further reduction of voluntary rests.

How Can Total Output be Increased by Shortening Hours of Work?

It may be wondered how it comes about that the *total* output sometimes shows a definite increase when the weekly hours of work are reduced. The matter is best explained by means of two examples, one hypothetical[1] and one actual. To take the hypothetical case first, let us suppose that each vigorous and healthy worker starts his day's work with 12 units of energy, all of which he can, if he pleases, put into his work without over-fatiguing himself, *i.e.*, without getting into a condition from which a good night's rest does not completely restore his initial vigour. Of these 12 units probably 1 unit is required by the worker to enable him to perform essential household duties and to get to his factory in the morning, whilst another unit is required for similar objects in the evening. He therefore has 10 units of energy left, all of which he can apply to his work if he so desires. Probably under normal circum-

[1] Cf. " Life and its Maintenance," p. 257. London, 1919.

stances he does not utilise more than 7 units in such a way, but he keeps 3 units in hand, and utilises them for other purposes, such as for playing games, or digging in his garden. Frequently he does not utilise them at all, but ends the day with a considerable supply of unexhausted vigour. Let us suppose, however, that for some reason such as patriotic endeavour or the desire for high wages he desires to put every particle of energy possible into his work, and to expend the whole of his 10 units in this way. How can he use them to the best advantage?

There can be no doubt that a great deal of energy is expended if a man stands idly all day in a factory without doing any work whatever. The effects of noise, which is often very great, and sometimes of inefficient ventilation, added to the physical effort of standing, would account for a good many of the units of energy. Let us suppose that they require half a unit per hour. Then in a 10-hour day the worker would have 5 of his 10 units of energy exhausted in this way, and he would have 5 units left to put into active work. In an 8-hour day, on the other hand, he would lose only 4 out of his 10 units unproductively, and he would have 6 units left for active work. In a 6-hour day he would lose only 3 units, and he would have 7 left for active work. That is to say, the shorter the hours worked the greater the amount of energy available for productive work, and the less the amount spent unproductively. Hence the total output would increase more and more as the hours of work were shortened, were it not for another factor which is acting in the opposite direction. Supposing it needs 1 unit of energy to produce 1 article in an hour, it does not need only 2 units of energy to produce 2 articles in the hour, but distinctly *more* than 2 units. The greater the speed of production, the relatively greater the call upon the physical energies of the body. The best proof of this statement is afforded by a simple physiological example.

When a man is absolutely at rest, he absorbs oxygen from the air he inspires, and he breathes out carbonic acid, at a steady rate. But directly he begins to move about he expends more physical energy, and he needs a greater supply of oxygen. It is easy to measure with accuracy the amount he absorbs under various conditions, by allowing him to breathe into an indiarubber bag carried on his back, and as the result of a number of observations of this kind,[1] made when the subject

[1] Cf. Douglas, Haldane, Henderson and Schneider. Phil. Trans. B. 203, p. 185. 1912.

was walking at a steady rate of 2 to 5 miles an hour, the following average values were obtained :

Rate of Walking.	Volume of oxygen con- sumed per minute in cubic centimetres.	Increase.	Increase per mile walked.	Miles walked per 60,000 c.c. of oxygen consumed.
Standing at rest	334	—	—	—
2 miles an hour	648	314	157	3.1
3 ,, ,,	898	564	188	3.3
4 ,, ,,	1185	851	213	3.4
4½ ,, ,,	1532	1198	266	2.9
5 ,, ,,	2125	1791	358	2.4

Here we see that when the subject was walking at two miles
an hour he consumed nearly twice as much oxygen as when he
was standing at rest, and the extra amount of oxygen needed
for each mile of ground covered came to 157 c.c. per minute.
When he walked at three miles per hour instead of two, the
consumption of oxygen per mile of ground covered increased to
188 c.c., and the faster he walked the greater the increase, till
at five miles per hour he was consuming oxygen more than
twice as fast, per mile of ground covered, as at two miles per
hour.   The oxygen consumption is an approximate measure of
the physical energy exerted, so one may say that the extra
energy needed for walking varied in the proportions mentioned.
    Supposing that the subject desired to get to a certain destina-
tion with a minimum expenditure of energy, how fast should he
walk ?   He is always consuming oxygen at 334 c.c. per minute,
even if he stands absolutely still, and this large unproductive
expenditure of energy has to be allowed for.   In the last column
of the above Table is recorded the distance the subject would
cover for a total consumption of 60,000 c.c. of oxygen, and it
will be seen that if he walked at 2 miles per hour he would
achieve 3.1 miles, but if he walked at 3 or 4 miles an hour he
would manage a distinctly greater distance, and it can be calculated that he would have got the greatest distance of all, viz.,
3.5 miles, if he walked at the rate of 3.7 miles per hour.   On
the other hand, the higher speeds of walking are so expensive
that at 5 miles per hour his 60,000 c.c. of oxygen would have
enabled him to cover only 2.4 miles.
    In the simpler forms of manual labour not dependent on
machinery, such as shovelling up earth and wheeling it in
barrows, in digging, and so on, there would be a very similar
parallelism between expenditure of energy and productivity to

D

that observed in walking, and the same parallelism would probably apply to the previously mentioned operation of sizing fuse bodies. In more skilled operations, and in those dependent on machinery, the expenditure of energy per unit of product would increase more rapidly as the rate of production was accelerated, but in every instance there is always the considerable dead weight of unproductive expenditure, incurred even during absolute idleness, which has to be allowed for. Hence it invariably follows that a very slow rate of production is uneconomical, just as a very fast rate is uneconomical. To produce a maximum output the worker must shorten his hours of work so as to reduce waste of energy from much standing about, but he must not shorten them so much as to necessitate a very great speed of production with its much more than proportionate call upon his energies. He must endeavour to hit off a happy mean involving *some* reduction of hours and *some* speeding up of production, but what the best hours of work and the best speed actually consist in can be ascertained only by prolonged observation and experiment.

The Optimum Hours of Work in Fuse Operations

What hours of work would have yielded the greatest output in the four fuse operations above described? The workers were full of patriotic enthusiasm, and were probably expending nearly all their store of available physical energy on their work. The fact that the output of the men engaged in sizing fuse bodies was so considerably greater when they worked a $55\frac{1}{2}$ hour week than when they worked a 60 hour week, suggests that they would have attained an even bigger output in a 50 hour week. Unfortunately they were kept on their 10-hour day throughout the war, though they got a Saturday half-holiday after a time. Had their working day been reduced to 9 hours (with a half day on Saturday), I believe that their output would have increased, and even on an 8-hour day it would probably have been maintained. Again, the women engaged in turning fuse bodies would in all probability have produced as much in a 9-hour day as in a 10-hour day, and nearly if not quite as much in an 8-hour day, but the other two groups of workers referred to are in a different category. It will be remembered that they were working on semi-automatic machines, which were run at a uniform speed. The mill-thread women could save a little time by inserting and removing the fuse bodies more quickly, but the top-cap youths had not even this advantage. They could save time only by applying themselves more persistently to their work, and it is probable that if they had worked a longer week than the 60 hours recorded, *e.g.*, 68 hours, their output would have approached, or equalled, that attained by them in their 77-hour week. The mill-thread women attained only slightly less output in a 57-hour week than in a 64½-hour week, but it is probable that in a 50-hour week they would have attained considerably less.

So far as the available evidence can show, therefore, it seems likely that the optimum hours of work of the men sizers and the women fuse turners would have been about 50 a week, but those of the mill-thread women would have been about 60 a week, and those of the top-cap youths 70 per week. Evidently no hard and fast rule can be laid down as to optimum hours of work for the various occupations in an industry. Each occupation is a law to itself, though we can generally predict that the greater the importance of the human element the shorter the hours required, and the greater the importance of the mechanical element the longer the hours required.

It is to be borne in mind that the hours mentioned are those suitable for workers determined to exert the maximum energy of which they are capable, and for employers who are determined to obtain a maximum output regardless of expense. They are by no means the most suitable hours for ordinary times and conditions. Supposing, for instance, it were found that the top-cap youths had a total output of 100 when they worked a 70-hour week, but one of 98 when they worked a 65-hour week, it would probably pay the employer much better to let them work the shorter hours, as the extra five hours a week produced such a small improvement of output.

Again, under ordinary conditions, we cannot expect for a moment that the workers should utilise all their available ' units of energy ' in the prosecution of their work. They ought to have quite a considerable margin left over which they can apply to other purposes if they wish. That is to say, if 50 hours per week be the optimum hours of work of men sizers and women fuse body turners, it is probable that a 44 hour week is long enough for them to do as much work as could reasonably be expected of them, and if 60 hours be the optimum for mill-thread women, then 54 hours would be a reasonable length. It would also be a reasonable length for the top-cap youths, in spite of the fact that their optimum hours of work are about 70 per week, for anything over 54 hours would leave insufficient leisure time.

The principle of giving the workers on light operations a longer working week than those on heavier operations does not appear to be adopted at all widely, though it seems the most reasonable and equitable one. In practice it would merely mean that, whilst all of the workers were nominally on, *e.g.*, an 8-hour day, a certain proportion of them would regularly be kept for 1 or 1½ hours a day on 'overtime.' That is to say, they would be paid at a higher rate for this extra work.

THE EVILS OF OVERTIME

The term 'overtime' is a very indefinite one, as it depends on what are reckoned to be the normal hours of work. In Great Britain, before the war, the normal hours of work in the textile trades were usually 55 a week, and in the engineering trades they were usually 53 or 54, and less frequently, 48. In associated trades such as those of the boiler makers, iron founders and ship builders, and in the boot and shoe trade, they were likewise 53 or 54 hours,[1] and any time worked over these hours was reckoned as overtime, and was paid for at a higher rate. Since the war the normal hours of work have dropped to 48 or 47 a week, or even to 44 in some instances. Hence, even after the imposition of several hours' overtime, the working week may be shorter than the normal week worked before the war.

However, one of the pernicious effects of overtime persists whatever the number of hours normally worked, even if they be reduced to 36 a week. Equilibrium between output and hours of work is upset, and it may take the worker a long time to regain it. We have seen that when the hours of work are reduced, it takes the operatives two months or more before they get their increasing output into equilibrium with the shortened hours, and it is probable that when they have reached equilibrium, they usually tire themselves out as much by their day's work as they previously did during the longer hours. Under all conditions of hours they unconsciously get into the way of doing the best day's work of which they are capable, with a reasonable margin of energy left to them for other than industrial labour. Not only is there a condition of approximate equilibrium between output and hours of work for each working week, but for each working day as well. In order that a man may work according to the law of 'maximum output with minimum effort,' he should work the same number of hours per day, and at the same speed. The more irregular his habits, the less his efficiency.

The methods of imposing overtime vary greatly. Sometimes an extra hour of overtime is put on to each day of the week, but it is more usual to impose two hours or more of overtime

---

[1] Cf. A. Shadwell. "Industrial Efficiency," p. 349. London, 1913.

(in shipbuilding, $3\frac{1}{2}$ hours) for two or three evenings a week, and allow the operative to work his normal hours for the rest of the week. Thereby his daily equilibrium of work is upset as well as his weekly equilibrium. Supposing that he has got into the habit of putting in a really good 8-hour day of work, at the end of which he has exhausted nearly all his 'units of energy,' and suddenly two hours of overtime are imposed. If he continues to work at the rate appropriate to the 8-hour day, he must draw on the *capital of his energy* for the extra effort required, as by hypothesis he has already nearly exhausted his daily income of energy. Such a draft on capital is very expensive, and fatigues the worker much more than corresponds with the work done. It induces a state of over-fatigue which cannot be fully recovered from in a good night's rest, and next day the worker begins without his normal supply of 'units of energy' at his disposal. If he continues to work at the same rate he gets into a worse condition of over-fatigue than ever, and before long he will find that he must either slow down, or he must stop altogether, in order to recuperate. As a matter of actual practice, he usually does not utilise the whole of his 'units of energy' in his normal day's work, so that he can still do a small amount of extra work without incurring over-fatigue, but he very soon begins to slow down his rate of production so as to prevent himself from lapsing into more than an incipient stage of over-fatigue. He usually does this unconsciously, as he is following the law of maximum production with minimum effort, but he may have learnt by experience to do it consciously, in order to avoid even a small amount of over-fatigue. If the overtime be continued, his production rate soon sinks to a level which is in equilibrium with the 10-hour day, instead of the 8-hour day.

This picture of what happens when overtime is imposed is by no means a fanciful one, as its main points can be substantiated by statistical evidence. The expensiveness of performing manual work with muscles already fatigued is best illustrated by an example taken from laboratory practice, as a suitable one from workshop practice is not available. It was obtained by means of Mosso's *ergograph*. In working this instrument the middle finger of one hand raises a heavy weight (*e.g.*, $6\frac{1}{2}$ lbs.) at regular intervals (*e.g.* every two seconds), as far as it can by means of a cord working over a pulley. The extent of each movement is recorded, and it is found that after a short time the muscles get so fatigued that they are unable to raise the heavy weight at all. In one instance[1] the subject of experiment (Dr. Maggiora) found that after 30 contractions

[1] Cf. Mosso. " Fatigue," p. 150. London, 1915.

his muscles were completely exhausted, and he had to wait two hours before every trace of the fatigue induced had disappeared, and he could move his finger as vigorously as before. If, however, he contracted his finger 15 times instead of 30 times, the fatigue induced was so much smaller that he recovered completely in half an hour instead of the hour one might have expected. That is to say, the last half of the 30 contractions, though they were much smaller in extent than the first half, caused a very much greater degree of fatigue.

The slowing down of production rate which follows on the imposition of overtime, is well shown by an observation of Abbé at the Zeiss Optical Works.[1] When the men were on a nine hour day they were occasionally required to work one hour of overtime in seasons of pressure. One November, when the men themselves were eager to earn more money for Christmas, the overtime was imposed, but the extra output deteriorated in a week, and by the third or fourth week it was practically non-existent.

Even more rapid was the reduction of output observed by me in tinplate millmen.[2] The rolling of red-hot tinplate bars into thin plates of steel, which are subsequently tinned, is a continuous process lasting from Monday morning till Saturday

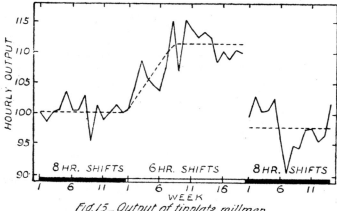

Fig. 15_ Output of tinplate millmen

afternoon. The work is very heavy, and is done under trying conditions of temperature. The millmen usually work three 8-hour shifts per 24 hours, but if there is a break-down of machinery or a shortage of material they may be made to work four 6-hour shifts, and I obtained output data under these two

[1] Abbé. Gesammelte Abhandlungen, Vol. 3, p. 223. 1906.
[2] Reports Nos. 1 and 6 of Industrial Fatigue Research Board, 1919 and 1920.

systems of shift at three different factories. The averages of six sets of data are reproduced in Fig. 15, and it will be seen that the relative hourly output is recorded for 14 consecutive weeks during which the men were on 8-hour shifts, and for the subsequent 19 weeks when they went on to 6-hour shifts. In the second week after the reduction of hours the output began to mount up, and from the 8th week onwards it averaged 111.4, as against a value of 100.2 during the 8-hour shift period. After various periods of time the men went back again to the 8-hour régime, and the curve to the right of Fig. 15 shows what happened to their hourly output. It is rather irregular, but it shows that the hourly output fell immediately to a value only slightly above that observed when 8-hour shifts were previously worked. Instead of taking two months to adapt their output to the change of hours, as they did when they changed from 8-hour to 6-hour shifts, the men got into approximate equilibrium with their longer hours at once.

This principle of very slow adaptation to a reduction of hours, but quick adaptation to an increase of hours, is most important in its application to overtime. If the overtime is imposed intermittently, then it is highly probable that the workers will unconsciously get into the habit of working permanently at a rate adapted to the longer hours worked, rather than to the *average* of the longer and shorter hours. Supposing, for instance, that a 10-hour day is imposed in alternate fortnights with an 8-hour day, it is very likely that the workers will get into the habit of working always at a speed appropriate to a 10-hour day rather than to a 9-hour day. Even a single fortnight of overtime work (*e.g.,* 10 hours per day instead of 8 hours), may lower the speed for several weeks to come almost to the 10-hour rate. Again, the imposition of two hours overtime on two or three nights a week may likewise lead to a reduction of speed to the rate appropriate to the longer hours worked.

It is evident, therefore, that if overtime be imposed at all, it should be evenly distributed over the whole period for which it is necessary, and not be concentrated on two or three days in each week, or on a few successive weeks. Otherwise there is a heavy penalty to pay in the form of reduced output when the overtime hours are remitted.

Supposing that overtime is imposed on hours of work which are already nearly as long as the workers can stand, then it is evident that the effects of over-fatigue will speedily develop. Instances of excessive overtime will be quoted in a subsequent chapter.

The evil effects of overtime on output may be strikingly in

evidence if the men in charge of the operatives are kept on over-time, even if the operatives themselves are working quite short hours. A case in point was observed by me at an ordnance factory, where the 1800 workers were employed exclusively in manufacturing 9.2 inch shells.[1] The output of considerable groups of women on typical operations was studied for a year, during the first half of which they were on a three shift system under which they averaged $44\frac{1}{4}$ hours of work a week, whilst the men in charge of the women were on a two shift system under which they averaged $63\frac{1}{4}$ hours of work a week. In the second half of the statistical period both men and women went on to the same modified two shift system, under which they averaged 54 hours of work a week. That is to say, the men were now putting in $9\frac{1}{4}$ hours less than before, but the women, $9\frac{3}{4}$ hours more. Since the women were working the lathes, and were dependent on the men only for the setting of their tools and the provision of an adequate supply of material, it might be supposed that the increase of working hours would reduce their hourly output rather than increase it, but it was not so. In the operation of "groove and wave" the hourly output of the women gradually increased by 42 per cent. : in that of 'rough turning' it increased by 10 per cent., and in that of 'boring' it increased by 12 per cent. Evidently the men, when they were working their long hours, were too tired to set the tools of the women promptly, and to keep them well supplied with material. Just as the strength of a chain depends on its weakest link, so the output of a factory depends on the capability of the managing staff, the skilled men, the semi-skilled workers and the labourers conjointly. Over-fatigue in any one of the interdependent groups of workers, brain workers no less than manual workers, may largely neutralise the working capacity of the whole body.

FATIGUE, PRACTICE-EFFICIENCY, AND END-SPURT IN WEEKLY OUTPUT

Weekly output records may show the same features of fatigue, practice-efficiency and end-spurt as were observed in the daily and hourly records, only they are spread over longer time intervals.

A diminution of output as the result of fatigue is sometimes seen when the workers are in need of a holiday. In 1916 the munition workers were asked to forego their usual Whitsuntide and August bank holidays, and they worked continuously from April 27 till August 20, when they had a full week off. The

[1] Report No. 6 of Industrial Fatigue Research Board, 1920, p. 21.

tendency of their output to flag may be gathered from Figs. 11 and 12. The hourly output of the women turning fuse bodies averaged only 122 between July 31 and Aug. 19, whilst it averaged 133 in the preceding 13 weeks. Again, the hourly output of the men sizing fuse bodies averaged 117 between June 26 and July 16, as against 122 in the preceding 13 weeks. After July 16 output began to go up in this latter operation, owing to the abolition of Sunday labour.

The influence of end-spurt on weekly output is frequently seen in the two or three weeks before a holiday. It appears to be due to the desire of the workers to earn a little more money to spend during the holiday, and to compensate them for the loss of working days. The bank holidays were usually observed at the fuse factory, and the workers had two or three days off in addition, so it generally happened that two consecutive working weeks were partly broken into by the holiday. The

INFLUENCE OF A HOLIDAY ON SPEED OF PRODUCTION

Operation	Clear weeks before holiday	Broken week before holiday	Broken week after holiday	Clear weeks after holiday
Women turning fuse bodies	123 120 126 123 131 137 123 134	126	118	141 135 134 138 135 139 137 137
Men sizing fuse bodies	116 114 121 125 122 126 115 123	111	109	125 121 123 119 120 124 126 123

accompanying Table shows the average of the output values recorded at Christmas, 1915 and 1916, and Easter, 1916. They are quoted for the six weeks before the two broken holiday weeks, and the seven weeks after. It will be seen that the speed of production (i.e., output per hour) of the fuse-turning women was considerably higher in the two weeks immediately before the broken holiday weeks than it had been in the preceding month (viz., 134 on an average as compared with 123), whilst that of the sizing men was considerably higher for four weeks before the holiday time (viz., 123 as compared with 115 in the preceding fortnight). In both of the broken holiday weeks the speed of production was low. It was low in the week before the holiday was taken because the workers were apt to get distracted by thoughts of the approaching holiday, and also for the material reason that any work they did would not be paid for till after the holiday was over. It was low in the broken week after the holiday was over because of lack of practice-efficiency, and general disinclination for work.

Once practice-efficiency had been acquired, the favourable effect of the holiday showed itself in full force. It will be seen that in the seven weeks after the holiday the fuse-turning woman had an output of 137, *i.e.*, distinctly more than that observed in the end-spurt weeks preceding the holiday, whilst the men sizers had the same output as in the end-spurt weeks.

The capacity of the workers to put on a spurt before a holiday is considered by some employers to show that they are not doing their best at other times. I do not think that this conclusion follows for a moment. The workers do not mind incurring a little over-fatigue before a holiday, as they know they will have an opportunity of recuperating. If they put on a similar spurt during a period of continuous work, their only method of recovering from the over-fatigue induced would be to go slow for a bit, or knock off altogether. Such a spurt, followed by a period of diminished work, would be contrary to the law of maximum production with minimum exertion.

CHAPTER IV

OUTPUT AND HOURS OF WORK IN VARIOUS INDUSTRIES

CONTENTS

Introduction—Industries dependent chiefly on Human Labour (Coal Mining, Granite Cutting)—Industries dependent more or less equally on Human Labour and on Machinery (Manufacture of Optical Instruments, Engineering, Boot and Shoe Manufacture, Manufacture of Chemicals)—Industries dependent chiefly on Machinery (Cotton Manufacture, Wool and Silk Manufacture, Iron and Steel Manufacture)—Overtime in various Industries.

INTRODUCTION

The question of output in relation to hours of work has been hotly debated for a hundred years or more. In the early days of factory life, it was usual for the cotton mills to be worked 90 to 100 hours per week, or 15 to 16 hours per day, though there were a few notable exceptions. Robert Owen ran the cotton mills of New Lanark $10\frac{1}{2}$ hours a day for the twelve years from 1816 to 1828, and it was found that the output did not sensibly fall below its previous amount, owing to the greater personal exertions spontaneously elicited from the workers. The hours had formerly been 16 per day, and before the final reduction they were lowered first to $12\frac{1}{2}$ and then to $11\frac{1}{2}$ hours, this second reduction causing a very marked improvement in the cheerfulness and alacrity of the operatives.[1]

Legislation limiting the hours of work was gradually introduced from 1802 onwards, when the hours of work of certain apprentices were limited to 12 a day. In 1819 an Act was passed which prevented the admission of children to cotton mills before the age of nine, and limited the hours of work of persons under 16 to twelve a day. In 1831 night work in cotton factories was prohibited for persons under 21, and the working week for persons under 18 was limited to 69 hours. This legislation did not apply to wool factories, where children

---

[1] John Rae. " Eight Hours for Work." London, 1894.

were still being terribly over-worked, but in 1833 an Act was passed which applied practically to all the textile trades. It limited the hours of children aged 9 to 13 to 48 per week, and those of young persons aged 13 to 18 to 68 per week. More important still, it provided for the appointment of factory inspectors to watch over the working of the law.

At each stage of factory legislation it was usual for many of the employers to maintain that restriction of hours would deprive them of their margin of profit, and ruin the industry. In 1837 Senior, a political economist, endeavoured to prove that the whole profit of a textile factory, running 12 hours a day, was derived from the last hour's work, and he was strongly supported in Parliament by many of the members. In 1844 Mr. Milner Gibson maintained the doctrine to be 'sound and indisputable'; and the leaders of the Manchester School, Bright, Hume, and Cobden, opposed the interference of the Government as certain to bring ruin upon manufacture.[1] In 1847 the celebrated Ten Hours Bill was passed, which restricted the hours of work of women and young persons to 60 per week, and fixed the legal working day from 5.30 a.m. to 8.30 p.m. No legislation at that time or subsequently was made to control men's hours of work, but in textile and other industries which were run by men and women working conjointly, it meant that the men generally kept the same hours as the women. In 1850 and 1851 legislation provided that women and children were to work only between 6 a.m. and 6 p.m., i.e., $10\frac{1}{2}$ hours work and $1\frac{1}{2}$ hours for meals, and were not to work after 2 p.m. on Saturday. Bleaching, dyeing, and lace manufacture were subjected to similar restrictions by the Acts of 1860 and 1862. A few years later night work in bake-houses was prohibited to young persons under 18, and the manufacture of earthenware, machinery, cartridges and matches was legally controlled, as were iron and copper works, glass works, printing and book-binding shops.

In spite of all this legislation, many industries are still uncontrolled, and it is said[2] that "the state of the sweated trades in 1912 is closely parallel to that of the Lancashire cotton mills in 1802." Other countries have always lagged behind England in industrial legislation, for France did not begin to legislate for the workers till the late forties, Switzerland following in the seventies, Austria, Holland, and Germany in the next two decades, and Italy at the close of the century[3]. In

[1] Cf. Josephine Goldmark. "Fatigue and Efficiency," p. 124. New York, 1913.
[2] Op. cit., p. 122.
[3] Op. cit., p. 7.

the United States of America the legislative protection of working children was mooted as early as 1825, but the first law applying to adult women was not passed till 1874.

Statistical information relating to excessive hours of work is not readily obtainable in this country, but the 1910 Census Reports of the United States (Vol. X) afford striking evidence that in America many of the most important industries still, at that date, exacted far too long hours from their employees.

WEEKLY HOURS OF WORK IN THE UNITED STATES (1910).

Industry.	Total employees in 1909.	Percentage of employees working every week for			
		60 hours.	Between 60 and 72 hours.	72 hours or more.	60 hours or more.
Cotton	378,880	31.4	17.1	0.1	48.6
Hosiery & Knitted Goods	129,275	38.6	0	3.8	42.4
Woollen Goods	168,722	26.8	0.6	0	27.4
Silk	99,037	13.0	0	0	13.0
Blast Furnaces	38,429	3.0	10.6	85.9	99.5
Steel Wks.& Rolling Mills	240,076	34.2	12.6	21.8	68.6
Slaughtering	89,728	72.1	.7	.6	73.4
Ice	16,114	12.5	12.2	65.4	90.1
Canning and Preserving.	59,968	71.5	4.8	4.2	80.5
Lumber	695,019	67.5	13.1	.3	80.9
Gas	37,215	15.6	15.5	57.4	88.5
Steam Laundries ...	109,474	33.7	.5	.1	34.3
Boots and Shoes ...	198,297	14.7	0	0	14.7
Paper and Wood Pulp ...	75,978	30.2	19.6	21.6	71.4
Printing and Publishing.	258,434	4.2	.2	.1	4.5
Brick and Tile	76,528	66.1	2.6	.6	69.3

This abbreviated Table shows that in many industries the great majority of the employees regularly worked for 60 hours or more per week, and in a few instances the majority worked 72 hours or more per week. The blast furnace men worked the longest hours of all, for 86 per cent. of them put in 72 hours or more. In fact 63 per cent. of them were on a 12-hour day for seven days a week, (i.e., an 84 hour week), as the iron smelting process is necessarily a continuous one. In this country, until 1919, there were likewise a good many blast furnace men on a 12-hour day, but in my experience they did not put in more than $10\frac{1}{2}$ hours of actual work, and usually a good deal less.[1] Still, their hours were undoubtedly excessive, and the almost universal adoption of the 8-hour shift in the

[1] Cf. Report No. 5 of Industrial Fatigue Research Board, 1920.

iron and steel trade, which came into force early in 1919, was a long-deferred act of justice.

We shall see that the effect of a reduction of hours upon output follows on the lines laid down in the previous Chapter. Reductions from 10 or 11 hours a day down to 8 or 9 hours vary very greatly in their effects in different industries, according as they are dependent chiefly on human labour, or upon machinery. Hence it will be convenient to classify and describe the chief industries about which we have information under three main headings, viz., those dependent chiefly on human labour, those dependent on human labour and machinery conjointly, and those dependent chiefly on machinery.

INDUSTRIES DEPENDENT CHIEFLY ON HUMAN LABOUR

COAL MINING.—The most important industry coming under the category of industries dependent chiefly on human labour is coal mining. In this country all but about 10 per cent. of the coal is cut by hand, though in the United States the proportion of machine-cut coal is much larger. In fact, the total amount mined by machine is nearly ten times greater than in Great Britain.[1]

There are no accurate statistics available showing the effect of reduction in hours of work on coal output in this country, as there has been no well defined reduction of working hours until July, 1919, when the 7-hour day was substituted for the 8-hour day. It is too early as yet to say what the effect of this change upon output will be, but in any case it will be impossible to determine what allowance should be made for the alteration of wage scale which was made simultaneously with the reduction of hours. The wages were raised sharply, and it is well known that such an increase may produce a fall in output,[2] which might neutralise some or all of the improvement due to shortened hours of work.

In the United States the hours of work in the four leading Eastern coal States were reduced from 10 hours a day to 9 or 8 hours in 1897. The output figures in most of the States are difficult to interpret owing to the gradual increase in the proportion of coal cut by machine, but in one of them, Illinois, the amount so cut was nearly steady during the statistical period quoted.[3] In the first three years of this period the

[1] Cf. Sir R. Redmayne's Evidence before the Coal Commission. 1919.
[2] Cf. Chapter VIII., p. 151.
[3] Final Report of U.S. Industrial Commission, Vol. XIX., 1902. For this summary, and for several of those quoted in this chapter, I am greatly indebted to "The Case for the Shorter Work Day," by F. Frankfurter and J. Goldmark. National Consumers' League. New York, 1915.

miners were on a 10-hour day, and in the last three, on an
8-hour day. In October, 1897, they changed over from one
system to the other, so it is best to ignore this year, but the
other data show that the average output of coal in short tons
per man per day was 17 per cent. greater when the shorter
hours were worked. Also the men worked on an average for
198 days a year as against 184 days, so their total yearly output
was no less than 26 per cent. greater. This improvement is
ascribed solely to the increased energy and promptness of the
workmen who were stimulated "to do a good, honest 8 hours'
work," but it is probable that there were some improvements
of plant, which may have accounted for a share of it.

OUTPUT OF BITUMINOUS COAL, ILLINOIS

Year		Average days worked per year		Average output in short tons		Percentage of coal cut by machine
1894	⎫	183	⎫	2.5	⎫	?
1895	⎬ 10-hr. day	182	⎬ 184	2.6	⎬ 2.7	?
1896	⎭	186	⎭	3.0	⎭	19.6
1897	... ...	186		3.4		19.7
1898	⎫	175	⎫	3.2	⎫	18.4
1899	⎬ 8-hr. day	206	⎬ 198	3.2	⎬ 3.2	24.9
1900	⎭	214	⎭	3.1	⎭	19.7

There is no evidence to show what would have been the effect
on the coal output if the hours of work had been reduced still
further, but if a reduction of hours from 10 to 8 produced an
improvement of something like 26 per cent., it seems highly
probable that the miners could have maintained their output
in a 7-hour day, and perhaps even in a 6-hour day. The
diminution of absenteeism above noted would presumably have
been still more marked, if the working day had been shorter.
There was plenty of room for improvement, as the men
averaged only 198 days' work a year, though in other industries
the workers generally average about 300 days. In this country
the time lost by the miners is, or was, much smaller, for it
averaged 10.7, 10.3, 9.9, 9.7, 8.9, and 11.0 per cent. respectively in the years 1913 to 1918.

GRANITE CUTTING—The work of cutting granite is done
chiefly by hand labour, and it requires a good deal of intelligence as well as muscle. A granite-cutting firm in the United

States[1] kept accurate records of the work done by each granite cutter from 1880 onwards, showing the time taken over the work, the wages paid, and so on, and they were able to compare the output of the men at the time they were on a working day of 10 hours, with what they subsequently accomplished, under identically the same conditions, in 9 and then in 8 hours. They found that the men accomplished more in 9 hours than in 10 hours, and considerably more in 8 hours, but actual figures are not quoted. The president of the Company believed that any good granite cutter could do just as much work in 7 hours, or even in 6 hours, as he did in 8, but he does not appear to have put his surmise to a practical test.

To sum up, it appears that in both the hand-labour industries referred to the output was considerably greater in an 8-hour day than in a 10-hour day, and it seems probable that as good an output would be attained in 7 hours as in 8 hours. It is possible that almost as good an output would be reached in 6 hours, but there is no direct evidence to support this suggestion.

INDUSTRIES DEPENDENT MORE OR LESS EQUALLY ON HUMAN LABOUR AND ON MACHINERY

MANUFACTURE OF OPTICAL INSTRUMENTS.—The results obtained by Abbé[2] at the Zeiss Optical Works should have been described partly in the previous section and partly in the present one, but it is more convenient to take them together. They show the effect of reducing the hours of work from 9 to 8 a day, and they relate to twelve different groups of piece-workers, numbering 233 men in all. All these men were steady workers, who had lost less than 300 hours during the year from sickness and other causes. They had been in the employ of the firm four years or more, and were over twenty-two years of age. Their output was estimated from their earnings for the last year of the 9-hour system (April, 1899, to March, 1900), and for the first year of the 8-hour system (April, 1900, to March, 1901). The hourly output of all the workers increased considerably in consequence of the reduction of hours, and their percentage increase is recorded in the Table.

---

[1] U.S. Congress, Senate Document, No. 1,124, 1913. Cf. " The Shorter Working Day." p. 690.
[2] Abbé. Gesammelte Abhandlungen, Vol. 3. 1906.

OUTPUT OF OPTICAL INSTRUMENT WORKERS

Occupation.		Number of persons.	Per cent. increase in hourly output during 8-hour day.	
Hand work	Lens-setters	21	16.6	
	Microscope Grinders ...	20	9.4	
	Grinders and Centerers...	59	16.7	
	Workers in adjusting room	22	17.1	16.0
	Polishers and Lacquerers	17	17.7	
	Engravers	5	19.3	
	Moulders	6	14.9	
Part hand and part machine work	Case Makers	6	12.7	
	Workers in mounting room	20	17.9	17.0
	Carpenters	15	20.3	
Machine work	Machine Grinders ...	19	18.8	
	Men Turning and Milling	23	18.1	18.4

It will be seen that on an average the output of the men engaged entirely on hand work increased 16.0 per cent. That of men engaged on work which was done partly by machine, but chiefly by hand, increased 17.0 per cent., and that of men entirely on machine work increased 18.4 per cent. Hence there was most improvement in the machine workers, but the difference is too small to be significant. In any case we must conclude that in highly skilled work, such as the manufacture of optical instruments, the hand worker is not able to speed up his output any more than men employed on lathes and grinding machines.

The hourly earnings of all the men, taken as a group, showed an increase of 16.2 per cent., and their total earnings, after allowance for the shorter hours worked, showed an increase of 3.3 per cent. The improvement of output was practically uninfluenced by the age of the men, being 18, 17, 15, 16, and 17 per cent. respectively in men aged 22-25, 25-30, 30-35, 35-40, and over 40.

ENGINEERING.—Several careful comparisons of output have been made at engineering works. The first relates to the Scotia Engine Works, Sunderland,[1] where the men changed from a 54 hour week to a 48 hour week. When on the longer day, they started work at 6.0 a.m. and continued till 8.30, when they had a break, but they were found to miss so many of these early morning 'quarters' that it was decided to start

[1] Cf. "A Shorter Working Day," by R. A. Hadfield and H. de B. Gibbins. London, 1892.

E

them at 7.30 a.m., and have only one break in the working day instead of two. The hours of work were thereby reduced to 48 a week, *i.e.*, to 8¾ hours for four days a week, 8½ hours on another day, and 4½ hours on Saturdays. The labour cost of the engines was taken out in detail under the two systems of hours, and it was found that in the six months after the reduction of hours the cost of the engines was rather decreased than increased. It had previously been found that a reduction of hours from ten to nine a day likewise caused no fall of output, so that the output in the 8-hour day was if anything greater than in a 10-hour day. Under the shorter system of hours the men lost much less time, and were in better physical condition.

Again, the hours of work at Hadfield's Steel Foundry Co. were reduced from 9½ to 9 a day (*i.e.*, from 54 to 51 a week), and the reduced hours did not add to the cost of production, so far as could be ascertained. However, alterations of method and of organisation prevented a very exact comparison.

The best known experiment at Engineering Works, viz., the adoption of the 48 hour week at the Salford Iron Works, Manchester, was mentioned in the previous Chapter, so it need not be described again. The practical application of the results of the experiment to other industries may now be referred to. Sir William Mather laid them before various Government Departments, and in consequence the hours of labour of 43,000 workers in Government factories and workshops were, in 1894, reduced to 48 hours a week. The 18,600 workers in the ordnance factories, and the departments of ordnance stores, army clothing, inspection, and small arms inspection, had their working week shortened by 5¾ hours, and it was subsequently stated[1] that the output was not diminished. The men on piece work earned as much as before, and those on a time rate, who were paid as much for 48 hours' work as for 54 hours, maintained their output likewise.

BOOT AND SHOE MANUFACTURE.—A detailed inquiry into this industry in the United States has recently been made by the 'National Industrial Conference Board.'[2] This is an association of employers, who sent schedules of inquiry to a large number of manufacturers, and made numerous personal visits. They obtained information from 190 establishments, representing 98,000 employees, and the opinions expressed are of considerable value if due allowance be made for two facts. Firstly, that they represent the view of employers, who would, as a rule, be very cautious in risking a fall of output by reducing

[1] British Board of Trade Labour Gazette, July, 1905.
[2] Report No. 7 of Nat. Industrial Conference Board, Boston, Mass., 1918.

hours of work. Secondly, that when hours of work were shortened, many or most employers compared the output in the few months *immediately* after the change with the output just before it, instead of waiting six months or so in order that true equilibrium between output and shortened hours might be attained.

Of the 190 factories, 77 reported their experience of reduced hours of work. The average hours before reduction were 56.4 per week, and after it 52.2, or 4.2 hours less. In 27 factories the reduction of hours was distributed evenly over the week, and it was found that output was maintained in 15, and reduced in 12. On the other hand, in the 50 factories in which the reduction of hours was effected by introducing a Saturday half-holiday, output was maintained only in 9, and was reduced in 41. This striking difference in the proportions of factories showing maintained output, viz., 56 per cent. and 18 per cent. respectively, seems to show that the immediate and direct effect of a Saturday half-holiday is unfavourable to output, whatever it may be in the long run.

More than two-thirds of the employees were on piece rates, and it was found in several factories that on reduction of hours the output of the piece-workers was maintained, but not that of the time workers. The effect on output varied a good deal in different operations, as can be gathered from the accompanying Table, which shows the output of piece-workers at one factory for the last two months of 1916, when a 54 hour week was worked, and for the first three months of 1917, when a $49\frac{1}{2}$ hour week was worked. It will be seen that output went up in one operation, and was maintained in two of them, but in three others it fell almost in proportion to the reduction of hours (viz., 8.3 per cent.).

OUTPUT OF BOOT AND SHOE OPERATIVES

Operation.	Average number of operatives.		Percentage change of output.
	54-hour week.	$49\frac{1}{2}$-hour week.	
Upper cutting	40	38	− 7.3
Sole cutting	19	19	− 8.6
Stitching	102	104	0
Stock fitting	26	26	− 7.0
Lasting	51	49	0
Making	48	48	− 2.4
Finishing	26	24	+ 1.6
Packing	43	45	− 5.2

There can be little doubt that if the output of these workers had been determined for a longer period under the shorter hours, a much more favourable result would have been observed. The manager at one factory said that "if hours of work are reduced gradually, it is possible for any well conducted boot and shoe establishment to secure maximum production in 50 or even 48 hours per week." It is true that the general conclusion of the Conference Board is against this view, for they stated that whilst a 54 hour week is long enough to maintain a maximum production, and a 52 hour week is long enough in some factories, "a 48 hour week will not maintain production at a maximum under present conditions." However, they thought that "a 50 hour week may be feasible for a limited number of establishments."

The experience of this country is much more limited, but such as is available supports the 48 hour week, or even a shorter working time. Thus in 1917 a boot and shoe firm at Rossendale reduced hours from $55\frac{1}{2}$ to 48 a week, and in 1918 to $46\frac{1}{2}$ hours.[1] It was found that output was maintained during the 48 hour week, and it was fairly well maintained even in the $46\frac{1}{2}$ hour week. A free cup of tea was provided at 10 a.m. and 3 p.m., a break of 7 minutes being allowed to the workers who were seated, and it is probable that this concession helped appreciably to stimulate production.

The work of boot and shoe making is for the most part done with machinery, but the speed of production is mainly dependent on the dexterity of the operative. It is essentially 'hand-time' work, not 'machine-time' work. For instance, in the operation of a clicking machine, which cuts out the various parts of the upper leather, a good deal of time is spent in carefully arranging the leather so as to insure economical and accurate cutting, whereas the machine operation of actual cutting is almost instantaneous. Again, in lasting the operative must manipulate the shoe during the entire process.[2] The heavier work is done by men, and the lighter work by women. Of the employees under investigation in the United States, 65 per cent. were men, 33 per cent. women, and 2 per cent. boys and girls.

MANUFACTURE OF CHEMICALS.—A striking experience of the effects of a considerable reduction of hours was obtained at the Engis Chemical Works near Liège.[3] The work of the men consisted in the reduction of zinc blende by roasting it in ovens,

---

[1] Report of Chief Inspector of Factories, 1918, p. 9.
[2] Cf. Report No. 7 of Nat. Industrial Conference Board, p. 5, and Report No. 10 of the Industrial Fatigue Research Board, p. 11, 1920.
[3] Cf. Goldmark. " Fatigue and Efficiency," 1913, p. 144.

and the conversion of the liberated gases into sulphuric acid. Productivity was estimated exactly by weighing the ore roasted. At first the men were on two 12 hour shifts per 24 hours and they put in 10 hours of actual work ; but their physical debility increased so alarmingly owing to the severity of their work, that in spite of their bitter opposition—for they feared a reduction of earnings—it was decided to change to a three shift system.

The men now put in $7\frac{1}{2}$ hours of actual work, or $22\frac{1}{2}$ hours out of each 24 instead of 20 hours as before. Fromont, the engineer and manager in charge, found that the output gradually increased, and in less than six months the men were producing as much in $7\frac{1}{2}$ hours as they had previously turned out in 10. Hence the total output of the factory was increased by 50 per cent., though all the conditions of production, other than the hours of work, were unchanged. The health of the men greatly improved, and they showed a new spirit of self-respect.

This instance of chemical manufacture is classified under the heading of industries dependent on human labour and machinery conjointly, as human labour was necessary for charging and emptying the ovens, but the rate of roasting, i.e., the mechanical part of the process, could not be much accelerated.

Another industry which may conveniently be grouped under chemical manufature is soap making, for the essential processes are chemical in nature. The only evidence I have met with relates to a large soap factory where the hours were reduced from 53 a week to $48\frac{2}{3}$, and then to 44.[1] Output was maintained under the shorter hours, but in the case of the machine workers it was necessary to speed up the machines. However, the fatigue of the work was diminished, and the time keeping was greatly improved.

Another industry coming under the heading of human and mechanical labour may be briefly described here. It concerns the manufacture of insulating apparatus. A manufacturer[2] reduced the hours of work in one department from 8 to 7, in spite of the objections of the men, who thought that their earnings would be diminished. However, after a few days they found that they could produce as much as before, but it appears probable that with these hours they reached their limit of speed.

Taking together the industries which have been included in the human and mechanical group, I think we may conclude that with them an eight hour day, or a 48 hour week, yields as good an output, or nearly as good a one, as any longer number

---

[1] Report of Chief Inspector of Factories, 1918, p. 10.
[2] Reports of Factory and Mines Inspectors for 1905, Vol. I., Prussia. Berlin, 1906.

of hours.   It seems probable, in the light of what was observed in the boot and shoe industry, that a 44 hour week, with a half-holiday on Saturday, would not yield as good an output as an eight hour day spread evenly over the whole week.

It appears unlikely that a seven hour day would yield as good an output as an eight hour day in most of the industries referred to, in spite of the direct evidence, just quoted, of the success of such reduced hours in one manufacture.

INDUSTRIES DEPENDENT CHIEFLY ON MACHINERY

The most important group of industries falling in this class are the textile industries.   The majority of the processes involved are dependent chiefly on machinery, though in some of them, such as weaving, the human element plays a more considerable part.   In *spinning,* for instance, a single operative tends the frames on both sides of a passage, and sometimes has to take care of as many as 1,000 spindles.   The spinner has to join together the ends of any yarns which become broken, but the work is not continuous, and there is occasional opportunity for sitting down.   The spindles are rotated at a fixed speed, sometimes more than 10,000 times per minute, and the spinner has no control over the speed of the machinery. The average time lost from breakage of yarn is said to represent probably less than 1 per cent. of the total spindle time, and except for loss of time in replacing the full bobbins by empty ones (doffing), in breakdowns and accidents, the only condition which interferes with the maximum production of a spindle is breakage of the yarn.   Even the temporary absence of the worker does not affect the output of most cotton machinery, unless there is a breakdown.   Indeed, automatic looms are sometimes run without attendance during the midday dinner interval and for a period after the closing hour.   If the yarn breaks or runs out, the loom automatically stops.[1]

In *carding* the work is likewise almost entirely a machine process.   The carding machines have cylindrical rolls covered with wire teeth which clean and straighten the staple and remove much of the short cotton fibre.

In *weaving* the threads of the warp are alternately raised and lowered, and an automatic shuttle, containing filling thread, shoots backwards and forwards between them.   Meanwhile the reed moves forward, pressing each weft thread into place so as to make a close fabric   The work of the weaver consists in mending broken threads, and in non-automatic looms he has likewise to refill the shuttles with bobbins, draw filling yarn

[1] Report No. 4 of Nat. Industrial Conference Board, Boston, Mass., 1918.

through the eye of the shuttles, and replace them in the looms. Looms which automatically perform the last three operations are rapidly coming into general use, and a single weaver may tend twenty such looms. The work of weaving is exacting, as it is very noisy and it requires constant attention, though the weavers have occasional opportunity of sitting down.[1]

COTTON MANUFACTURE.—In the United States the National Industrial Conference Board have recently collected evidence by the previously mentioned method of questioning manufacturers.[2] Of the mills situated in the Northern States concerning which useful information was obtained, 70 (employing 49,000 workers) have had their hours of work reduced within recent years. The average reduction of hours was from 57.2 a week to 54.4, or 2.8 hours. Only in six factories, employing 11 per cent. of the total workers, was the output said to be maintained when hours were reduced, and in two of them the reduction was only from 55 to 54 hours a week. In the remaining factories output was reduced, and in most cases the reduction was said to be about proportional to the reduction of hours. Thus in 12 factories a reduction of hours from 56 to 54 (= 3.6 per cent.), produced an average reduction of 3.3 per cent. in output. In three factories a reduction of hours from 58 to 55 (= 5.2 per cent.) produced an average reduction of 4.2 per cent. in output. About 55 per cent. of all the workers were on piece rates, and in a few instances piece-workers practically maintained production when the hours of work were reduced, although the output of the whole factory showed a falling off.

Of twenty mills in the Southern States, which employed 15,000 workers, 4 reported a maintenance of output when hours of work were reduced, and 16 reported a decrease of output. The average hours before reduction were 64.7, and after it, 59.7, or 5.0 hours less, and the conclusion is drawn that hours in excess of 60 per week do not necessarily yield a larger output than 60 hours.

In Great Britain the available evidence is rather more favourable to the shorter working week. The Chief Inspector of Factories reports (1918) that when the hours were reduced from 55 to 49½ a week, the output in some factories (at Macclesfield) showed a reduction proportionate to the reduction of hours, but at other factories it was proportionate to about half the reduction of hours, and in one factory there was practically no reduction in the output of the looms, as the weavers kept so much better time. In Scottish factories, again, a similar

[1] Cf. op. cit.   [2] Cf. op. cit.

reduction of hours caused an almost proportionate fall of output in carding, but a smaller fall in spinning, whilst in ' finishing ' there was no reduction of output.   Time keeping was said to have improved greatly.   At a Yorkshire thread works a reduction of hours from $55\frac{1}{2}$ to $49\frac{1}{2}$ at first caused output to fall in proportion to the reduction of hours, but it gradually rose during the four subsequent years till it reached the old maximum, which has been maintained ever since.   No information is vouchsafed as to the cause of the very gradual rise of output, other than that time-keeping improved.   Presumably there were some improvements of plant and organisation, and some speeding up of machinery.

In Wales a firm reduced the hours of work from $52\frac{1}{2}$ to $49\frac{1}{2}$, and the result was so satisfactory in the weaving department that the system was extended to the spinning department. The day workers were told that if the output was not reduced their wages would be maintained at the old level.   Time keeping immediately improved, and it is considered that the output is now fully up to that previously obtained.   On the other hand the Belfast employers were universally of the opinion that the output of the spinners will be reduced almost *pro rata* to the reduction of hours, though the weavers are in very different case.

It is to be remembered that the whole of the above-recorded evidence relating to cotton manufacture was furnished by employers, and in many instances it is undoubtedly vitiated by the fact that the comparison of output was made immediately after and before the change of hours.   The only independent investigation known to me is that by C. D. Wright,[1] who found that when the hours of work in Massachusetts were reduced to ten a day, the output calculated either per man, or per loom, or per spindle, was as great as in other States where eleven hours or more were worked per day.

The varying importance of the human and the mechanical factors in the different processes of cotton manufacture is well shown by the recent observations of Wyatt[2] on the individual differences in the output of cotton workers. The piece rate payments (usually for an eight week period) were taken as a measure of output, for the standard piece rates are accurately adjusted to the character of the work; but in order to reduce to a minimum the error which would arise from inaccurate fixation of piece rates, the figures used for comparison purposes were obtained, so far as possible, under approximately similar

[1] Report of Massachusetts Bureau of Statistics of Labour, 1881, p. 457. Cf. Goldmark, " Fatigue and Efficiency," 1913, p. 131.
[2] Report No. 7 of Industrial Fatigue Research Board, 1920.

conditions of work. A summary of the results obtained is recorded in the Table. It will be seen that the output of 423 men engaged in fancy weaving was determined, and that if the

VARIATIONS IN WAGES IN DIFFERENT PROCESSES COMPARED

Process.	No. of Cases.	Wage.			Mean Variation
		Maximum.	Minimum.	Average.	
Weaving (Fancy)	423	132	65	100	10.0
Winding ...	46	119	75	100	8.3
Weaving (Plain)	752	126	73	100	6.0
Slubbing ...	17	109	91	100	4.7
Drawing ...	22	108	89	100	4.0
Intermediate ...	15	108	94	100	3.2
Roving ...	27	109	92	100	2.9
Spinning (Ring)	51	109	92	100	2.0
Spinning (Mule)	32	107	91	100	1.9

average output is taken as 100, there was a variation of 132 to 65 in extreme cases. The mean variation of output was ascertained by calculating the mean of the differences between individual wages and the average wage. It amounted to 10.0 (*i.e.*, 10 per cent. on the average wage) in the weavers of fancy cloth, and 6.0 in the weavers of plain cloth, whilst it was 8.3 in the winders. In the cotton spinners, however, it was only 1.9 or 2.0, and the extreme variations of output observed ranged only from 109 to 91.

As Wyatt points out, these results suggest that as the human element is of such great importance in weaving and winding, it is in these processes, rather than in spinning, that efficiency may be increased and fatigue reduced by the elimination of waste in method and movement. It was found, for instance, that even in a cotton mill where an unusually large number of labour-saving devices were in use, the winders were engaged in actual winding for only half to two-thirds of the total working hours in which winding was possible.

WOOL AND SILK MANUFACTURE.—The National Industrial Conference Board came to almost the same conclusions with regard to wool manufacture as those arrived at for cotton manufacture.[1] This is what one would expect, as it is so largely dependent on machinery. The Board obtained information from 111 establishments, employing 71,600 workers. A reduction of hours from 57 to 54 a week almost always resulted

[1] Report No. 12 of Nat. Industrial Conference Board, 1918.

in a decreased output, for only 6 factories reported an increased output, and 7 factories a maintenance of output.

Silk manufacture stands on a somewhat different basis, as it is less mechanical than cotton and wool manufacture. Information was obtained by the Conference Board from 84 factories.[1] The hours of work had been reduced by 2 to 5 a week, and they are now 50 per week in two-thirds of the factories. Of 58 factories with a 50 hour week, 9 maintained the same output as was observed when longer hours were worked, and in two of them there was an increase of output. However, 19 factories reported a loss of output almost proportional to the reduction of hours, and 23 reported one somewhat less than proportional.

It is concluded that maximum production in the silk industry is reached somewhere between the 50 and the 54 hour week, or in a nine hour day. On the other hand cotton and wool manufacture, taken as a whole, appear to need 56 to 60 hours, or a ten hour day, to yield the greatest output possible. Weaving, considered apart from the other operations in cotton and wool manufacture, is probably best suited by an $8\frac{1}{2}$ to 9 hour day.

IRON AND STEEL MANUFACTURE.—In many of the processes of iron and steel manufacture, the rate of production is so greatly limited on the mechanical side that it is best to include them in the category of industries dependent chiefly on machinery. Most of the processes are continuous, so that it is necessary to run them by means of two 12 hour shifts, or three 8 hour shifts. A few years ago it was the usual custom to observe the longer shifts, but the shorter ones gradually came into operation, and in the spring of 1919 they were adopted almost universally by arrangement between employers and employees. Hence it is possible to ascertain the effect on output of this clear-cut reduction of working hours, and I have recently collected statistical information on the subject.[2]

Cast iron is produced entirely by smelting iron ore in blast furnaces with coke (or coal), and limestone. The furnaces are run continuously for years, and are almost always kept nearly full of material. Hence it is usually impossible for the men to increase production by charging the furnaces at a greater speed. Absolutely reliable evidence as to the effect of reduction of hours on output is not obtainable, because the conditions of production, such as quality of iron ore and of coke, vary somewhat from time to time, but the available data show that, practically speaking, the reduction of hours caused no improve-

[1] Report No. 16 of Nat. Industrial Conference Board, 1919.
[2] Report No. 5 of Industrial Fatigue Research Board, 1920.

ment of output. It is true that in some instances it was possible to carry on the work with a smaller number of men per shift when shorter shifts were in force, as the men worked harder and kept better time. For instance, at one works the 18 furnace fillers on 12 hour shifts were replaced by 21 men on 8 hour shifts, and not by 27 men. In another instance the 90 men of various categories required to run six small furnaces, were replaced by 102 men and not by 135 men. However, in the larger blast furnace plants, run chiefly by mechanical methods, little if any saving in man power was possible.

Wrought iron, as distinct from cast iron, is produced entirely by hand labour, though the men (the puddlers) are limited by the custom of working a practically fixed number of 'heats' per day. When they went on to an 8 hour day the number of heats to be worked by the three shifts instead of the two shifts was increased by 15 per cent., as the result of an arrangement with the employers, but there is reason for thinking that they could be increased by 23 per cent. if the men desired it. Even in this case the output per 8 hour shift would be 18 per cent. less than in the previous 12 hour shifts.

Steel production by the open-hearth process was investigated at one works over a four year period, during the first two years of which the men were on 12 hour shifts, and in the last two, on 8 hour shifts. The conditions of production were the same throughout, and the total weekly hours of work were likewise the same. It was found that the average output of the ten 40 ton furnaces in the last two years was only 7 per cent. greater than in the first two years, but we saw in a previous Chapter[1] that when the outputs were plotted out month by month it took over a year for the maximum value to be attained, and this value was 18 per cent. greater than that observed immediately before the reduction of hours.

At another works the output of six 30 ton furnaces was ascertained for one year of 12 hour shifts, and for the succeeding year of 8 hour shifts, and the average output was found to increase only 2 per cent.

The production of steel by the Bessemer process was not investigated under the 8 hour shift system, but it is unlikely that the rate of production will be much greater than that observed in 12 hour shifts; *i.e.,* the output per shift will fall considerably.

Rolling Mill production was investigated at a number of steel works, but at most of them the 8 hour shifts have been adopted so recently that output data were not available. At one works

[1] Chapter III., p. 36.

the output was ascertained for a year under the 12 hour shift system, and for the subsequent two years of 8 hour shifts. In the first year of the 8 hour shifts it was .5 per cent. *less* than before, and in the next year, 2.0 per cent. more, but as the weekly hours of actual work were 2.1 per cent. longer under the 8 hour shift system, the hourly output was slightly diminished. The conditions of production were unaltered, the same products (tin plate bars) being rolled throughout from 14 cwt. steel ingots.

At another works the output was ascertained for 8½ months when the men averaged 61⅓ hours of work per week, and for the subsequent 15½ months when they averaged 57 hours. In spite of the shorter hours of work, the total output increased 16 per cent., but this was due in large part to the advent of a new manager, who introduced improvements of organisation. However, the plant was unaltered, so it is evident that in some instances there is a possibility of improvement, apart from alteration of the mechanical conditions of production. A more striking instance has recently been recorded in open-hearth steel production.[1] The interest of the men in their work was stimulated by the formation of a Men's Society. Lectures relative to steel production were given by workmen and by managers, new methods of working were suggested and discussed, and if, after due trial, they were found to be of practical value, they were permanently adopted. In consequence of these improvements, and of the extra keenness of the men in working the furnaces, the output of the hand-charged furnaces gradually increased to about 70 per cent. above its previous value. This striking result, be it noted, was achieved without any substantial alterations of plant whatever. Moreover, the casting of the steel was so much improved that the net final yield of saleable steel was raised some 30 per cent. above the old level.

OVERTIME IN VARIOUS INDUSTRIES

There is undoubtedly a good deal of overtime worked in certain industries in this country, but I have discovered very little exact statistical information about it. Overtime in the munition industry has been referred to in a previous Chapter, though it was not designated as such. In the iron and steel industry there appeared to be very little of it except at week ends, when some of the men had to work a double shift in order that the shifts might change over. Under the 8 hour shift system this means a 16 hour shift for most of the men engaged on blast furnaces. Under the 12 hour system it implied a 24

[1] "The Organiser," November, 1919.

hour shift, but in practice this terribly long shift was often avoided.[1] At one works substitutes were obtained in two cases out of three, so the men worked a 24 hour shift only once in six weeks. At another works one of the changing shifts worked for 21 hours, and the other, for 15 hours. There can be little doubt that even a 16 hour shift imposes a considerable strain on men engaged in the heavy work of charging blast furnaces by hand, and it would be much better if two of the changing shifts worked 12 hours each, instead of 16 and 8 hours respectively.

In the shipbuilding industry overtime is very prevalent, and some of it is unavoidable, owing to the urgency of repairs at short notice. The men engaged on the ironwork of the ship, viz., the riveters, platers, caulkers, and drillers, work overtime with considerable frequency. Most of the data I obtained[2] were at shipyards engaged on government naval work during war time, but the peace-time data likewise show a large amount

PERCENTAGES OF RIVETERS WORKING VARIOUS HOURS PER WEEK

Weekly hours worked	Sep.–Oct. 1914	Jul.–Aug. 1915	Dec.–Jan. 1916	Aug.–Sep. 1917	Mar.–Apr. 1918	Mean 1914–1918	Mean relative hourly output
26¾ or less..	13	11	12	6	6	10	102.5
27 to 35¾ ..	15	8	13	9	12	11	102.7
36 to 44¾ ..	13	15	17	19	26	18	100.8
45 to 53¾ ..	22	26	19	27	37	24	98.4
54 to 62¾ ..	20	29	25	28	21	25	95.5
63 or more	17	11	14	11	8	12	97.6
No. of data	613	303	479	642	462	2499	100.0

of overtime. Until 1919 the normal hours worked were 54 per week, or 9¾ hours from Monday to Friday, and 5¼ hours on Saturday. When overtime is worked, it is customary to put in an extra spell of 3½ hours. At one very large yard I sampled the hours of work of about 100 hand-riveters over periods of 3 to 6 weeks on five different occasions, and in the Table are shown the frequencies with which various times were worked. The data are fairly consistent, though they are spread over five years, and relate to all seasons of the year. It will be seen

[1] Report No. 5 of Industrial Fatigue Research Board, 1920.
[2] These data are here published for the first time.

that on an average 10 per cent. of the riveters put in 26¾ hours
or less of work per week (*i.e.*, less than 3 days), and 11 per
cent. of them 27 to 35¾ hours (3 to 4 days) : 25 per cent. of them
put in 54 to 62¾ hours, and 12 per cent. of them put in 63 hours
or more, but none of them exceeded 71¾ hours.   Hence one
may say that about a quarter of all the riveters put in some
overtime, but it is evident that this overtime could have easily
been reduced if only the men, taken as a whole, had been better
time keepers.   There was no excuse for such a large proportion
of them losing two, three or four whole days of work a week,
and if they had averaged a five day week almost the whole of
the overtime could have been avoided.

In the last column of the Table is recorded the mean relative
hourly output of the men (as judged by piece payments) when
they were working the various hours, and it will be seen that
when they were on overtime their rate of riveting was only
about 6 per cent. less than when they were working two or
three days a week.   It must be remembered, however, that the
men were practically never on overtime for a number of consecutive weeks, so that their output was not to any great extent
subject to the effects of cumulative fatigue.

In another large yard engaged on naval construction the
hours worked by about 100 riveters in the spring of 1918 were
ascertained.   During the 9 week period investigated, 80 per
cent. of the weekly hours worked were 54 or less, 12 per cent.
of them ranged from 54¼ to 59¾ hours : 5 per cent. from 60 to
69¾ hours : 2 per cent. from 70 to 79¾ hours, and 1 per cent.
of them amounted to 80 hours or more.   Hence the number of
men on overtime was not quite so great as in the other yard,
but the overtime hours worked were somewhat longer.

The hours of work of groups of about 100 caulkers (who
make the riveted plates water tight) and 200 drillers (who drill
the rivet holes), were ascertained on two occasions, and it will
be seen from the Table that the caulkers worked less overtime
than the riveters, whilst the drillers worked considerably more
overtime.   In fact, nearly half of the drillers put in a certain
amount of overtime, and 2 or 3 per cent. of them worked for
72 hours and upwards per week.   During these hours the men
employed (who may have been quicker workers than the
average, though there is no information on this point) fully
maintained the usual rate of drilling, but the caulkers showed a
distinct deterioration when working overtime.   At another
yard, which was situated in a different area of the United
Kingdom, the drillers were at one period kept on overtime for
a number of consecutive weeks.   Between January 13 and
April 13, 1915, a group of 60 men averaged 66.0 hours of work

per week, and in one week they averaged 84 hours. Yet their hourly output during the 13 weeks was the same as in the subsequent 9 months, when they averaged 51.9 hours of work per week. Hence drilling, which is a comparatively simple operation, does not easily induce a state of over-fatigue.

PERCENTAGE OF CAULKERS AND DRILLERS WORKING VARIOUS HOURS PER WEEK

Weekly hours worked.	Caulkers.			Drillers.		
	Aug.-Sept. 1915.	April, 1918.	Mean relative hourly output.	Aug., 1915.	Dec., 1918.	Mean relative hourly output.
26¾ or less ...	5	14	107.4	5	5	96.4
27 to 35¾ ...	8	21	99.6	8	10	99.8
36 to 44¾ ...	20	26	101.8	16	18	99.0
45 to 53¾ ...	35	22	101.1	24	25	99.5
54 to 62¾ ...	22	10	97.6	31	31	99.4
63 to 71¾ ...	10	7	92.5	13	9	100.9
72 or more ...	0	0	—	3	2	105.0
Number of data	678	639	—	725	795	—

In order to obtain a measure of overtime hours during pre-war conditions, I averaged the hours of work in the two years immediately before the war (viz., June, 1912, to June, 1914), of the iron workers employed at the shipyard concerning which the above tabular information is recorded. There were on an average 82 squads of riveters (four men per squad), and they put in 35.3 hours of normal time per week out of their nominal 54 hours, and 4.6 hours extra of overtime per week. The platers, 100 in number, put in 42.2 hours of normal time, and 4.7 hours of overtime per week. The caulkers, 60 in number, put in 36.3 hours of normal time, and 4.4 hours of overtime, whilst the drillers, 130 in number, put in 42.9 hours of normal time, and 6.2 hours of overtime. Hence the *average* overtime was not excessive, especially considering the bad time keeping of the men in general, but it naturally tended to come in rushes. In one period of three months, for instance, the drillers averaged 49½ hours of normal time, and 18 hours of overtime; *i.e.*, 67½ hours per week altogether.

In the United States many flagrant instances of overtime

have been recorded.[1] Women are sometimes kept in canneries till after midnight, and in 1907 some of the women were employed in one New York cannery for 85 hours a week. In California, labellers and stampers who handled the tinned fruit after it was hermetically sealed and no longer perishable, were known to work as much as 12 to 15 hours a day, or 72 to 98 hours a week. Again, in one fruiting establishment in New York girls were employed once and sometimes twice a week, during a period of 16 to 26 weeks, for $20\frac{1}{4}$, $22\frac{1}{2}$, and $24\frac{1}{4}$ consecutive hours. In a number of box factories, employing over 1,000 workers altogether, the average duration of overtime was fifteen weeks a year, and in one factory it was continued for more than nine months in the year.

[1] Cf. Goldmark. " Fatigue and Efficiency," pp. 85 and 185.

CHAPTER V

THE SIX HOUR DAY AND MULTIPLE SHIFTS

Contents

Introduction

In fixing the most suitable length for the working day, two opposing factors have to be reconciled, the economic factor and the human factor. We saw in the last Chapter that from the point of view of maximum output, the hours of work of the manual labourer, such as the coal miner, who was not limited by machinery, might be fixed at about 7 per day. The hours of work of the labourer, such as the engineer, who was largely dependent on machinery as well as on his manual skill and strength, might be fixed at 8 per day, whilst those of the operative who was dependent chiefly on machinery, such as the textile worker, might be fixed at 9 or 10 per day. These figures do not represent the economic optimum, for that can be attained only by running the mechanical plant continuously. Still, the cost of the plant and the overhead charges in general vary enormously in different industries, and we are bound to take them into consideration. It is well known that they are particularly high in textile industries, and especially in spinning, where a single operative may control a thousand spindles. On the other hand they are very low indeed in industries such as stone quarrying, which require very little plant, and are mainly dependent on human labour. Hence it is of special importance that industries which require an expensive plant should be kept running as many hours as possible per week.

On the other hand the industrial worker is expecting, nay demanding, that his hours of work be diminished rather than increased, and there can be no doubt that in the future he will expect them in many cases to be reduced below their present figure, which in most industries is about 8 hours per day, or 44 to 48 hours per week. The tendency of production is more and more towards standardisation and specialisation, to the production of articles in bulk by repetition work, and this mass production inevitably increases the monotony of industry.

MONOTONY OF INDUSTRIAL WORK

Monotony is stated by the Health of Munition Workers Committee[1] to be "analogous to, if it does not represent, a fatigue process in unrecognised nerve centres." Münsterberg[2] states that "the problem of monotony comes very near to the question of fatigue. But we must see clearly that these two questions are not identical." Speaking from personal experience, which is almost limited to mental work, a feeling of monotony is sometimes quite independent of fatigue. For instance, when engaged in looking over a large number of examination papers I often experienced a feeling of irritation at the wearisomeness of the task when I first started work in the morning, but this soon wore off, and was replaced by a feeling of apathy. Later on in the day, when mental fatigue gradually developed, the feeling of wearisomeness began to return with increasing force. The mere thought of a monotonous task ahead of one may induce a feeling of monotony, so that this sensation is psychical, and is not necessarily bound up with fatigue of nerve centres.

Whatever the definition of monotony adopted, and whatever the intimate nature of the phenomenon, everyone from personal experience is to some extent familiar with the sensation, whether the monotony be caused by mental work or by physical work, or by a combination of the two. A few concrete instances will help to illustrate the monotony of much of our modern industrial work. In shoe making, for instance, a well-made shoe has to pass through the hands of about 100 workers, and about 60 different kinds of shoe-making machinery are employed on it. These figures do not include the work of the stitching room, where a separate group of workers are employed on specially constructed sewing machines. The men who work the trimming machines have to handle 5,200 shoes a day, whilst women operating eye-letting machines can finish 2,000 pairs of ladies shoes in a day.[3] There is no variety, for a given individual seldom performs more than a single operation. So great is the monotony that "the mere changing from coarse to

[1] Memo. No. 7 of Health of Munition Workers Committee, 1916.
[2] Münsterberg. "Psychology and Industrial Efficiency," p. 192. New York, 1913.
[3] Cf. Goldmark. "Industrial Fatigue and Efficiency," p. 64. 1913.

fine leather is a source of pleasure to the operative."[1] However, in the stitching rooms there are frequent pauses which break "the wearisome monotony of making the same number of stitches hour after hour on bits of leather identically the same." The monotonous character of the work often causes the workers to throw up their job and try for other work under different conditions. "Of 300 women interviewed, nearly 80 gave as a reason for leaving a job, ' tired of it.' On the whole, however, there is as much variety in the shoe work as in the clothing trades, and far more than in the textile mills or in the majority of other factory trades."[2]

Münsterberg[3] has made a careful study of monotony in the industrial worker, and he has become more and more convinced that the scientific psychologist should not endorse the popular view of the monotony of industrial labour. He believes that the feeling of monotony depends much less upon the particular kind of work performed than upon the disposition of the individual performing it. He says that in every large factory which he has visited he has tried to discover the particular job which from the point of view of the outsider presents itself as the most tiresome possible. When he found it, he had a full frank talk with the man or woman who performed it. To take a few chance illustrations :—In an electrical factory he observed a woman whose sole task was to pack incandescent lamps in tissue paper. She wrapped up 13,000 lamps a day, and she had been doing it for 12 years. The packing of each lamp demanded about 20 finger movements, and 25 lamps, which filled a box, took her 42 seconds to pack. She stated that she found the work really interesting. She constantly felt an inner tension, thinking how many boxes she would be able to fill before the next pause. There was continuous variation, as she sometimes grasped the lamp or paper in a different way, and sometimes the packing did not run smoothly.

Another instance relates to a man who was feeding an automatic machine with metal strips in which holes were punched. He had to push the strips slowly forward, and if the strip did not reach exactly the right place he could stop the machine by a lever. He made about 34,000 uniform movements daily, and had been doing that for the past 14 years. He found the work interesting and stimulating. At first he sometimes found it quite fatiguing, but later he began to like it more and more. This was not because the work had slowly become

---

[1] Report No. 7 of National Industrial Conference Board, 1918.
[2] "The Boot and Shoe Industry in Massachusetts as a Vocation for Women." U.S. Bureau of Labour, 1915.
[3] *Op. cit.*

automatic, allowing him to turn his thoughts to other matters, as he still had to concentrate his mind entirely on the work in hand.

Much of the work on automatic machines is so easily and mechanically performed as to require very little attention on the part of the operatives, but this quality is not always considered to be in its disfavour. Some women prefer such work, as they are free all day to think of anything that takes their fancy. In fact, women as a whole are much more immune from the feeling of monotony than are men, and very few men will consent to perform work of a very monotonous type for any length of time.

In contrast to the instances above quoted, Münsterberg points out that many industrial workers who seemed to have really interesting and varied activities complained bitterly of their monotonous, tiresome factory labour. The same phenomenon is observed in intellectual work. Some school teachers constantly complain that it is intolerably monotonous to go on teaching immature children the rudiments of knowledge, whilst other teachers with exactly the same task find their work a constant source of inspiration. Some actors feel it a torture to play the same rôle every evening for a few weeks, whilst others repeat their parts with undiminished interest many hundred times.

Granted the truth of Münsterberg's contention that some industrial workers do not mind the monotony of their task, the fact remains that many of them, perhaps the majority, do mind it, and they are likely to mind it more in the future than in the past, owing to the almost unavoidable increase of repetition work. How can the effects of monotony be best neutralised? It seems probable that it will be difficult in many cases, if not impossible, to introduce much variety of occupation. The alternative, is to reduce the number of hours worked per day, and to institute shorter work spells with longer rest pauses between them. It seems likely that the majority of industrial workers would prefer to do six hours of monotonous work each day rather than eight hours of somewhat varied work, and the question to be decided is whether a six hour day is economically possible.

THE SIX HOUR DAY

During the last two or three years the possibility of a six hour day in industry has been frequently discussed by Lord Leverhulme.[1] On his scheme, as first propounded, the workers

[1] Leverhulme. "The Six-Hour Day," London, 1918. Also articles in "The Organiser," April and May, 1918; "The Glasgow Herald," March 29, 1919.

were to start one shift at 7 a.m., and continue till 1.30 p.m., with half-an-hour's break in the morning for breakfast. A second shift was then to come on and continue till 8 p.m., with half-an-hour's break in the afternoon for tea. If each shift worked six days a week they would put in 36 hours' work, whilst the machinery would be running for 72 hours a week, instead of the 44 or 48 hours experienced under the usual eight-hour day. In fact it would be possible to organise three, or four, shifts per 24 hours, and thereby keep the machinery running for a maximum of 132 hours per week. The overhead charges for machinery and factory buildings are so great that in some industries they represent 90 per cent. of the cost of production, apart from the cost of raw materials, whilst the human labour engaged represents less than 10 per cent. of the cost. Supposing that the overhead charges represented only 50 per cent. of the cost of production, it would still be possible to pay the workers as much for a six-hour day as for an eight-hour day, even if their hourly rate of production remained the same, because these overhead charges vary very little with the time for which the machinery is run. It is true that the machinery wears out faster when run more continuously, but in most industries it becomes obsolete long before it is worn out, and is replaced by improved machinery. Lord Leverhulme believes that the worker will be able to produce as much in six hours as in eight hours, and consequently it will be possible to pay him bigger wages than under the old system.

It is hoped that this multiple shift scheme will shortly be introduced at the soap works, Port Sunlight, but it is found desirable to modify in some particulars the six hour a day system above described. The morning shift is to come on at 7 a.m., and work till 8.45. Then, after 15 minutes for light refreshment—which is provided free by the management—it is to work till 1.15 p.m. Hence this shift will work six hours, and it will continue to do so for six days a week. The afternoon shift, however, will work only five days, in order that the workers may have a free Saturday afternoon. They will work from 1.15 till 4.45 p.m., and after half-an-hour's interval for food, will continue till 9 p.m.; i.e., they will work for 7¼ hours daily, except that on Friday they will stop at 8.45 p.m., so as to keep their weekly total of hours down to 36.

A certain number of continuous shifts have to be worked in the industry, and as it is inconvenient that a man's household should be disturbed between 10 p.m. and 6 a.m., it has been arranged that for one week in four the men should put in eight hours' work by night, whilst for the other three weeks they have to put in only 5⅓ hours by day. They thereby work for

36 hours a week on an average. In other words, the nominal six-hour day amounts in practice to anything between $5\frac{1}{3}$ hours and 8 hours.

In his scheme Lord Leverhulme lays special stress on the principle of multiple shifts, which would enable the machinery to be run for a greater number of hours per week, but such shifts are not necessarily bound up with a 6-hour working day. They could be, and have been, adopted in conjunction with a 7-hour, 8-hour, and 9-hour day. We are told that in Germany[1] a number of manufacturers have adopted the plan of running their factories with two shifts of men in order to utilise the plant to the full extent, and the factories are closed only from midnight to 6 a.m. Some of the coal mines in this country work two 7-hour shifts, and almost all the iron and steel works now work three 8-hour shifts. Hence, before deciding on the applicability of the 6-hour day scheme to industries in general, we have to determine the effects of the two independent features contained in it, viz., (a) the influence on output of working for 6 hours a day instead of for 8 hours ; (b) the possibility of a general adoption of multiple shifts.

The effect of a 6-hour day on output can roughly be deduced from the data described in the last Chapter. It can be gathered that the substitution of such a day for the usual 8-hour day would probably induce only a small reduction of total output in industries such as coal mining, where the getting of coal is for the most part independent of machinery. In industries such as engineering and shoe manufacture, which are dependent more or less equally on machinery and on human labour, the 6-hour day would almost certainly produce a fall of output, but it might be proportional to not more than half the reduction of hours. In industries such as the textile trades, which are chiefly dependent on machinery, the 6-hour day would reduce output to very little more than three-fourths that yielded by an 8-hour day.

In one industry alone, so far as I am aware, has a 6-hour day been actually tried so far. This is in the tinplate industry already referred to. The millmen, who are rolling red-hot tinplate bars into thin sheets of steel, are not infrequently put temporarily on to 6-hour or even to 4-hour shifts, instead of their usual 8-hour shifts. At one factory[2] I obtained the output every week for 18 consecutive months of 6-hour shifts, and in another, for 10 months of 4-hour shifts. I found that on an average the hourly output of the men on 6-hour shifts was only 10 per cent. greater than that observed when they were on

[1] Reports of the Factory and Mine Inspectors for 1905, Vol. I., Prussia. Berlin, 1906.
[2] Report No. 1 of Industrial Fatigue Research Board, 1919.

8-hour shifts, whilst it was 11.5 per cent. greater when they were on 4-hour shifts. The men were on piece rates, and were almost certainly doing their best, but they were quite unable to speed up their rate of production sufficiently to maintain their total output when the hours of work were reduced.

It is to be remembered, again, that on Lord Leverhulme's scheme the day shifts are to work for 6 hours and $7\frac{1}{4}$ hours in alternate weeks, whilst the continuous workers put in $5\frac{1}{3}$ or 8 hours. If the conclusions arrived at in Chapter III are valid, it follows that the speed of production of the workers would tend to become adapted, not to an average 6-hour day, but to the longer hours worked; i.e., it would be but little greater than that observed in a steady $7\frac{1}{4}$ or 8-hour day.

THE OBJECTIONS TO DOUBLE SHIFTS

The adoption of double shifts raises several questions. Firstly, are the workers themselves prepared to accept them? They accepted double and treble shifts whole-heartedly in munition industries during the war, but admittedly the conditions were abnormal, and many expedients for increasing output were temporarily adopted, under the express proviso that they would not be continued in peace times. Trade unionists, as a whole, appear to object strongly to a double shift system on the ground that their Union meetings would be interfered with.[1] Such meetings are usually held in the evenings, after the day's work is over, and if the second shift worked on till 9 p.m., it would not be possible for the workers in this shift to attend. The difficulty does not seem a very serious one, as by hypothesis Saturday evening would be free for everybody, and if another evening meeting were required it would be possible to release the afternoon shift an hour earlier than usual, and make up for the lost time by adding on 15 minutes extra per shift to the other four working days.

Again, it is argued that a double shift system would upset home life, for where a family has members working on different shifts, meal times and bed times would spread themselves over day and night. We have seen that on Lord Leverhulme's scheme even continuous shift workers leave their household undisturbed from about 9.45 p.m. to 6.15 a.m., whilst double shift workers would reach home by about 9.15 p.m. and would not leave earlier than about 6.45 a.m. They would have so much additional leisure from their work that they could assist considerably in household duties, and thereby more than make up for the extra labour caused by the double shifts.

[1] Cf. "The Organiser," February, 1918.

Again, it is contended that the education of the workers would be greatly upset by the double shift system, in that it would be impossible to get the same people together for two consecutive weeks. It is true that the classes would have to be run double, but so far from interfering with education, Lord Leverhulme's scheme offers it very strong support. In fact, one of the salient points of the whole system is that the worker should use his extra leisure from industrial work in self improvement. It is proposed that (1) From the age of fourteen every boy and girl should receive for the next four years educational and physical training for two hours a day. (2) From eighteen to twenty-four years of age they should have technical and other education and further physical training for two hours a day, whilst the women should learn sick nursing and household management. (3) From twenty-four to thirty years of age two hours a day should be devoted by the men to military and physical training, and to training in the duties of citizenship.

After the age of thirty the workers would be allowed to spend their extra leisure as they pleased. Some of them would waste it, but probably the majority would take up gardening, further education, or other useful work, as they would have acquired the habit of regular work from their previous training.

We may conclude, therefore, that there is no inherent objection to a two-shift system, provided that the second shift is finished by 9 p.m., or in exceptional circumstances, by 10 p.m. It does not follow, however, that if a two-shift system is adopted a 6-hour day must be observed at the same time. It would be quite easy to squeeze in two seven-hour shifts, if one shift worked from 6 a.m. till 1.30 p.m., and the other shift from 1.30 p.m. till 9 p.m., each shift having a half-hour break in the middle for food. As the afternoon shift would not want to work on Saturday afternoon, it might be thought necessary to make up for the lost time by working till 10 p.m. on the five nights per week, but this hour would be inconveniently late, especially for women, so it would be better frankly to forego the sixth shift, and get the workers to put in 42 hours and 35 hours in alternate weeks. The plant would thereby be kept running for 77 hours per week instead of the usual 44 or 48 hours.

It does not follow that two 7-hour shifts are necessary or even desirable, but their adoption might serve as a half way house between the present 8-hour system and the 6-hour day recommended by Lord Leverhulme. Supposing this country were competing in the open markets of the world against another country which had adopted two 7 or 7½-hour shifts per day, it might find that it was impossible, on economic grounds, to reduce working hours to six a day.

The recently published report of the Chief Inspector of Factories[1] describes the existence of multiple shifts in a number of industries. The employment of women and young persons on multiple shifts is prohibited by the Factory Acts, but the Secretary of State for the Home Office has obtained powers to authorise such shifts in suitable cases, and at the end of May, 1920, the two shift method of working was in operation in about 200 works employing in aggregate 15,000 women and 3,400 young persons. The double shifts were found to secure greatly increased production at a lower cost, and to prevent unemployment. In an iron foundry, where, during the war, the work had been carried on in an unsatisfactory manner by men, the employment of women on two short shifts proved to be such a success that the managing director desired to continue it permanently. In a glass works it was arranged that the women should work the two day shifts, whilst boys worked the third (night) shift.

The usual hours worked on the two shift system, where women were concerned, were from 6 to 2, and 2 to 10 p.m., but in some instances they were from 6 to 1.30 and 1.30 to 9 p.m., or from 6 to 1, and 1 to 8 p.m. Men worked at a wire drawing mill from 6 to 2.30, and from 2.30 till midnight. In certain lace factories alternating spells of work and rest were tried. One set of workers came on at 4.30 a.m., and continued till 9 a.m.; then a second set worked from 9 till 2 p.m. The first set resumed work and continued from 2 till 7 p.m., when the second set came on and worked from 7 till midnight. By this means each set of workers put in a $9\frac{1}{2}$ or 10-hour day, and the machinery was kept running for $19\frac{1}{2}$ hours a day.

The question of a third or fourth shift in each 24 hours stands on quite a different footing from that of a second shift. It means the definite adoption of night work, and this is a problem which requires detailed discussion.

A COMPARISON OF NIGHT WORK AND DAY WORK

The question of night work has to be considered in several aspects besides the material one of its economic value. As has been mentioned in a previous Chapter, night work in cotton factories for persons under 21 was prohibited by law as long ago as 1831, and in 1844 night work was prohibited for all women. Other countries were slow to follow our example, but in 1864 one of the Swiss cantons made a similar prohibition

[1] Annual Report of Chief Inspector of Factories for 1919, p. 91.

as regards women, and in 1877 a Swiss Federal law was passed to the same effect. In 1906 representatives of 14 European powers met at Berne, and agreed to prohibit the industrial night work of all women. A minimum period of eleven consecutive hours was set for the duration of the night rest, to include the time between 10 p.m. and 5 a.m. in all cases.[1] One or two minor exceptions were permitted, but by 1910 twelve out of the fourteen participating States had ratified the convention, and a number of British and French colonies did so as well. The one striking exception was the United States of America, where several States specifically legalised night work for women, and 40 States legalised it for women employed in laundries, canneries, restaurants, candy stores, and telephone exchanges.[2]

The basic objection to night work depends on the fact that it is unphysiological. Man is a diurnal animal, and not a nocturnal one. It is found that during each 24 hours his body temperature shows a regular rhythm. It rises to a maximum at about 6 p.m., and falls gradually to a minimum at about 5 a.m., which is one to two degrees Fahrenheit below the maximum. This variation is dependent on his bodily habits, for if he completely reverses them, his temperature cycle is reversed too. For instance, Linhard[3] found that during the long polar night the temperature varied as usual during the periods of artificial light, which corresponded to day time, and of darkness, which corresponded to night, but if these periods were reversed the temperature rhythm was reversed too. If, on the other hand, the reversal of habits is not complete, the temperature rhythm may be modified, but it is not completely changed. A night watchman with five years of uninterrupted night service to his credit, still showed a minimum temperature in the early morning.[4]

The average industrial worker finds it impossible to effect a genuine reversal of habits when he is on night shift. The other members of his household are almost always day workers, and his sleep is disturbed by them. Besides being broken and irregular it often is quite insufficient in duration. The New York State Factory Investigating Commission found in one large factory that the married women on night shift obtained only about 4½ hours' sleep by day. Night work tends to press much more hardly on women than on men, as they have more household duties to attend to, and these duties can be carried

[1] Cf. Goldmark. " Fatigue and Efficiency," 1913, p. 260, et seq.
[2] Cf. Goldmark, loc. cit.
[3] Linhard. Skand. Arch. f. Physiol., 8, p. 85, 1898.
[4] Benedict. American Journal Physiology, XI., p. 143, 1904.

out only in the day time. Again, night work implies deprivation from the health-giving effects of exposure to sunlight. The night workers at an Italian spinning mill showed marked signs of anæmia and debility, and it is generally agreed by physicians and factory inspectors that women habitually employed at night suffer from symptoms betokening lowered vitality, such as anæmia, headache and loss of appetite.[1]

Night work for women is objectionable also on moral and social grounds. This is especially the case if the women are not working a full night shift, but have to return home after midnight, e.g., from the night-restaurants where they are employed. Again, shocking abuses were occasionally found in connection with night work by the agents of a Government Committee who were investigating the cotton mills of North Carolina.[2]

In many industries there is necessarily a certain amount of night work, and in a few of them, such as in the iron, steel and tinplate trades, night work is unavoidable, as most of the operations are continuous. The men employed change shifts every week, so they used to be on night shift in alternate weeks when 12-hour shifts were in vogue, whereas now, under the 8-hour régime, they have to go on night shift for one week in three. This alternation of shifts is advantageous in that the men still live for half or two-thirds of their time under normal physiological conditions. On the other hand their habits of life are completely upset once a week and it might be maintained that if they kept continuously to night work they would settle down to a steady mode of existence with a consequent reversal of their physiological state. They might, in fact, become nocturnal animals instead of diurnal animals.

In support of the principle of continuous night shifts it was known that many hospital nurses worked continuously at night work, even for years on end, and they apparently experienced no harm from it. On the other hand it was realised that these nurses did get uninterrupted sleep by day, which the majority of industrial workers could never do. Hence it followed that though everyone is agreed that night work should be avoided when possible, there was great difference of opinion as to what system of night shifts should be adopted during the war, when night work was essential for hundreds of thousands of women, as well as of men. The available plant was so limited that in order to obtain a maximum output it was necessary to run it almost continuously, even though the productivity of the night

[1] Report No. 2 of New York State Factory Investigating Commission, 1913.
[2] Cf. Goldmark, op. cit., p. 274.

shifts might prove greatly inferior to that of the day shifts. In order to obtain decisive evidence on the points at issue, the Health of Munition Workers Committee asked four investigators to collect information independently at a number of munition factories, and they combined this information in a report on 'The Comparative Efficiencies of Day and Night Work in Munition Factories.'[1] As the evidence is rather voluminous, it will be possible to quote only samples of it.

THE OUTPUT OF MUNITION WORKERS BY NIGHT AND BY DAY

With regard to women on "discontinuous work,"—i.e., alternating periods of day and night work—in which the day and night shifts changed over every week, Capt. M. Greenwood observed the output of 50 girls engaged on cartridge case operations over a 12-week period. They worked 52 hours by day and 55 by night, and their mean hourly output by night was 1 per cent. greater than that by day. In another group of 339 girls, who were observed over a 5-week period, the output was 1.3 per cent. less by night than by day. I myself observed the output of 112 women on various cartridge case operations for 22 weeks, there being 29 women on 'second draw,' 39 on 'head-trimming,' 24 on 'second cut-off,' and 20 on 'reamering.' The mean hourly output by night was +2, −2, 0, and +2 per cent. above or below that experienced by day in the respective groups of women. This meant practical equality of output for the whole group of women concerned, though they put in 55.9 hours per week of actual work by night, as compared with 51.7 hours per week by day. Mr. P. S. Florence observed the output of 171 women engaged on cartridge operations for two weeks, and he found that the night output was 5 per cent. less than the day output.

Other observations were made by Capt. Greenwood and Mr. S. H. Burchell on the output of women engaged in manufacturing 9.2 inch shells, and fuses, and the Committee came to the conclusion that the evidence, taken as a whole, showed that in monotonous processes which call for little physical effort, such as those concerned with cartridge making, discontinuous night work in women gives an output which rarely falls more than 10 per cent. below, and usually closely approximates closely to, that obtained by day.

In men, Capt. Greenwood and Mr. Burchell studied the output of 138 workers engaged on 6-inch shells, for a period of 12 weeks. The men worked for four consecutive weeks on day or night shift before changing over, and their mean output by

[1] Interim Report of Health of Munition Workers Committee, 1917, p. 26.

night was 3.8 per cent. greater than by day. Another group of 53 men, engaged on 9.2 inch shells, was observed for three months. These men changed over week by week, and their output by night was found to be .6 per cent. greater than by day. Arguing from these and other data the Committee concluded that in men "there is no significant difference between the rate of output in night and day shifts managed on the discontinuous system." I might add, incidentally, that I came to the same conclusion as regards the men employed in an entirely different industry. I observed the rate with which shifts of 12 men each hand-charged a blast furnace for a five month period (August-December, 1918). The men were on 8-hour shifts, and they changed over every week. I found that the rate of charging was exactly the same in the morning and the afternoon shifts, and was .8 per cent. less in the night shift.[1]

Passing on to the consideration of continuous night shift work, I found that when the output of groups of about 20 men engaged on various 3-inch shrapnel shell operations by night was compared with that of similar groups by day for 7 to 14 weeks, there was usually a distinct defect in the night shift output. Men engaged in 'boring the powder chamber' had a 10 per cent. smaller output, those engaged in 'finishing, turning and forming' the shells had 2 per cent. less output, and those engaged in 'rough turning' them, 6 per cent. less. Women yielded corresponding results. Capt. Greenwood observed the output of about 90 day workers and 30 night workers engaged on cartridge case operations for 11 weeks in the winter and 9 weeks in the summer, and of 130 day workers and 56 night workers engaged for similar periods on bullet operations. In the winter, the night workers in the case department showed a 17 per cent. inferiority of output, and those in the bullet department, a 10 per cent. inferiority. In the summer the inferiority was 12 per cent. in the former department, whilst in the latter department output was the same by night as by day.

Arguing from these and other data, the Committee concluded that both with men and with women "continuous night work is productive of definitely less output than is the discontinuous system."

It is to be borne in mind that the practical equality of output observed during night and day work conducted on the discontinuous system does not necessarily prove that night work does no harm. The evil effects of night work may gradually accumulate towards the end of the week, and exert their adverse influence on output, not only then, but during the first few days of the subsequent day shift week. Thereby the favourable

[1] Report No. 5 of Industrial Fatigue Research Board, 1920, p. 10.

influence of day shift work would be neutralised. Definite proof that the harmful influence of night work does continue into the day shift week was obtained by me at a fuse factory where the employees worked alternate fortnights of day and night shift.[1]

Operation and Workers.	Relative Hourly Output.			
	Day Shift.		Night Shift.	
	1st week.	2nd week.	1st week.	2nd week.
21 to 70 women turning fuse bodies for periods aggregating 8 months	138	142	154	150
		140		152
90 men sizing fuse bodies for 7 months	138	143	145	143
		140		144
26 to 42 women milling a screw thread for 2 months	134	133	132	134
		134		133
15 to 24 youths boring top caps for 11 months	128	127	131	123
		128		127
Mean	134	136	140	137
		135		139

The mean results summarised in this Table show that in two of the operations the night shift output was larger than the day shift output, but this was due to a better arrangement of work spells and breaks.[2] Making allowance for this factor, it will be seen that as a rule the output was distinctly lower in the second week of the night shift fortnight than in the first week, whilst on the other hand it was distinctly higher in the second week of the day shift fortnight than in the first week. In other words, the harmful effect of night shift work persisted to a considerable degree for the first week of the day shift fortnight, whilst the good effect of day shift work persisted for the first week of the night shift fortnight.

Again, I ascertained[3] the output of 72 women on various cartridge case operations (a) for six weeks when they were on

[1] Cf. Final Report of Health of Munition Workers Committee, p. 156, 1918.
[2] Cf. Chapter VI., p. 102.
[3] Interim Report of Health of Munition Workers Committee, p. 33.

day and night shift in alternate weeks, (b) for the subsequent four weeks when they were on continuous day shift, and (c) for a further ten weeks when they reverted to the discontinuous shifts. I found that their hourly rate of output during the continuous day shift period, so far from being greater than that in the preceding and succeeding periods, was .9 per cent. less. When, on the other hand, I compared the output of 72 cartridge women who went on to night shift for a continuous period of five weeks with their output in the preceding and succeeding periods of discontinuous shifts, I found that it averaged 4.4 per cent. less. That is to say, continuous night work was definitely less advantageous than discontinuous day and night work, but continuous day work was not—to put it at its best—appreciably more advantageous. The explanation of this unexpected result may depend on the extreme monotony of cartridge case manufacture. Even a weekly change of shift may afford a welcome break in the conditions, although it is accompanied by disturbed and irregular sleep. The healthy worker who loses some sleep in her night-shift week can probably make up for the loss very speedily during her subsequent day-shift week, but naturally a fortnight of disturbed sleep would be much more trying, and would take longer to recover from.

The general conclusion to be drawn from observations on day and night workers, is that night work for women is only permissible in very exceptional circumstances, such as in war time, and should not be allowed in peace times, however much the economic value of a factory plant be increased by its more continuous running. The same objections do not apply to night work for men, though even in their case it should be adopted only exceptionally. The day and night shifts should change over once a week, and not at fortnightly or longer intervals.

The Hourly Output During Night Shift

The somewhat greater fatigue produced by night work than by day work is to some extent indicated by the variations of output experienced from hour to hour throughout the shifts. I ascertained the variations exhibited by the workers at a 6-inch shell factory over five consecutive nights and days in August, 1916, by taking power records. These records were corrected for the power required to drive the machinery, and the excess power values were averaged over hourly (or $\frac{3}{4}$ hour) periods.[1] They represent the approximate output of the whole factory, where there were in all 1,300 men and 700 women at work.

[1] Memo. No. 21 of Health of Munition Workers Committee, 1918, p. 13.

Half of them were on day shift and half on night shift, and they worked a 63 hour week in each case. The shifts started at 6 a.m. and 6 p.m., and the hours of work and meal breaks corresponded almost exactly.

From the curves reproduced in Fig. 16 it will be seen that in the first spell of work the night shift output was considerably

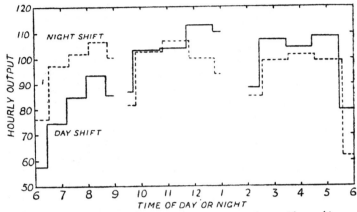

Fig. 16 — Output of 6 inch shell factory by day and by night.

greater than the day shift output. In fact it averaged 97.5 per cent. (per hour) on the mean hourly output of the whole night, whilst the day shift output averaged only 80 per cent. of the output of the whole day. As will be pointed out in the next Chapter, the low day shift output was due to the day shift operatives starting work without taking a substantial meal beforehand, whilst the night shift operatives did have a good meal. In the middle work spell the day shift output continued to rise, and reached a maximum, 13 per cent. above the average hourly output of the whole day, in the last full hour of work. Then it fell away slightly in the third work spell. The night shift output, on the other hand, reached its maximum, which was 6.7 per cent. above the average of the whole night, in the middle of the second work spell, and then fell away distinctly. In the third work spell the average night shift output was 6.7 per cent. *less* than that of the whole night, whilst the average day shift output was 1.1 per cent. *more* than that of the whole day.

These observations were repeated a year later, and, as before, the day shift output got to its maximum in the last full hour of the middle spell of work. The night shift output, however, got to its maximum more rapidly, for it reached it in the last full hour of the first work spell, and then declined. Power records obtained at another factory, where 9.2 inch shells were being manufactured, showed that in August, 1917, the day shift output got to its maximum in the middle of the third work spell, and then fell away, whilst the night shift output got to a maximum in the first hour of the second spell, and then showed a much more considerable fall.

Hence in both shell factories the hourly output of the night shift fell away more rapidly than that of the day shift. Presumably this was due in large part to the greater fatigue induced by night work, though it may have been in some degree owing to the usual nocturnal fall in the physiological activity of 'diurnal' men.

G

CHAPTER VI

WORK SPELLS AND REST PERIODS

CONTENTS

Introduction—Two-Break and One-Break Systems—The Adverse Effect of Five-Hour Work Spells—The Efficacy of brief Rest Periods—The Spontaneous Adoption of Rest Periods—The Influence of Rest Periods combined with other improved Conditions—Sunday Labour.

INTRODUCTION

After the weekly number of hours to be worked in an industry has been decided upon, there still remains the important question of the distribution of these hours through the week. For several reasons, to be referred to subsequently, it is universally agreed that so far as possible Sunday work should be completely avoided, hence it remains for us to determine how the hours should be apportioned to each of the six week days, and what alternating periods of work and rest should be adopted on each of these days.

If the working week be 54 hours, it would be simplest to assign 9 hours of work to each day, and if it be 48 hours, 8 hours of work to each day. If an immediate maximum output be the sole consideration, this even distribution of hours would probably be the best one, for we saw[1] that when the hours of work in American boot and shoe factories were reduced from 56.4 to 52.2 a week, the output was maintained in the majority of factories where the reduction of hours was distributed evenly over the week, but it was maintained only in 18 per cent. of the factories where the reduction was effected by introducing a Saturday half-holiday. In almost all industries in this country, however, it is the custom for the workers to have a Saturday half-holiday, and it is not at all likely that they would consent to forego it in the interests of improved output. If Saturday afternoon work were forced upon them against their wish, the psychological effect of compulsion would much more than neutralise the favourable effect of the even distribution of working hours through the week.

We saw in a previous Chapter[2] that the output on Saturday

---

[1] Cf. Chapter IV., p. 67. [2] Chapter II., p. 30.

mornings is sometimes poor, as the workers are disturbed by the half day, and the thoughts of their prospective week-end relaxation, so that the abolition of all Saturday work has been suggested. This scheme finds favour with some employers, as it enables them to shut down their factories from Friday evening till Monday morning, with a consequent saving of expense in running the furnaces and boilers for half a day. However, the plan does not appear to be very successful where it has been put into operation. At one large textile factory where it was tried for some time the output fell off so much that the firm adopted a 6-day week with an after breakfast start at 8 a.m. Notwithstanding the shorter weekly hours, the output increased again.[1] In the jute industry the 5-day week has been adopted more widely, but its effect on output is not recorded. When it is adopted, it is usually the custom to spread the weekly hours of work equally over the five days, so a 54-hour week would practically mean a $10\frac{3}{4}$ hour day, and a 48-hour week, a $9\frac{1}{2}$ hour day of work.

Though a free Saturday is a great boon to most women employed in industry, as it gives them time for household duties, it is not so desirable for men, unless they can devote part of the day to gardening or other useful work. A two day rest is not really necessary for recuperation from the effects of five days' labour, and the longer the week-end rest, the greater is the disinclination to start work again on the Monday morning. Again, a half-day's work on Saturday reduces the working time on other days by nearly an hour, and we saw in Chapter IV. that in most industries it is possible to work at a considerably greater speed in a 9-hour day than in a 10-hour day, or in an 8-hour day than in a 9-hour day. Hence a 5-day working week is not to be recommended either on theoretical or practical grounds.

Two-Break and One-Break Systems

The principle of a $5\frac{1}{2}$ day week of work being admitted, it follows that a 54-hour week implies $9\frac{3}{4}$ or 10 hours of work per day on five days a week, whilst a 48-hour week implies $8\frac{3}{4}$ hours a day. If an 8-hour day be desired, only 44 hours of work can conveniently be worked. How are the 8 to 10 hours of work best distributed over the day? There are two main schemes of distribution adopted in this country, the so-called 'two-break' system, and the 'one-break' system. On the two-break system the workers start at 6 a.m., or less frequently at

[1] Report of Chief Inspector of Factories, 1918, p. 12.

6.30 or 7 a.m., and work for about two hours, when they have a breakfast interval of half-an-hour. There is a dinner interval of an hour's duration from 12.30 to 1.30, or from 1 to 2, so that the working day is cut up into work spells of 2, 4, and 4 hours' duration, or sometimes of $2\frac{1}{2}$, $3\frac{1}{2}$, and 4 hours' duration. At many shipyards the hours of work were until recently from 6 to 9 a.m., 9.45 to 1 p.m., and 2 to 5.30 p.m., or the work spells came to 3, $3\frac{1}{4}$ and $3\frac{1}{2}$ hours. The essential point of the two-break system is a rest interval sometime between 8 and 9.30 a.m. The majority of the workers then partake of a substantial breakfast, as they have had little or no food before starting work at 6 a.m.

On the one-break system the workers start at 7, 7.30, or 8 a.m., and they have only a single break in the course of the day, viz., an hour for dinner. Hence if they are on a 10-hour day they usually work two 5-hour spells; if on a 9-hour day, two $4\frac{1}{2}$-hour spells, and if on an 8-hour day, two 4-hour spells, though sometimes the length of the spells differs by a quarter or half hour. The workers are supposed to have had a substantial breakfast before starting work, but they often get a cup of tea and a little food at about 9 a.m., whilst remaining at their work in the shops, and there is a tendency for some of them to take very little breakfast before starting work, and to rely on this chance of light refreshment for their bodily needs. Thereby they defeat the main advantage of the one-break system, which is *food before work*.

The importance of the one-break system in improving output during the first few hours of the working day, as compared with the two-break system which reduces output, can be established by direct measurement. At the fuse factory which has been mentioned in previous Chapters, the day shift workers were on a one-break system. They started work at 7 a.m., and continued till 12, or for five hours, and though most of them had a cup of tea at 9 a.m., they were not allowed to leave their machines. Probably, therefore, the great majority of the workers had had a good breakfast before leaving home. I compared[1] the output of seven sections of lathe workers (some 1,000 to 1,800 individuals), with that of the night shift workers on the same machines for three consecutive days and three consecutive nights in January and July, 1917. These night shift workers undoubtedly had a substantial meal before starting work, for they began work at 6.30 p.m., and did not get their first meal break till 10.30 p.m. In Fig. 17 is seen the relative hourly output of the day and night workers for the first $3\frac{1}{2}$ hours of

[1] Final Report of Health of Munition Workers Committee, 1918, p. 154.

their shifts, the average hourly output throughout the shift being taken as 100 in each case. It will be seen that output corresponded closely both in winter and summer, and on the whole the day shift operatives worked up their output rather more quickly than the night shift operatives.

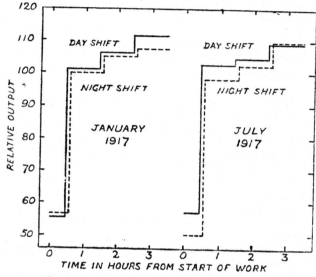

Fig. 17. Output at factory working on one-break system.

Very different is the comparison of day and night shift output shown by workers on the two-break system. In the last Chapter the output of the day and night shift workers at a 6-inch shell factory was recorded (Fig. 16), the operatives in each case working for $10\frac{1}{2}$ hours, and putting in a 3-hour spell when they came on to work (*i.e.*, 6 to 9 a.m., and 6 to 9 p.m.) We saw that the output of the day shift during this spell was much less than that of the night shift. In fact it averaged 18 per cent. less, whilst a year later, when another comparison was made, it was 7 per cent. less. It can be seen in Fig. 16 that for the first $2\frac{1}{4}$ hours after the meal break the day shift output corresponded closely with the night shift output, and there can be little doubt that the improvement was due to the stimulating influence of food, whilst the preceding defect of output was due chiefly to lack of food.

The better time-keeping observed under the one-break system than under the two-break system will be referred to in a subsequent Chapter.

THE ADVERSE EFFECT OF FIVE-HOUR WORK SPELLS

The chief objection to the adoption of a one-break system when a 10-hour or 9-hour day is being worked, depends on the length of the two spells. As the result of conversations with workers, and of my own limited experience of 5-hour spells in munition work, I am convinced that 5 hours of continuous work are too much for a man, and considerably too much for a woman. Even $4\frac{1}{2}$ hours are too much, and all work spells ought, if possible, to be reduced to four hours or less. Direct numerical proof of the evil of 5-hour work spells is difficult to get, but I obtained an indirect proof[1] which seems to me convincing.

It was pointed out in the last Chapter that when day and night shifts are changed over every week, the average hourly output of the two shifts is practically equal. As a mean of the eight sets of statistical data on women munition workers, and the three sets on men, which were obtained by Capt. Greenwood, Mr. P. S. Florence and myself, the output of the workers when on night shift proved to be only 1 per cent. less than when they were on day shift. However, in a fuse factory where the workers changed over once a fortnight instead of once a week, the night shift output was found to be distinctly *greater* than the day shift output, in spite of the undoubted fact that the less the frequency with which the shifts are changed, the greater the tendency of the night shift output to fall off. The explanation of this contradictory result lies in the better arrangement of work spells followed by the night shift operatives. They started at 6.30 p.m. and worked till 10.30, or for 4 hours. After an hour's interval for supper they worked a second spell of $3\frac{1}{2}$ hours, and then, after a half-an-hour for breakfast, they worked a third spell of 3 hours. That is to say, they put in $10\frac{1}{2}$ hours of labour instead of the 10 hours (*i.e.*, two 5-hour spells) worked by the day shift, but they worked their longest spell when they were fresh and vigorous, and their shortest spell when they were most fatigued.

The hourly output of the women engaged in turning fuse bodies was 9 per cent. greater by night than by day, whilst that of the men engaged in sizing fuse bodies was 3 per cent. greater. That is to say, the *active* workers were distinctly benefited by the shorter work spells and longer rest intervals. The workers engaged on semi-automatic machines, however (women milling a screw thread, and youths boring top caps), had in each case a 1 per cent. smaller output by night than by day, for their work caused them much less physical

---

[1] Cf. Final Report of Health of Munition Workers Committee, 1918, p. 156.

fatigue than was experienced by the active workers, and they would not be likely to feel the long 5-hour spells of the day shift so much.

How can 5-hour or 4½-hour work spells be avoided? The 9 or 10-hour day can be cut up into three work spells, as on the two-break system, provided that the first break does not come so early in the morning as to serve for a breakfast interval. If the workers come on at 8 a.m., and have their dinner hour from 12 to 1 p.m., they can put in the remaining five hours of a 9-hour work day in the following way :

8 to 12	1 to 3.45	4 to 6.15
4 hours	2¾ hours	2¼ hours

By this scheme they get a 15 minute interval for tea. This is too short if they have to go to a canteen for their meal, but it suffices if the tea is brought to them in the shops. If a 10-hour day is to be worked, the operatives ought to start by 7.30 a.m., but even then they do not get finished till 6.45 p.m. if they have 1¼ hours for meal breaks; or till 7 p.m., if they have 1½ hours, and this is too late for them to have a chance of doing much shopping after working hours. The true moral is that a 10-hour day should not be worked under any circumstances, but if it has been imposed, it would probably be better to revert to the 5-hour work spells, provided that each of them is broken by a 10 or 15 minute rest interval in the middle.

THE EFFICACY OF BRIEF PERIODS.

The method of cutting up long spells of work by brief rest intervals has frequently been adopted in recent years. The National Industrial Conference Board in America[1] made inquiries of a large number of employers in various industries, and they obtained replies from 104 who had experimented with rest periods. Only 15 of these employers had discontinued the rests for some or all of the employees affected, the usual reason given being that the employees were indifferent to the change, or that they did not improve their time keeping when it was adopted. The duration of the rest interval was 10 minutes in 36 per cent. of all the instances tabulated, 15 minutes in 35 per cent. of them, and 5 minutes in 18 per cent. of them. The other rest intervals tried varied between the extremes of 3 and 30 minutes.

The employers reported that the system of rest intervals diminished fatigue, sometimes to a marked extent. In some cases it saved time, as at a foundry where, previous to the

[1] Report No. 13, 1919.

introduction of a rest at 9.0 to 9.10 a.m., the men were observed nibbling food at almost any time between 8 and 11 a.m. Again, rest periods were introduced at a tobacco factory " on account of the tendency of part of the girls frequently to stop work and go to the rest room on one excuse or another." In a large minority of cases the employers reported that there was no perceptible difference in the amount of fatigue after rest periods were introduced, and some employers pointed out that in certain industries there was no need for them, as the character of the work inevitably admitted of frequent rests. In a machine-tool factory, for instance, it was stated by the manager that " the operator works intensely for a short period of time, making the set-up or putting a new piece in the machine, and then rests for a time while the machine does its work." Again, it was stated that in the various cotton mill operations the following amounts of the total working time were unoccupied, and might be spent in resting :

Twisting and weaving 10—20%
Carding 20—40%
Spinning 20—50%
Warping 40—60%

The employees generally appreciated the rest periods greatly. For instance, at a laundry five-minute rests were allowed at 2-hour intervals throughout day, but as an experiment they were temporarily abolished, with the result that " without exception the workers wished to have them retained—they were not nearly so tired." However, at a silk mill 80 per cent. of the piece-workers did not favour regular rest periods, on the ground that they involved a loss of earnings. At a hosiery factory the piece-workers, though at first they objected to losing the time involved in the rests, gradually came to understand that " a rest helps the production." At another factory " the tannery operatives, 90 per cent. of whom were piece-workers, were unanimously in favour of rest periods."

It was practically the universal custom to supplement the usual ventilation of the factories by opening windows and doors at the time of the rest pause, and when suitable rest room facilities were lacking, an effort was often made to induce employees to go into the open air. In some factories physical exercises, supervised by trained instructors, were introduced, but " the manner in which pauses are filled should obviously be dependent upon the character of the preceding work. Sedentary workers profit from change of position and move-ment ; those engaged in muscular work need opportunity to relax and rest."

The accurate estimation of the effect of brief rest periods on output is somewhat laborious, and I myself have attempted it only at one factory, where the women and girls concerned were employed on cartridge case and bullet operations.[1] The output of five groups of experienced workers, or 150 in all, was studied for 38 consecutive weeks, during the first 23 of which a two-break system was in vogue. The usual hours of work then followed were :

7 to 8.30	9 to 1	2 to 4.15	4.30 to 6 or 7
$1\frac{1}{2}$ hours	4 hours	$2\frac{1}{4}$ hours	$1\frac{1}{2}$ or $2\frac{1}{2}$ hours

In the latter half of the statistical period a one-break system was adopted, when the usual hours of work were :

7.30 to 10	10.15 to 12.30	1.30 to 4.15	4.30 to 6.30
$2\frac{1}{2}$ hours	$2\frac{1}{4}$ hours	$2\frac{3}{4}$ hours	2 hours

The operatives worked on day and night shift in alternate weeks, and the night shift hours during the two periods were the same as the day shift hours, with p.m. substituted for a.m., and *vice versa,* except that on Sunday night the full hours were worked whereas no work was done on Saturday afternoon. Under both systems of work a $\frac{1}{4}$-hour rest period was observed in the latter half of the day or night, but in the second system there was in addition a $\frac{1}{4}$-hour period in the first half of the day or night. Thereby the working hours were cut up into two nearly equal work spells of $2\frac{1}{4}$ or $2\frac{1}{2}$ hours' duration, and the long 4-hour spell previously worked was got rid of.

The hourly output remained very steady and consistent from week to week (Cf. Table V. in *op. cit.*), but it rose immediately after the adoption of the extra $\frac{1}{4}$-hour rest period, and showed an average improvement of 5 per cent. The average hours of actual work were 52.4 per week when the rest period was adopted, and 53.8 hours a week previous to its adoption, so that the total output showed a 2 per cent. increase. This was in spite of the fact that the $\frac{1}{4}$-hour rest period was reckoned as working time.

During the $\frac{1}{4}$-hour rest periods at the cartridge factory the machinery was stopped, and travelling canteens were brought round to the shops, at which the workers could purchase tea and light refreshments. As the result of repeated observation, I found that the average amount of working time lost on each occasion was between 20 and 25 minutes, but no doubt this interval could have been abbreviated if the management had insisted on it. At several other munition factories where travelling canteens were brought round, the machinery was not

[1] Final Report of Hours of Munition Workers Committee, 1918, p. 159.

stopped at all, and the working time lost was not more than five minutes. Such an interval is probably too short in most industries, and the 10 or 15 minutes usually adopted in the American factories is more suitable. However, no hard and fast rule can be laid down, as the frequency and duration of the rests should obviously vary with the character of the work done. At a certain factory, the character of which is not mentioned,[1] the workmen were found to produce 16 pieces per hour when allowed to work at their own pace. When they were made to work for 25 minutes and rest for 5 minutes alternately, they produced 18 pieces per hour. When they worked for 17 minutes and rested for 3 minutes they produced 22 pieces, and when they worked for 10 minutes and rested for 2 minutes they produced 25 pieces. Thus the amount of time taken in the form of rests was nearly constant in each case, as it ranged only from 15.0 per cent. to 16.7 per cent., but the short work periods followed by short rests gave a considerably better result than the long work periods followed by the long rests.

The employers reporting to the Industrial Conference Board gave instances in which the adoption of rest periods increased the output of dictaphone operators and clerical workers, of employees in a paper mill, in a corset factory, in a hosiery factory, in munition factories, and in other machine trades. In the accounting department of a printing establishment there was a very marked increase of accuracy, and in another establishment the quality of the proof-readers' work was improved. Only in one instance, that of a munition factory, was it held that rest periods actually decreased the total output. On the other hand an industrial specialist, speaking from his experience in German factories, claimed that "a shorter work day with more intensive work secured a greater output than a longer day with rest pauses." It should, however, be remembered that the average hours of work in Germany were considerably longer than in Great Britain or America.

Other evidence in favour of rest periods has been obtained by the U.S. Public Health Service.[2] A recess of ten minutes in each 5-hour spell of the 10-hour day was introduced at a munition factory, and in 11 out of the 12 operations studied it was found that the average daily output per worker increased after the recesses were put into effect. Increases amounting to 3.3 per cent., 7.1 per cent., and 25.9 per cent. were observed in women engaged in various operations, but no adequate proof is offered that these increases were not the result of increased practice. In some operations in which men of long experience

[1] Quoted from Report No. 13 of National Industrial Conference Board, p. 29.
[2] Public Health Bulletin, No. 106, 1920.

were engaged, improvements of 0.9 per cent. and 1.1 per cent. were observed. In other operations, with men of less experience, the improvements were 1.1 per cent. and 7.9 per cent. Hence the men more than made up for the daily loss of 20 minutes of working time.

The 10-minute recesses were introduced into four departments of the motor car works, where an 8-hour day was in force. In some cases only one recess was adopted, and in other cases, two. There was some improvement of *hourly* output, but not sufficient to maintain the total output of the shift.

At a large match factory in this country, a system of rest periods was introduced by stopping all machinery from 9.0 till 9.10 a.m., so as to allow the workers to eat food brought with them from home. In the afternoon they were sent to the canteen for 15 minutes in three detachments, and were given a free mug of tea. The hours of work were from 7 to 12 and from 1 to 6 (Saturday being free), so the rest periods broke up the 5-hour spells into spells of 2 to 2¾ hours. The girls employed are now in much better spirits towards the end of the spells than they were before the change, and the output has been well maintained.[1] Again, at a munition factory the manager gave a break of 15 minutes daily at 11 a.m. to the girls engaged in sedentary work of a monotonous repetitive kind. During the break the girls had recreation in the open air. In spite of this deduction of time from their working hours, the output per day was increased.[2]

THE SPONTANEOUS ADOPTION OF REST PERIODS

The necessity for rest periods during working hours is proved by the fact that workers engaged in active manual labour habitually take considerable rests, even when they are undoubtedly striving to attain the maximum productivity within their physical powers. Prof. W. Neilson Jones and I[3] made a number of observations on munition workers, in order to obtain an accurate numerical measure of these spontaneous resting periods. The workers knew that their hourly output was being counted, but they did not know that any note was taken of their rests from work. Rests were not counted if under 3 minutes in duration.

In the heavy operation known as ' hand-tapping fuse sockets,'

[1] Report of Chief Inspector of Factories, 1918, p. 10.
[2] Memo. No. 7 of Health of Munition Workers Committee, 1916.
[3] Final Report of Health of Munition Workers Committee, 1918, p. 161.

which has already been referred to,[1] four men were kept under observation for two days. In the Table is recorded the average duration of rest pauses, calculated per hour (*i.e.*, the total time lost in the half-hour intervals is doubled), and it will be seen that between 8.30 and 11.30 a.m., and again between 2.30 and 5.30 p.m., the men rested for about 8 minutes per hour, the extreme times varying only from 7.1 to 9.4 minutes. That is

AVERAGE DURATION OF REST PAUSES, CALCULATED PER HOUR

Time.	Men hand-tapping fuse sockets.	Men sizing fuse bodies.	Women turning fuse bodies.		
			Avoidable pauses.	Unavoidable pauses.	Total pauses.
7 to 7.30 ...	25.7	26.8	30.6	4.0	34.6
7.30 to 8.30 ...	2.6	12.0	3.9	12.0	15.9
8.30 to 9.30 ...	9.4	10.5	4.4	12.6	17.0
9.30 to 10.30...	9.4 8.6min.	6.2 8.7min.	0.4	9.2	9.6 7.8min.
10.30 to 11.30..	7.1	6.0	3.5	2.4	5.9
11.30 to 12.0...	11.3	9.9	3.6	2.7	6.3
1 to 1.30 ...	13.2	15.9	20.4	4.9	25.3
1.30 to 2.30 ...	2.4	4.9	2.0	6.3	8.3
2.30 to 3.30 ...	7.4	9.0	4.5	4.9	9.4 8.1min.
3.30 to 4.30 ...	8.2 7.8min.	11.4 8.2min.	4.8	2.9	7.7
4.30 to 5.30 ...	7.8	7.4	2.2	4.7	6.9
5.30 to 6.0 ...	20.3	34.6	20.2	2.6	22.8

to say, for six hours out of the 10-hour working day they spontaneously rested for a nearly constant interval. In the first hour of full work in each spell they naturally rested much less, whilst in the initial and final half-hours of the spells they lost much more time, owing to delay in settling down to work, and in making preparations for departure.

These nearly constant spontaneous rest pauses are *average* values, but when we come to individuals a very different condition of affairs is revealed. In Fig. 18 are shown the actual times when rests were taken, and we see that the best workman, whose output was 34 per cent. more than that of the worst workman, took frequent rests at fairly regular intervals in the morning of both the days he was under observation, but he was not so regular in the afternoon. The next best workman, however, though he took regular rests in the morning of one day, worked continuously for four hours in the afternoon, whilst

[1] Cf. Chapter II., p. 15.

workman C on one day worked continuously for $2\frac{3}{4}$ hours in the morning and $3\frac{1}{4}$ hours in the afternoon. Workman D took an

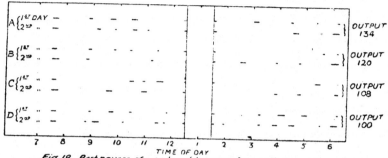

Fig. 18— Rest pauses of men hand-tapping fuse sockets

unnecessary number of rests on both days, and accordingly had a low output.

There can be practically no doubt that if these men had followed a regular system of work spells and rest pauses their output would have been greater, and their fatigue less. They might have worked for 52 minutes and rested for 8 minutes alternately throughout their nominal work spells, or perhaps still better, have worked for 26 minutes and rested 4 minutes. There can be little doubt that as workmen of considerable experience they were unconsciously trying to follow the law of ' maximum production with minimum effort,'[1] but they fell far short of the ideal, which could in truth be attained only by obedience to a definite and ordered scheme of work spells and rest pauses.

In the operation of sizing fuse bodies observations were made upon 16 men, *i.e.*, four on each of four days, and it will be seen from the above Table that these men likewise tended to take rests of about 8 minutes per hour, though they did not keep them at so steady a level as the hand-tappers. Both in hand-tapping and sizing the men are free from machinery, and can work or rest just when they please, but in lathe operations a certain amount of time is unavoidably lost, as the machines need a good deal of attention at the hands of the tool setters. However, such 'unavoidable' rest pauses fulfil their object almost as well as the spontaneously taken 'avoidable' pauses. This can be gathered from the observations recorded on the right side of the above Table. These observations were made for five days on 27 women engaged in turning fuse bodies, and it will be seen that for 6 hours out of their 10-hour day the

[1] Cf. p. 26.

women likewise took rest pauses which averaged about 8 minutes per hour. This 8 minutes might be made up almost entirely of unavoidable pauses (*e.g.*, between 9.30 and 10.30), or chiefly of avoidable pauses (*e.g.*, between 3.30 and 4.30.)

It is not to be imagined that there is any special significance in the fact that a rest period of about 8 minutes was observed in all the operations described. The duration of the rests naturally depends a good deal upon the severity of the work, and is greater in heavy operations, and less in light ones. In the hot and heavy work of rolling red hot tinplate bars the millmen take longer rests.[1] When the men were working on shifts of eight consecutive hours, with no fixed meal break at all, I found that their average rest pauses amounted to 11, 13, 14, 14, 13, 12, 11 and 13 minutes respectively in the successive hours of the shift : *i.e.*, they were nearly constant, in spite of the fact that only four squads of men were kept under observation (two on each of two days). All the men were very experienced workers, and presumably for this reason they unconsciously kept so accurately to the law of maximum production with minimum effort. The men lost no time whatever from slow starts at the beginning of the shifts, as each squad of men was waiting to take over the work when the shifts changed.

When the tinplate millmen were on 6-hour shifts they took somewhat shorter rest pauses, the average time taken in the successive hours of the shift being 10, 11, 12, 11, 10, and 7 minutes. This final figure is almost certainly too low, as in the last hour of the preceding 6-hour shift the men took a 10-minute pause.

In comparatively light lathe work the workers may take practically no rest pauses whatever. For instance, Mrs. E. A. Osborne found[2] that the total rests taken by women engaged in 'rough turning' 9.2 inch shells averaged only 1.0 minute per hour when they were on day shift, and 2.6 minutes when on night shift. The women were putting in 48 hours' work a week by day, and 60 hours a week by night, in alternate weeks.

THE INFLUENCE OF REST PERIODS COMBINED WITH OTHER IMPROVED CONDITIONS

A good deal of evidence in support of rest periods has been adduced which is much more striking than that recorded above, but it suffers from the defect that other conditions of production were altered at the same time as the rest periods were intro-

[1] Report No. 1 of Industrial Fatigue Research Board, 1919, p. 10.
[2] Report No. 6 of Industrial Fatigue Research Board, 1920, p. 32.

duced. However, it is desirable to discuss this evidence at some length, as much of it has gained wide currency, and is accepted by the uncritical as the direct result of the rest periods, and of them alone.

The most remarkable and widely quoted instances of all are due to the late F. W. Taylor. The first relates to the pig iron gang at the Bethlehem Steel Works.[1] The men had to pick up a pig weighing 92 lbs. from a dump, carry it for an average distance of 36 feet, and after walking up an inclined plank, pitch it into a railway truck. They did this all day long, and on an average they loaded 12½ tons of iron a day. Taylor picked out a man, one Schmidt, who appeared to him the most suitable for the experiment, and told him that if he would do just what he was told he would have his wages raised by 60 per cent. He was made to load 10 to 20 pigs, and rest for a short time, then load another 10 to 20 pigs, followed by another rest, and by the end of the day it was found that he had loaded 47½ tons of pig iron, or nearly four times his previous amount. It is sometimes assumed that this tremendous improvement was due to the system of work spells and rest periods adopted, but there is no actual proof that any of it was due to this cause. It is true that Taylor was able to induce a number of men to load the 47½ tons per day regularly by his method, but as far as one can gather from his account he put all these men on to his differential piece rate of payment, instead of their previous day rate. That is to say, they only got their full 60 per cent. increase of wages if they loaded 47½ tons of iron per day. Anything short of this would have been paid for at a considerably lower scale, though the total wages paid would have been higher than under the old day rate system. So severe was Taylor's standard that out of the original gang of 75 men, who were said to be "good, average pig-iron handlers," "only about *one man in eight* was physically capable of handling 47½ tons per day. With the very best of intentions, the other seven out of eight men were physically unable to work at this pace."[2]

Taylor maintains that if Schmidt had been allowed to attack the pile of iron without guidance and direction, in his desire to earn high wages he would probably have tired himself out by mid-day. He would have worked so continuously that his muscles would not have had the proper periods of rest absolutely needed for recuperation, and would have become completely exhausted early in the day. I do not admit this contention for a moment, as it is directly opposed to the results

[1] F. W. Taylor.   "The Principles of Scientific Management," p. 42. New York, 1915.

[2] *Loc. cit.*, p. 61.

described in the preceding section, and to the law of maximum production with minimum effort. I quite admit, however, that Schmidt would probably not have managed to load the iron so effectively if he had unconsciously followed the dictates of his bodily sensations.

Taylor also maintains that he worked out a law, according to which a first-class labourer, loading 92 lb. pigs, can be under load for only 43 per cent. of the day, and must be free from load for 57 per cent. of the day. When, on the other hand, he is loading half-pigs, he can be under load 58 per cent. of the day, and has to rest only 42 per cent. of it. Taylor does not tell us how he arrived at these figures, and in fact no such calculation is possible. The figures necessarily vary with different men. For instance, a weakling might be able to load half pigs fairly comfortably, but be quite unable to load whole pigs.

The second of Taylor's instances relates to girls who were inspecting steel balls used in bicycle bearings, and picking out defective balls.[1] They were originally working a $10\frac{1}{2}$-hour day, but their hours were gradually shortened in successive steps to 10, $9\frac{1}{2}$, and $8\frac{1}{2}$ hours, and with each shortening of the working day the output increased instead of diminishing. The girls were then given a 10-minute rest interval at the end of each $1\frac{1}{4}$ hours of work, so that they had two 10-minute rests in each of the $4\frac{1}{4}$ hour morning and afternoon work spells. Ultimately 35 girls were able to do the work of the original 120, but how much of this tremendous improvement was due to the introduction of the rest periods? One cannot say, because of the simultaneous alteration of two other conditions of production. The picking out of defective balls needs good sight and a quick visual response, so Taylor had the 'visual reaction time' of the girls determined in a physiological laboratory. The method is well known, and it consists in suddenly bringing an object, such as the letter A or B, within the range of vision of the subject, and directly she recognises the letter she has to press a button. The time elapsing between the appearance of the signal and the appropriate reaction of the subject of experiment is accurately recorded, and it is found that different individuals show very different reaction times. All the girls with a long reaction time were dismissed, even if they had been particularly intelligent, hard working, and trustworthy, as they did not possess the quality of quick perception followed by quick reaction. The remainder were subjected to the differential piece rate system of payment,

[1] *Loc. cit.*, p. 88.

according to which they got a considerable bonus only if they attained the very high standard of output fixed by Taylor. Ultimately they reached his mark, and their wages were now 80 per cent. to 100 per cent. higher than before.

The next instance to be quoted is due to F. B. Gilbreth,[1] and it relates to the output of girls engaged in folding handkerchiefs. These girls worked throughout the entire day, except for an hour at noon, and they sat at low tables, in chairs of ordinary height. Gilbreth made them arrange the folded and unfolded handkerchiefs in the most convenient manner on the work table, and he got them to adopt various changes of posture. In each working hour the girls sat for 24 minutes, stood for 12 minutes, sat or stood (as they wished) for 18 minutes, and walked about and amused themselves for 6 minutes. Moreover, they took 1 minute rest pauses at 5 minute intervals, so the complete scheme of work and rest periods was as follows :

Posture of girls.	Work and rest periods (work periods in italics).
Sitting for 24 min. ...	*5*, 1, *5*, 1, *5*, 1, *5*, 1,
Standing for 12 min. ...	*5*, 1, *5*, 1
Sitting or standing for 18 min.	*5*, 1, *5*, 1, *5*, 1
Walking about for 6 min....	*6*

In every 60 min. = 45 min. work and 15 min. rest.

It is stated that at the end of the day's work under these conditions the girls accomplished more than three times the amount of their previous best work, and with no more fatigue. It looks as if this tremendous improvement were due chiefly to the introduction of the rest periods, but this may not have been so, for we are told that "all the variables of the work had been studied, and the results of the study standardised," though no details are given of the standardised conditions.

A somewhat similar instance relates to the girls employed on rather monotonous work in a bleachery.[2] They were allowed two periods of ¾-hour rest in the day besides their dinner time of ¾-hour. Under Mr. H. L. Gantt's management they were given spells of 80 minutes' work, 20 minutes' rest, throughout the working day, with an arrangement of 'spare-hands' which obviated any break in the work of the machines. Their output was increased by about 60 per cent., but it is impossible to say

[1] F. B. and L. M. Gilbreth. "Fatigue Study," p. 127. London, 1917.
[2] M. and A. D. McKillop. "Efficiency Methods," p. 102. London, 1917.

H

how much of this improvement was due to the rest pauses, and how much to the other changes of conditions.

A striking instance of the effect of rest periods is recorded by the health of Munition Workers Committee,[1] though not in exact numerical terms. "Two officers at the front recently, for a friendly wager, competed in making equal lengths of a certain trench, each with an equal squad of men. One let his men work as they pleased, but as hard as possible. The other divided his men into three sets, to work in rotation, each set digging their hardest for five minutes and then resting for ten, till their spell of labour came again. The latter team won easily."

We are not told the number of men per yard of trench, but this experiment suggests that when all the men were working together, they tended to get in one another's way. If so, the success of the latter team was due partly to the effect of rest periods, and partly to greater freedom of movement.

It is evident that the more arduous the work, the greater the need of rest periods, which should increase both in frequency and duration. One of the most trying forms of modern industrial work is that of controlling telephone exchanges. The telephone girl "must be continually at the top-notch of expectancy, watching intently for the flash of the signal lights, responding instantly to the clicking sounds heard whenever impatient subscribers move their hooks up and down, making and severing connections with all the speed she may."[2] The girls often suffer severely from over-strain, and a Royal Commission, which sat at Toronto in 1907, reported that in view of the medical evidence before them, which was submitted by 26 physicians, the women ought not to work for more than six hours a day. Even these six hours should be spread over a period of 8 to $8\frac{3}{4}$ hours by the interposition of suitable rest periods. When the girls were working for seven hours, their working and resting periods were spread over nine hours, thus (the work periods italicised) :

$$2 \quad \tfrac{1}{2} \quad 1\tfrac{1}{2} \quad 1 \quad 2 \quad \tfrac{1}{2} \quad 1\tfrac{1}{2}$$

The general conclusion to be drawn from the evidence adduced in this and the previous section is that regular rest periods ought to be adopted very widely in industries. Irregular and unsuitable rests are usually taken spontaneously by the workers, and the more experienced the workers become, the more nearly they tend, by unconscious instinct, to take rests which conform to the theoretical ideal. They

---

[1] Memo. No. 7, 1916, p. 5.
[2] Goldmark. "Fatigue and Efficiency," p. 47. 1913.

must always fall far short of this ideal, however, so it is better to try various schemes of work spells and rest periods experimentally, and find out by practice which gives the best result. No one scheme would be best suited to everybody, so the most suitable scheme for the largest number of workers in a shop or factory should be followed. A good scheme may be expected to increase output by 10 per cent. or 20 per cent., without increase of fatigue to the workers, but improvements of 100 per cent. or 200 per cent. can never be expected of experienced workers, merely from the introduction of rest periods without any other improvements of working conditions. Such a result would be diametrically opposed to the law of maximum production with minimum effort.

Sunday Labour

We have seen the advantage of taking brief rest periods in every hour of work, and longer rest periods between the spells of work. The principle of rests is no less advantageous when applied over longer time intervals. There should be at least one day's complete rest from industrial work per week, and longer rests of three (or more) days' duration at three monthly intervals.

The weekly day of rest is almost always taken on Sunday, so it is worth while to record what evidence we have in favour of abolishing Sunday labour. During the first 1½ years of the war Sunday work was very widely adopted in munition factories, under the mistaken idea that it promoted an increased output, but employers gradually became disabused of the idea, and there was a steady diminution of Sunday labour during the last three years of the war. The Health of Munition Workers Committee were emphatic in their condemnation of it. In their first Memorandum, published in November, 1915, they state that the evidence before them has led them to hold strongly that if maximum output is to be secured and maintained for any length of time, a weekly period of rest must be allowed. They quote the case of an important firm where heavy machine work was done. Working hours were reduced by 13 at the week-end, so that they nominally came to 65½ instead of 78½. Time keeping so much improved that the average number of hours actually worked, viz., 60, exceeded those worked in the six months preceding the change, and hourly output was—in the opinion of the manager—improved likewise.

Exact evidence as to the effect of abolishing Sunday labour in a large fuse factory has already been recorded in Chapter III, so that it is unnecessary to do more than briefly re-capitulate it here. It was shown that in women engaged in turning aluminium fuse bodies the advent of a regular Sunday rest caused the total output to improve 13 per cent., in spite of the loss of 8 hours' Sunday work. In men engaged in sizing fuse bodies the abolition of intermittent Sunday labour caused the total output to improve 13 per cent., in spite of the average loss of 4.7 hours of work. Such results more than confirm the statements made to the Health of Munition Workers Committee that "seven days' labour only produces six days' output."

Sunday labour is uneconomical not only because of the physical strain involved, but because of the monotony of continuous work, unrelieved by any relaxation. The Health of Munition Workers Committee record[1] the case of a skilled toolmaker who had had only eight days' holiday in 14 months. He complained of the strain on his nerves.

The improvement of output induced by a few days' holiday has already been recorded and described in Chapter III. Our present system of Bank Holidays ensures the workers getting one free day at Whitsuntide and in August, and (usually) two free days at Easter and Christmas, but these holidays do not cut up the year into equal work periods. The continuous period between the beginning of August and Christmas is too long, and it should be broken by an extra holiday in October, or perhaps on armistice day, November 11th. Also it would be well to make a regular custom of giving industrial workers three clear days' holiday at Christmas, Easter and in August, whenever possible.

[1] Memo. No. 7, p. 9.

CHAPTER VII

LIMITATION OF OUTPUT

CONTENTS

Introduction—The Extent of Output Limitation in various Industries—The Investigation of Output Limitation—Output free from Limitation—Output showing intentional Limitation—General Limitation of Output—The Causes of Output Limitation, and the Remedies.

INTRODUCTION

When, in previous Chapters, the question of hourly, daily, or weekly output has been discussed, the workers referred to were always, except in one or two instances specifically mentioned, employed on piece work. Moreover, it was assumed that in every case they were doing their best, and were not practising any artificial limitation of their output. This assumption is a very large one, and it is desirable that an adequate proof of its validity should be afforded, as far as possible. Most of the industrial operations I have myself investigated relate to the output of munitions, and for this reason alone, apart from all others, one might feel justified in assuming that by reason of patriotic enthusiasm the workers would really attempt the maximum production of which they were physically capable. So far as I could judge by frequent observation of the workers themselves, this was actually the case, and I never saw any slacking on the part of the piece workers, though the same statement by no means holds for the time workers. However, personal impressions are very misleading, so that it is much more satisfactory to obtain a numerical proof, when it is possible, as to the presence or absence of output limitation. Such a proof is frequently obtainable, as I shall demonstrate in subsequent sections of this Chapter.

It will be realised that the discussion of hourly, daily, and weekly output statistics is absolutely futile if the workers under consideration are not really doing their best. A fall of output at the end of a work spell may not indicate any fatigue whatever, if the worker is in the habit of slowing down when he has done what he considers to be enough work. A fall of output in the latter part of the week may similarly be due to intentional limitation rather than to fatigue. The reduced output sometimes observed when hours of work are increased may be due to the determination of the worker to take it easy, as some compensation for being deprived of a further part of his few daily hours of leisure. It is therefore a fundamental assumption that in all output statistics worthy of discussion the worker must not intentionally be practising any restriction of his output.

THE EXTENT OF OUTPUT LIMITATION IN VARIOUS INDUSTRIES

To what extent is limitation of output practised in various industries? Information on this matter is very hard to obtain, and such as does exist is almost always biassed and exaggerated. The employers naturally tend to magnify the evidence, and the employees to minimise it. But almost everyone is agreed that it is widespread, and is a serious danger to economic prosperity, especially in this country. The value of goods produced per worker in this and other countries strongly suggests limitation, though it does not prove its numerical extent. The figures in the Table[1] show that whilst in 1886 the average value per industrial worker in the United Kingdom was £312, it fell to £244 by 1912, or 22 per cent. lower. This fall may have been due in part to depression of trade, frequent strikes, and similar causes, but it seems highly improbable that it could be due wholly to these reasons, for we see that in America and in our Colonies the productivity of the workers increased very largely.

VALUE OF GOODS PRODUCED BY EACH WORKER PER YEAR

	In 1886.	In 1906.	In 1912.	Per cent. change between 1886 & 1912.
United Kingdom..	£312	£275	£244	− 22
United States ...	400	596	600	+ 50
Australia ...	333	462	542	+ 63
New Zealand ...	359	470	503	+ 40
Canada ...	341	—	472	+ 38

Between 1886 and 1912 we find an improvement varying from 38 per cent. to 63 per cent., and the value of the goods produced in 1912 was two to two-and-a-half times greater in America and the Colonies than it was in this country. In fact it is maintained[2] that, after suitable corrections are made, the

[1] Cf. Leverhulme. "The Six-hour Day," p. 48. 1918.
[2] Ellis Barker. Nineteenth Century, November, 1918.

American industrial production is at least three times as great as the British. The net output per worker is greater in almost every typical industry. For instance, the yearly production of coal in the United Kingdom was 312 tons per wage earner in 1886-90, and 260 tons in 1911. In the United States it was 400 tons in 1886-90, and 613 tons in 1911, or nearly $2\frac{1}{2}$ times the British figure.[1] Coincident with this greater productivity, the wages paid in America were, in 1918, about three times as high as in Great Britain.

The greater productivity of the worker in America is due in part to the much wider utilisation of mechanical power, but it is frequently maintained that it is also due to the absence of limitation of output. Mr. Gompers, President of the American Federation of Labour, representing many millions of working men, said recently,[2] " There has not been any restriction of output for over thirty years in America. We, in the United States, have followed an entirely different policy." In contrast with this statement, F. W. Taylor said that with English workmen it is almost a religion to turn out as little work as possible each day.

THE INVESTIGATION OF OUTPUT LIMITATION

It is evident that in any inquiry into output in relation to hours of work and other conditions, the possibility of limitation must never be lost sight of. But how can the limitation be detected, when it exists? It would be useless to cross-examine the workers themselves, and to consult the employers might give one an exaggerated or erroneous idea of the extent of the mischief. However, it is possible to obtain reliable and unbiassed internal evidence by a detailed study of the weekly output of the individual workers; but before describing the procedure to be adopted, it is necessary to explain the basis of the method on which it is founded. This method is an application of the laws of probability, and it will be most easily explained by a few concrete instances.

Supposing that the stature of the whole of the men working at a large factory were measured, and the men were sorted into a small number of groups, say five, according to their height. It would be found that only a very small proportion of the whole were very tall men, a moderate proportion were tall men, a large proportion were men of medium height, a small proportion were short men, and a very small proportion were very short men. Supposing that a still larger number of men were

[1] Leverhulme. " The Six-hour Day," p. 256.
[2] Cf. Leverhulme, p. 46.

measured, and they were sorted out into a large number of groups, of narrower range, it would be found that on passing from very tall men to medium sized men, there was a regular increase in the proportion of men in each group, and on passing in turn from medium sized men to very short men, a regular decrease in the proportion. For instance, in Fig. 19 is shown graphically the number of men of various heights amongst 25,878 recruits examined for the United States Army.[1] Only 2 out of this huge number of men had a height of 77-78 inches, and 6 had a height of 76-77 inches, but no less than 4,054 of

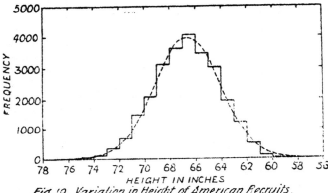

Fig. 19. Variation in Height of American Recruits.

them had a height of 66-67 inches. Passing on to the men below medium height, we find a rapid dwindling in the proportion, so that only 7 men were found to be 57-56 inches in height, and only 2 were 53-51 inches in height.

Supposing that a very much larger number of men were measured, and that they were sub-divided into height groups of narrower range, the curve of stature would approximate to the dotted line drawn in Fig. 19. Now this line is a probability curve, or a diagrammatic representation of Gauss' Law of Frequency of Error,[2] and it is found that the variations in the characteristics of man and other organisms are usually distributed approximately according to this law. For instance, in Fig. 20 is shown the distribution of a group of 1,497 men classified according to their physical strength. This strength was tested by a dynamometer, which had to be pulled in the same way that an archer pulls a bow, and it was found that whilst 4 men out of this number could exert a maximum pull of

[1] J. H. Baxter. "Medical Statistics of the Provost-Marshal-General's Bureau," Vol. I., 1875.
[2] Cf. Vernon. "Variation in Animals and Plants," p. 12. London, 1903.

155-145 lbs., the average pull was only 77.5 lbs., and no less than 522 men (or 35 per cent. of the whole) exerted a pull of 75-65 lbs. The weakest men, 3 in number, could exert a pull

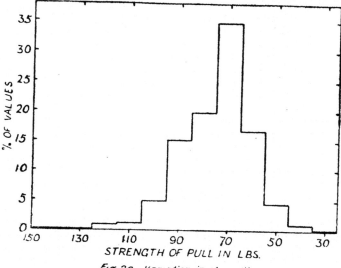

Fig 20 - Variation in strength.

of only 35-25 lbs., and from the form of the curve it will be seen that the gradation in the numbers of men capable of various strengths of pull roughly follows the general contour of the probability curve in Fig. 19.

When, however, the weights of 5,552 men (aged 23 to 50) from various districts in England are plotted out,[1] as in Fig. 21. it is seen that the curve is not quite symmetrical. There is a tendency for many men to put on flesh as they get older, and this excess of heavy men makes the curve project on the left side more than it projects on the right : but in spite of its slight asymmetry, there is quite a regular gradation from very heavy men to medium men, and from medium men to very light men. Galton[2] has shown that if groups of men and women are sorted out in accordance with other qualities, such as keenness of eye-sight and swiftness with which they can aim a blow, they still fall into groups distributed approximately in accordance with the law of frequency of error, though it has since been shown by Karl Pearson and others that there is often a slight degree of asymmetry in the distribution. Other qualities

[1] Cf. British Association Report, 1883.
[2] Galton. "Natural Inheritance." London, 1889.

such as intelligence and manual skill are likewise distributed according to the laws of chance. Hence we are able to formulate the following rules for our guidance in respect to the output of industrial workers.

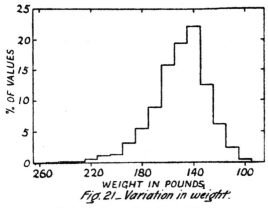

Fig. 21_ Variation in weight.

(1) In a group of experienced industrial workers, all of whom are doing their best, it will inevitably be found that there are distinct variations in skill, and in magnitude of output. (2) If a large number of (hourly) output values are sorted out, according to their magnitude, it will be found that the highest and the lowest values occur infrequently, the moderately high and moderately low values occur with moderate frequency, and the medium values occur with considerable frequency. (3) Any substantial departure from this distribution of output values is due to some limitation of output. Such limitation may be of mechanical origin, but it is usually due to the volition of the workers, i.e., it is an intentional limitation.

These rules form the basis of the method I have suggested[1] for testing the presence or absence of intentional limitation of output in industrial workers.

OUTPUT FREE FROM LIMITATION

I have applied the frequency curve method to a large number of output data, and I will first describe some of the results which show no indication of any intentional restriction of output. My first example relates to the output of 264 experienced drillers (i.e., journeymen) at a large shipyard. The output of these men was obtained for three consecutive weeks in 1917, in terms of piece payment per working hour. The men were engaged in drilling rivet holes of different sizes in steel plates

[1] Memo. No. 18 of Hours of Munition Workers Committee, 1917.

of different thickness, but the payments are accurately calculated in accordance with the character of the work, and they afford a reliable test of output. The 791 (relative) output values varied in magnitude from 11 to 33, though all but 2 per cent. of them varied between 17 and 29. They are plotted out in Fig. 22, and it will be seen that they are in close accord with

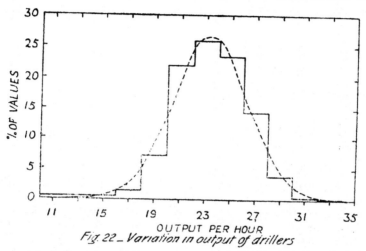

Fig. 22 _ Variation in output of drillers

the symmetrical probability curve which I have calculated, and inserted as a dotted line.[1]

My next example relates to the output of 100 women turning fuse bodies. In November to December, 1915, when the relative hourly output of these women averaged 100, the extreme values of the 540 outputs tabulated were found to range from 56 to 135. On sorting the values into five groups, I found that only 2.0 per cent. of them varied from 55 to 64 : 17.7 per cent. of them varied from 65 to 84 : 42.8 per cent. varied from 85 to 104 : 31.4 per cent. from 105 to 124, and 6 per cent. of them from 125 to 144. These values are plotted out in Fig. 23, and it will be seen that they form a fairly symmetrical frequency curve. Four months later the average hourly output of the women had increased to 121, but the distribution of the slow, medium and quick workers round this new mean still followed the same principle as before, though the output of the slowest worker was now 69, and of the quickest worker, 170. Eight months later the average output had risen to 148, and here again the distribution of the output values followed the same

[1] The mean output was 23.372 ± .072, and the standard deviation 2.999 ± .051.

principle, though these values now varied between the extremes
of 91 and 230. That is to say, there were still about the same
relative proportions of slow, medium and quick workers as

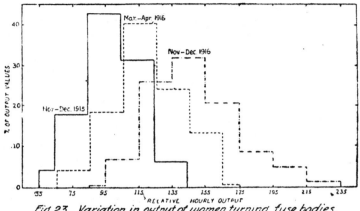

Fig. 23_ Variation in output of women turning fuse bodies.

were observed a year previously, in spite of the fact that all the
workers of every category had considerably improved their
output in consequence of a reduction in the hours of labour.

It will be seen that the numerical range of variation in the
outputs steadily increased during the three statistical periods
investigated, the differences observed being as follows :

Period.	Range of variation.	Ratio of extreme values.
Nov.-Dec., 1915	56 — 135 = 79	1 : 2.4
Mar.-April, 1916	69 — 170 = 101	1 : 2.5
Nov.-Dec., 1916	91 — 230 = 139	1 : 2.5

However, the ratio of the extreme values was practically
constant throughout, and at each period the quickest workers,
in their best weeks, achieved about $2\frac{1}{2}$ times the hourly output
of the slowest workers in their worst weeks. This steadiness
of variability is an important point, which ought always to be
borne in mind when output data are being tested for limitation.
The variability can roughly be determined by the method
recorded, and by examining the contour of the plotted frequency
curves, but in order to obtain an accurate measure of it the
' standard deviation ' of the series of values must be calculated
by a recognised mathematical procedure.[1]   The standard

[1] Cf. G. Udny Yule's "An Introduction to the Theory of Statistics,"
London, 1919; also Davenport's "Statistical Methods," New York, 1907; also
Vernon, "Variation in Animals and Plants," London, 1903.

deviation, when calculated as a percentage on the mean of the
output values, is called the 'coefficient of variability,' and this
coefficient varies greatly in different cases. Simply expressed,
the range of variation of a series of output values, which was
as 1 to 2.5 in the women turning fuse bodies, may be as low as
1 to 1.3 in some operations, and as high as 1 to 5 in others;
but whatever the actual range, the same kind of distribution
of slow, medium and fast workers is still exhibited.

It is unnecessary to describe any more normal frequency
curves in detail, but I have found that in all the operations
investigated, except those to be referred to shortly, the hourly
output data varied approximately in accordance with the law
of frequency of error, *i.e.*, they yielded nearly symmetrical
frequency curves of the type described. This conformation to
normal type held for the men in various shipyards who were
engaged in drilling, and, as a rule, for those engaged in caulk-
ing and riveting. It held for male munition workers engaged
in various operations on 3-inch shells, for women engaged on
9.2-inch shell operations, and for men and women engaged on
various operations in fuse production. It held also for women
in seven out of the nine cartridge operations investigated, but
in the remaining two operations there was a departure from the
normal owing to mechanical limitation of output. In Fig. 24

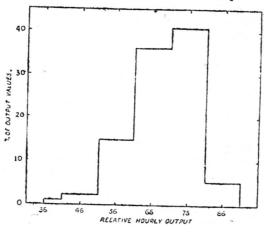

Fig. 24—Variation in output of women drawing cartridge cases

are plotted the hourly output values of 25 women engaged over
a period of 19 consecutive weeks in the operation known as
'second draw.'[1] It will be seen that whilst the frequency curve

[1] Cf. Memo. No. 18 of Hours of Munition Workers Committee, p. 16.

shows the usual contour on the left side, *i.e.,* it indicates that
there was a steadily increasing proportion of moderate output
values as compared with low values, it shows a rapid fall on the
right side. Most of the large output values which would be
observed under normal circumstances are lacking, and the
frequency curve is distinctly asymmetrical. Evidently there is
some limitation exerted on the output of the quickest workers.
However, this limitation was not a voluntary one on the part of
the workers themselves, but was mechanical in origin. In
cartridge-drawing operations the cartridge cases are inserted
one by one into a succession of holes at the periphery of a
horizontal wheel, which slowly jerks onwards about twice a
second. The pace of the wheel is always the same, and the
quickest workers not only have time to fill in all the holes, but
have even a little time to spare in which they could fill other
holes if they were available. The criticism may be made that
if 5 per cent. of the workers achieved the maximum output of
81-91 many others might have done likewise, but in all probability this small group of women owed their exceptional output
to greater promptness than the rest in starting work, and to
more steadiness in keeping it up during working hours.

In the operation of rectifying cartridge cases a similar though
less marked limitation of output was observed, but as far as my
own experience goes, this mechanical limitation is quite
exceptional. When present, there should not be much difficulty
in its identification.

OUTPUT SHOWING INTENTIONAL LIMITATION

If the workers engaged on a given operation depart from the
principle of always doing their best, and by some mutual
arrangement limit their output to an agreed figure, it is evident
that the distribution of their output values will no longer conform to the laws of probability. The biggest outputs being
eliminated, the frequency curves will become truncated on one
side, and the degree of truncation will afford a measure of the
limitation practised.

In order to test this method of identifying limitation, I
collected output statistics of the shipyard workers at five of our
largest shipyards, situated in three industrial areas of the United
Kingdom. Output can be ascertained only in terms of piece-
rate payments, but these payments are fixed so as to correspond
with considerable accuracy to the work done. They had, as a
rule, to be corrected for a number of bonuses and wage advances
so as to bring them to comparable terms, and the values quoted
may be taken to represent approximately the relative hourly

outputs of the workers concerned. They relate only to experienced journeymen workers, who had served their apprenticeship.

I made the majority of my observations on riveters, and at one yard (shipyard B), I sampled the output of groups of about 120 squads of hand riveters (each of four men) for periods of four to eight weeks during the years 1915 to 1918. I thereby obtained from 400 to 900 output values on eight occasions, and the frequency distribution of some of these sets of values is shown in Figure 25. The (symmetrical) probability curve giving the best fit is likewise indicated,[1] and it will be seen that in

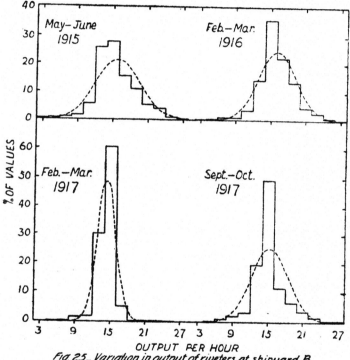

Fig. 25_ Variation in output of riveters at shipyard B

May-June, 1915, the values obtained conformed moderately well with theory, though there was rather an excess of the medium output values. In Feb.-March, 1916, the values obtained conformed still better with theory, but in February-March, 1917, there was a marked change. No less than 60.4

[1] I am greatly indebted to Mr. F. G. Brabant, M.A., for assisting me in calculating out these curves.

per cent. of the riveters now showed a (relative) output of 15 rivets, whilst on the previous occasions mentioned the proportion of men showing this output was 28.0 per cent. and 35.6 per cent. respectively. Only 6.9 per cent. of all the riveters achieved an output of 17 or more, and 1.8 per cent. an output of 19 or more, whereas, a year previously, 43.9 per cent. of the riveters achieved an output of 17 or more, and 21.6 per cent. one of 19 or more. There was evidently an intentional attempt on the part of the men to keep down their output to 15 rivets. This limitation was by no means a steady phenomenon, for in the next six months it diminished considerably. The Table

VARIATION IN OUTPUT OF RIVETERS AT SHIPYARD B

Statistical period.	Mean relative hourly output	Co-efficient of variability.	Per cent. of riveters showing output of	
			17 or more.	19 or more.
May-June, 1915 ...	15.81	23.6 %	37.2	21.9
Oct.-Nov., 1915 ...	15.25	21.4	34.2	15.9
Feb.-Mar., 1916 ...	16.04	20.1	43.9	21.6
Sept.-Oct., 1916 ...	14.93	15.4	16.6	7.1
Feb.-Mar., 1917 ...	14.37	10.9	6.9	1.8
April-May, 1917 ...	14.44	13.1	10.3	2.7
Sept.-Oct., 1917 ...	15.32	20.7	24.7	13.4
Feb.-Mar., 1918 ...	14.42	22.5	20.4	10.4

shows the percentage of riveters putting in 17 or more rivets, and 19 or more, and it likewise records the mean number of rivets put in. This number was 10.5 per cent. smaller in Feb.-Mar., 1917, when restriction was most marked, than it was a year previously, when it was least marked.

It will be seen that the 'co-efficient of variability,' which gives an accurate measure of the range of variation of the output values, fell gradually from a maximum of 23.6 per cent. in May-June, 1915, to a minimum of 10.9 per cent. in February-March, 1917, and then increased to a second maximum in February-March, 1918. Had there been no restriction, it would have remained practically constant throughout.

This irregular restriction practised by the riveters was a localised phenomenon. It was shown very little by the apprentice riveters working in the same yard, and not at all by the caulkers in the yard. Nor was it shown by any of the riveters employed in the adjoining shipyard, though these men at one time practised another kind of restriction which is

referred to in the next section. All the riveters and other iron
workers are paid at standard piece rates. Hence it could
scarcely have been due to any well-founded fear that piece rates
were going to be cut, though there may, of course, have been
a groundless panic to this effect.

A similar localised restriction of output was observed amongst
the riveters at a yard (shipyard A) situated in quite a different
industrial area. The riveters at this yard, though nominally
on pure piece rates, were to some extent guaranteed against
very low rates of payment, so that there was at all times a
deficiency of the low output values, and an excess of the medium
values, but it will be seen from Fig. 26 that between September-
October, 1914, and July-August, 1915, the application of this

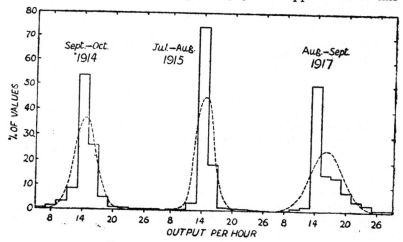

Fig. 26. Variation in output of riveters at shipyard A.

principle was increased, and at the same time there was a
diminution of the higher output values, the result of increased
voluntary limitation. Owing to these reasons, no less than
74.1 per cent. of the riveters showed a relative output of 14,
and only 3.8 per cent. of them had one of 18 or more. Two
years later the voluntary restriction had considerably
diminished, and 31 per cent. of the riveters had an output of
18 or more. The number of output values tabulated on each
occasion was over 600, or sufficient to give a reliable result. It
will be seen that in no instance did the output values correspond
well with the theoretical probability curve.

The habit of restriction at this yard extended to some extent
to the caulkers, but the drillers showed a perfectly normal

I

frequency curve (Cf. Fig. 22), and so did the riveters, caulkers, and drillers in the adjoining shipyard. Hence it follows that, just as in the former instance, a considerable restriction was practised by a portion of the men at certain periods without any real justification.

It should be mentioned that the relative output values obtained at different yards are not directly comparable with one another.

The output data of riveters obtained at the fifth yard, situated in still another industrial area, showed no signs of intentional limitation, so that taken as a whole, the shipyard data indicated that intentional restriction of output was the exception, and not the rule. Riveters were the chief offenders, whilst the drillers appeared to be quite free from blame. This was due, I believe, to the fact that the drillers were paid on a lower scale than the riveters, and their total earnings were only about two-thirds as great. Hence they could not afford to forego even a fraction of their maximum earning power.

It is evident that if the shipyard employers regularly plotted out the output values of their employees in the manner I have indicated, they would be able to tell at a glance if work was going on satisfactorily, and if at any time a wave of restriction affected one or other of their groups of workers, they might, by discreet inquiry, determine the cause, and try to rectify it. Still better would it be for them to take the men into their confidence, and demonstrate the evil to them by suitable diagrams and figures.

In the iron and steel trade, and in the tinplate trade, I have obtained no evidence whatever of intentional restriction of output, though I have not gone into the question very thoroughly. In another industry, at present under investigation, there appears to be a good deal of restriction, but it is not reprehensible like that mentioned above, as it is done with the consent of the employers. The workers on a given operation fix what they consider to be a fair day's work, and when they have achieved it they stop, and in some instances at least they are then allowed to go home. It is not etiquette to exceed the agreed limit, and I was told of a woman who on one occasion inadvertently did too much, and when this was discovered tearfully petitioned that the excess should not be counted or paid for. Again, P. S. Florence[1] observed that the girls employed on several of the operations on 18 lb. shell cases maintained an absolutely steady output in the four sample weeks which were investigated. Further inquiry elicited that the wage system of payment was not understood by the wage earners, and that the foremen,

[1] Interim Report of Health of Munition Workers Committee, 1917, p. 72.

unable to make it intelligible, indicated a standard of output which would satisfy the firm. Power observations showed that most of the girls completed their standard output about two hours before the end of the shift and then slacked off.

In the recently published report[1] of the United States Public Health Service, the practice of setting a standard day's performance is said to have been widely prevalent in the fuse factory where output was investigated. In the operation of drilling holes in the fuse, exactly the same number of fuses, viz., 3,600, were drilled night after night for a whole week by each of the 16 workers kept under observation. As the workers were on a 12-hour shift, they averaged 300 fuses per hour, and it was found that the day shift, who were on a 10-hour day, averaged the same hourly output, and thereby drilled only 3,000 fuses per shift. Again, in the operation of forming the large end of fuses on a capstan lathe, one man finished exactly 1,000 fuses on 44 nights out of 45, another the same figure on 47 nights out of 50, and another the same on 46 nights out of 51.

Any system of restriction, whether applied with the consent of the employers or not, is economically unsound, as it reduces the total output of a factory, and indirectly raises the price of the article produced. The fact that individual workers possess inequalities of skill and output capacity cannot be avoided or ignored. If all the workers on a given operation maintain the same output, it necessarily follows that they limit their productivity to that of the slowest workers. Even the medium workers must be producing less than they are easily capable of doing, whilst the quick workers must be producing considerably less. It is sometimes said that ill-feeling is created if one worker on a job is paid more than his neighbour, yet it is the almost universal principle in all trades and professions that the better man gets the better pay. If, however, the ill-feeling is genuine, it would be better to pay the group of workers on a collective piece-rate basis. On this system the quickest workers would probably not work so well as on an individual piece rate, as they would be inclined to slow down to the speed of their weaker brethren, but they would nevertheless do better than when their output was absolutely limited to the level of the slowest workers.

GENERAL LIMITATION OF OUTPUT

In a different category from intentional limitation exhibited by the naturally quick workers comes the general limitation of the whole body of workers. This is a more widespread

[1] Public Health Bulletin, No. 106, 1920.

phenomenon amongst workers paid on a time rate than in those paid on a piece rate. It has been stated[1] that in the building trade the men, almost all of whom are on a time rate, only work to half the extent of their power, and in many other trades if is generally considered that the time workers work to something between a half and three-quarters of their power, but sometimes it is considerably less than half. For instance, it was stated in evidence before the Dock Workers Inquiry[2] that the average rate of discharge of iron ore per ' grab' at Glasgow was 64 tons up to the end of July, 1918, when the men were working on a piece rate, but now that they were on a time rate it had fallen to 21 tons. The custom of working considerably below their real productive capacity has become so thoroughly ingrained amongst some classes of industrial workers that neither the men themselves, nor their employers, realise their latent powers. A case in point is recorded by the Health of Munition Workers Committee.[3]

"At one long established factory a new shop has been built and staffed so as to produce 5,000 of a particular stock article of warfare per week, that estimate being based upon the results of the older shops doing the same work. New hands were engaged, and these in the new shop are now, after six months, producing in spite of their inexperience not only 5,000, as expected, but 13,000 of these articles per week. The older hands in the other shops do not approach this output, though all the mechanical conditions of work are practically equal. As patriotic interest in their output appears to be shared here by all the men alike, the lower output by the more experienced hands appears to be assignable only to the effects of long standing customary restrictions upon habits or rhythm of work from which the newer hands are free."

At one of the shipyards previously referred to, I obtained striking evidence of general output limitation.[4] The workers at this yard were paid at a piece rate, but they were likewise guaranteed a somewhat liberal minimum wage, whatever their output. Before the war, when there were plenty of men available, this system worked fairly well, for if a worker persistently failed to earn his guaranteed time rate, he could be discharged. During the war, however, the demand for shipyard workers, and especially for riveters, became greater than the available

---

[1] Cf. " The Times," April 9, 1920.
[2] " The Times," March 3, 1920.
[3] Memo. No. 7, 1916, p. 8.
[4] Cf. " Life and its Maintenance," p. 263. London, 1919.

supply, and the men now controlled the situation. They found it easier to receive their guaranteed time rate than to try and earn their piece rate, and at one period scarcely a riveter earned the money he was paid. The figures in the second column of the Table show the extent to which the riveters on a battleship earned their guaranteed pay during a month's period when matters were at their worst. We see that 8 per cent. of the men earned less than 40 per cent. of their pay, and no less than 76 per cent. of them, or three-fourths of the whole, earned less than 60 per cent. of it. The second column of the Table refers to the riveters on torpedo boat destroyers, at a period when slackness was not so marked. It shows that 54 per cent. of these men earned less than 70 per cent. of their pay, whilst 5.5 per cent. of them earned it, and were therefore paid the genuine piece rate.

Percentage of wages earned on those paid.	Proportion of battleship riveters.	Proportion of torpedo-boat riveters.
39 per cent. or less	8.1 per cent.	1.8 per cent.
40-49	30.4	8.3
50-59	37.3	19.3
60-69	16.2	24.8
70-79	4.3	22.9
80-89	1.2	15.6
90-99	1.9	1.8
100	.6	5.5
	100.0	100.0

When the guaranteed time rate was abolished, the number of rivets put in by the men was very nearly doubled. Taking three trial weeks in 1915, 1916, and 1918, the relative number of rivets per hour put in by each squad varied thus :

	Nov. 1915	Nov. 1916	Nov. 1918
Relative number of rivets	100	185	198

That this improvement was the direct result of the change in the system of payment was proved by determining the output of 14 squads of torpedo-boat hand-riveters in the two months immediately before and immediately after the change. The relative output rose from 8.3 to 14.8, or by 78 per cent., and the riveters most frequently drove 13-15 rivets, instead of their previous 7-9, as can be gathered from the data in the Table.

Relative output per hour.	Percentage of output values.	
	Before the change.	After the change.
5	7.4	—
7	37.6	—
9	40.4	7.6
11	11.0	10.6
13	1.8	27.3
15	0.0	19.7
17	0.9	13.6
19	0.9	13.6
21	—	7.6
Mean output	8.3	14.8

It can be seen from Fig. 27, where the output values of the riveters are plotted, that their distribution varied roughly in accordance with the normal frequency curve both before and after the change of wage payment. Hence the frequency curve

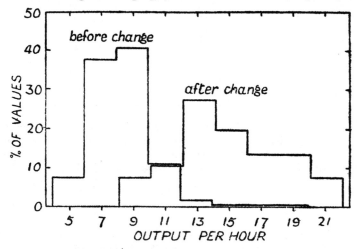

Fig. 27. Variation in output of riveters

method may not show any indication of restricted output when the whole of the workers involved are going slow. Amongst such a body there will still be small numbers of relatively slow and relatively fast workers, and a large number of medium workers. However, the distribution of output values may take a very abnormal form if it relates to a mixture of strenuous and non-strenuous workers. This is well shown by the curve on the left of Fig. 28, which shows the distribution of the output values of a group of 25 women over a period of 30 consecutive weeks. These women were sorting cartridge cases, and picking out the buckled and abnormal cases.[1] They were paid at a time rate, and it will be seen that whilst the majority of the women had an output of 22 to 52, a small proportion of them had an output of 62 to 92. The extremes of output varied as 17 to 92, or as 1 to 5.4, and there can be little doubt that this tremendous range of variation was due to part of the women working conscientiously in order to obtain a good output, and

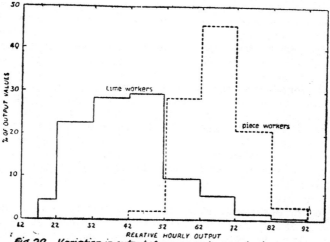

Fig. 28. — Variation in output of women sorting cartridge cases.

another part—the larger one—taking things easily. Confirmation of the truth of this hypothesis is afforded by the curve on the right of Fig. 28. This shows the distribution of the output values of a group of 18 women for a 25-week period. These women were situated in another block of the same factory, and they were likewise sorting cartridge cases, but they were paid at a piece rate. Unfortunately their output values are not directly comparable with those of the time workers, as the character of their sorting was slightly different, but in drawing the curve I have assumed that the maximum output of the two sets of workers was the same (though we may be sure that it would have been greater in the piece workers). On this assumption, we see that almost the whole of the piece work

[1] Memo. No. 18 of Hours of Munition Workers Committee, p. 17.

outputs greatly exceeded the time work outputs. The frequency curve is roughly of the normal type, and the range of variation of the extreme values, viz., 42 to 92, or as 1 to 2.2, is not half as great as in the time workers.

The Causes of Output Limitation, and the Remedies

It would be out of place for me to attempt a detailed discussion of the various causes conducing to limitation of output, and of the remedies for abating or abolishing the system, but I will endeavour to discuss the subject briefly in its relation to the prevention of fatigue and the increase of efficiency.

First and foremost among the causes of output restriction is the fact that all work means effort, and man is naturally prone to avoid unnecessary effort. Without a stimulus of some sort few men, if any, would do any work at all. The usual stimulus of the industrial worker is the need to earn a livelihood, though combined with this stimulus is often found the more honourable one of pride in his work and craftsmanship. Even this stimulus is chiefly founded on the desire for approbation by his fellows, and there can be few men who would deliberately take the trouble to finish off their work with unnecessary elaboration and care if they knew that it would never be seen by anyone save themselves. Closely related to the desire for approbation is the desire to excel other men, and in intellectual pursuits this form of stimulus often takes the form of social ambition, but probably the desire for increased creature comforts is still more widespread.

To get the best out of a worker we therefore need an adequate stimulus, but this stimulus must not be so powerful as to make him overstrain himself. He must not be induced to work so hard as to injure his health, and the work must not even absorb so much of his physical energy that he has little or none left, after his day's labour is over, to devote to amusement, relaxation and necessary duties. An instructive instance of a stimulus powerful enough to lead to overstrain may be quoted from F. W. Taylor's book on 'Shop Management.'[1] It relates to the men at an engineering works, who were engaged in turning standard steel forgings. They produced them at the rate of 4 or 5 a day, and they were paid 50 cents a piece. After methods of time and motion study were introduced, and the speed of the lathes was quickened, the men were able to turn out 10 forgings a day, provided that they worked "at their maximum pace from morning till night." They were now paid 35 cents a piece, so their total earnings came to about 14/- a day instead

---

[1] F. W. Taylor. "Shop Management," p. 81. New York, 1911.

of the previous 9/-. Supposing, however, that they failed to reach their ' standard task ' of 10 pieces, they were paid only 25 cents a piece, and for 9 pieces they would receive 9/- instead of 12/7. That the men were overstraining themselves in order to attain the standard task and earn the full ' differential piece rate,' is shown by the fact that when the higher rate was abolished, and they were paid 25 cents per piece whatever the number produced, their output immediately fell to 6 or 8 a day.

As the men would now be earning only 7/- a day, the chances are that in the endeavour to maintain their weekly wage they would be working rather harder than they did before ' Scientific Management' methods were introduced, as they then earned 9/- a day. Yet they produced 3 pieces less per day than under the differential rate system. Under this system they must have had to put every ounce of their available energy into their work, and have had none left for any other purpose. Such ceaseless work ' at maximum pace from morning till night' could not be maintained indefinitely. Sooner or later the strain would be too great, and the worker would drop out. Proof that this happened is given on several occasions by Taylor. His pig iron handlers were set such a tremendous standard task that only 1 in 8 of the men could achieve it. Of his original gang of 600 shovellers (of iron ore, coke, etc.), who were admittedly good workers, only 1 in 5 were up to the prescribed mark, and the others were rejected.

What is the best form of wage payment, which acts as sufficient incentive to stimulate the industrial worker to do a really good day's work, but not to overstrain himself? In most industries a time rate of payment is not a strong enough stimulus and, as has been stated above, it is considered that the time worker usually does only half to three-fourths as much work as the piece-worker. In some industries a piece rate is impossible, but it could be introduced in many instances where it is at present non-existent. However, the Trade Unions in a number of industries, so far from encouraging its introduction, have rules prohibiting it when it is not already established, and urging its abolition where it exists.[1] This is a short-sighted policy, like the objection to dilution of labour, and to the introduction of labour-saving methods and devices. The main cause of these objections appears to be the view that an increased speed of production will mean less work to ' go round,' and consequent unemployment. Whilst it is quite natural that the individual workman should adopt such an attitude, for he not infrequently has direct experience of the effects of a limited amount of work for distribution among an excess of would-be workers, the

[1] G. D. H. Cole. " The Payment of Wages," p. 23. London, 1918.

officials of the great trade unions ought to be alive to the economic fallacy involved. They ought to take the long sighted view, that the cheaper an article can be produced, the greater will be its sale, and the greater will be the employment created.

What is the best form of piece rate payment? The differential piece rate, as applied by Taylor, is sufficiently condemned by the instances above quoted, but there would be no objection to it if the ' standard task ' were fixed at so low a level that all but the really slack and thoroughly inefficient men could attain it. Such men deserve to be eliminated. In theory, the fairest form of piece rate is a graduated differential rate. In that the overhead charges of a factory are almost constant, whether the workers are producing much or little, it follows that the employers reap a relatively greater and greater profit the larger the output of the individual worker. Hence it would pay them to stimulate a maximum production by paying, e.g., at the rate of 1/- for the first dozen articles produced by an operative in his day's work, 1/2 for the second dozen, 1/5 for the third dozen, 1/9 for the fourth dozen, and so on, in increasing proportion. This system is very seldom adopted, and I have met with only one instance of it in this country.[1] It is not to be recommended, in spite of its intrinsic equitableness, as it is liable to lead to overstrain on the part of the workers. The stimulus of the excess pay for maximum output is apt to be too strong a one. Other systems such as the premium bonus system, which pay a relatively smaller and smaller piece rate the greater the output, are essentially unfair. Hence the straight piece rate system is probably the best one of all. It is readily comprehended by the workers, and this is an important point, as the instance previously quoted indicates.[2]

The straight piece rate may be compounded with a minimum wage, which is to be paid however low the output may be, but this minimum must not be fixed too high. We saw that, owing to a high minimum wage, the riveters at one yard scarcely ever attempted to earn the piece rate which was well within their powers, so that any fixation of a minimum wage ought to be accompanied with the proviso that if more than a small proportion of the workers fail to earn it, it will be withdrawn, or that the backsliding workers, after an adequate period of trial, and full warning, will be dismissed.

If a straight piece rate is adopted, the fixation of the most suitable rate per piece is often a matter of extreme difficulty. Too high a rate tends to diminish production, for most industrial workers become used to a certain wage expenditure

[1] Cf. Report No. 3 of the Industrial Fatigue Research Board.
[2] Cf. p. 130.

and its corresponding standard of living, and they strive to maintain this standard under all conditions. If the rate of pay goes up, they partly neutralise it by working less hard, and if the rate of pay goes down, they work harder than before. It is desirable, therefore, that increments of piece rates should be very gradual, so that the workers may at each stage have time to become used to an increasing standard of comfort and wage expenditure. They will then continue to experience the same strong incentive to work their best.

The Health of Munition Workers Committee point out[1] that the incentive to work exercised by a wage system must necessarily vary according to the physical condition of the workers. If their hours of work are too long or too continuous, the desire for rest may be strong enough to overcome any wage incentive. Hence it is of great importance that the system of working hours and of rest pauses adopted should be such as to maintain a reasonable inclination to work.

One of the most potent causes of output limitation is the rate-cutting sometimes adopted by employers. Finding that some of their men, by working really hard, are earning more than they think they are entitled to, they lower the scale of pay, perhaps with the subterfuge of slightly altering some of the conditions of production. A worker who has once been subject to such treatment is not likely to try and achieve a maximum output on any job to which he is subsequently put. In extenuation it may be said, with truth, that equitable rate fixing is a difficult business, in which mistakes are bound to be made. When this is the case the employers ought to bargain with the men, and arrange that if any particular piece rates are lowered, other piece rates are at the same time raised, whereby the total payments made to the men are not reduced, but are distributed more equitably.

The industrial worker is apt to argue that if he works harder, the lion's share of the profits goes to his employer, and not to him. This view has a considerable element of truth in it, so far as it applies to the individual employer for a short period after the rate of production is accelerated, but in the long run there is very little substance in it. When matters have adjusted themselves, the employer will probably be earning about as much profit as before, whilst the whole community, including the workers themselves, will be getting the benefit of the articles at a lower price. In some isolated instances schemes of co-partnership and profit-sharing have been adopted which have proved very acceptable to the employees no less

[1] Interim Report, 1917, p. 76.

than to the employers, but it must be admitted that so far they have not as a rule been a great success. Often this is because the employers have not given the workers a sufficiently liberal share of the profits. A fair system would be to guarantee the shareholders who had provided the capital a reasonable interest on their outlay, e.g., 6 per cent., and divide any profits over and above this figure equally between capital and labour. Labour may retort that as it has done the work it ought to receive *all* the excess profits, but capital would rightly point out that if it is not going to have a chance of extra profit from investing its money in somewhat risky industrial concerns, it prefers to put it into absolutely safe government bonds and loans.

It is unlikely that the habit of restricting output which has grown up in this country will be easily or quickly eradicated, nor is there any single or infallible remedy. In addition to the palliatives mentioned, an important measure lies in the better education of the industrial workers, and especially of their trade union officials. If once these men in authority can thoroughly grasp the economic fallacy of output restriction, they will do all they can to reduce it. However, the working man will be difficult to persuade unless a more sympathetic spirit springs up between him and his employer. He should learn that it is equally to his own interest, to that of the employer, and that of the general public, that all restrictive customs be abolished. A real spirit of sympathy can be established only when labour obtains a much greater share in management and control than it possesses at present. The recent introduction of joint industrial councils and works committees is a hopeful step in this direction.

CHAPTER VIII

LOST TIME AND ITS CAUSATION

CONTENTS

Introduction—Lost Time due to Sickness—The Influence of Fatigue on Sickness—The Causes of Avoidable Lost Time (Systems of Wage Payment, Seasonal and Weather Effects, The Monday Effect)—Two-Break and One-Break Systems—Time Keeping of Night Shifts and Day Shifts—General Conclusions.

INTRODUCTION

The subject of time-keeping is very important in its relationship to industrial efficiency and fatigue, but it has hitherto received very little systematic study. Probably this is because of its inherent difficulty. The causes of bad time-keeping are so numerous, and so difficult to disentangle, that the conclusions drawn from a study of time-keeping records are necessarily somewhat uncertain. We shall see, however, that if the records relate to large numbers of workers, and are of considerable duration, it is possible to draw valuable conclusions from them concerning the causation of bad time-keeping, and the methods of abating it.

The term 'lost time' is rather an indefinite one, as its significance varies in different industries and may change from year to year. Usually the length of the working week is fixed at a definite figure, which ranged from 48 to $55\frac{1}{2}$ hours before the war, but is now 44 to 48 hours. Any time short of the fixed hours is counted as 'lost time,' unless these missing hours of work are due to lack of material, break-down of machinery, and similar causes. Work done in other than the regulation hours is reckoned as 'overtime,' and is not taken account of in estimating lost time, though this system often leads to considerable anomalies. For instance, a man on a 54-hour week may put in only 48 hours of work during regulation hours, but 6 hours of overtime in extra-regulation hours, so that he has really done a full 54-hour week, though his official record states that he has lost 11 per cent. of his time. During the war it was the custom, in many munition factories, to fix the usual working week at a level considerably beyond that of pre-war normal hours and overtime hours combined; *e.g.,* an instance was recorded in Chapter III. in which the working week at a fuse factory was 78½ hours. Hence overtime, as such, might be very seldom worked. In speaking of lost time it is therefore necessary to bear in mind the possibility of overtime, though it is often difficult in practice to find out the exact numerical measure of this time.

Loss of working time falls under two main headings, unavoidable and avoidable. Unavoidable lost time is due to sickness and accidents, and this is the class of time which is specially interesting to the student of industrial fatigue. Avoidable lost time is due to the worker voluntarily absenting himself from his factory for reasons which may be good or bad. Systematic study of the avoidable time lost often reveals the chief causes of the loss, and suggests partial remedies, hence it is important to pay attention both to avoidable and unavoidable lost time. Unfortunately many or most employers who keep lost time records at all do not attempt to separate the time into the two categories, but we shall see that even the records of the total time lost often yield information of value.

Lost Time Due to Sickness

It is by no means easy for employers to determine how much of the time lost by a worker is genuinely due to sickness. In some factories only the time is so counted for which a medical certificate is produced, and as, under the National Insurance Act, employees receive no sick benefit for the first three days' illness, they may not trouble to get a medical certificate unless they are absent for more than the three days. Hence their absence is reckoned as avoidable lost time. Again, a worker may often feel off colour owing to overwork, and may take a day or two off, without being sufficiently ill to be certified as sick. On the other hand, as Loveday points out,[1] the medical certificates are often unsatisfactory, as in most populous districts a few unscrupulous medical practitioners exist who will give a certificate when it is not deserved. And there are others who not infrequently give it to men whom they have rarely if ever seen before, on the strength of their own statements. However, the employers soon get to know the degree of reliance they can place in their individual employees, and if they carefully question them, they can usually determine with fair accuracy whether absence is due to sickness or not.

As the result of examining a number of lost time records, obtained for the most part at engineering works, Loveday came

[1] Cf. Interim Report of Health of Munition Workers Committee, 1917, p. 45.

to the conclusion that " nearly all records understate, and most records understate greatly, the proportion of lost time due to sickness and other unavoidable causes." In order to afford other investigators of lost time a basis for testing this state- ment, he quotes a number of figures obtained at factories where the records of sickness were carefully kept. At a works employ- ing 1,200 men, where the men usually put in 55 to 59 hours a week of heavy work (inclusive of overtime), they lost 10.5 per cent. of time altogether, of which 6.6 per cent. was due to sick- ness. The records extended over 22 weeks, and they were very consistent. At a department of another factory, where 270 men and 290 women were engaged on light work, the total time lost came to 6.6 per cent., of which 4.7 per cent. was lost unavoidably, during the 16 weeks for which it was investigated. At two smaller factories, where the total time lost amounted to 7.3 per cent. and 5.0 per cent., the amount due to sickness came to 3.9 per cent. and 3.0 per cent. respectively. At all these four places, therefore, where time keeping was reason- ably good and records were carefully made, the unavoidable loss was more than half the total loss. If the time-keeping is bad, the relative proportion of time lost from sickness is naturally smaller. At an engineering works employing 21,000 operatives the total time lost during a week in March (when they averaged 53 hours work) came to 13.7 per cent., of which 4.3 per cent. was due to sickness. This amount is less than a third of the total time, but it almost coincides with the average time (viz. 4.5 per cent.) lost at the four factories just mentioned. Hence it appears that men (and women) engaged in fairly heavy work in the engineering trade for over 50 hours a week usually lose over 4 per cent. of their time from sickness.

At some factories the time said to be lost from sickness is considerably less than 4 per cent., and the inference is that some of the time reckoned as being avoidably lost is really due to sickness. Loveday suggests that this suspicion should be tested by comparing the curves of sickness and of avoidable lost time. If they are both observed to rise and fall more or less synchronously, it follows that a part of the time lost from sickness has been wrongly attributed to avoidable causes.

THE INFLUENCE OF FATIGUE ON SICKNESS

One of the most important contributory causes of sickness and of the loss of working time is fatigue arising directly from industrial work. I had an opportunity of testing this statement on a large scale at three National Shell Factories, all situated in the same district. The lost time was very carefully tabulated, and was divided up into (a) time lost avoidably, (b) that lost

LOST TIME IN RELATION TO WEEKLY HOURS OF WORK

Class of factory.	Statistical period.	Weekly hours of work.	Percentage of time lost by					
			Men.			Women.		
			Unavoidably	Avoidably.	Total.	Unavoidably.	Avoidably.	Total.
Factory A— 6-inch shells	July-Dec., 1916.	63 for men and women	7.9	2.8	10.7	7.5	5.4	12.9
	Jan.-June, 1917.	62 ,, ,,	6.0	3.5	9.5	6.1	4.8	10.9
	July-Dec., 1917.	61 ,, ,,	4.0	4.6	8.6	5.5	7.5	13.0
	Mean		6.0	3.6	9.6	6.4	5.9	12.3
Factory B— 9.2-inch and 15-inch shells	Aug.-Dec., 1916.	63 for men and 45 for women	4.4	8.8	13.2	3.3	7.1	10.4
	Jan.-June, 1917.	62 for men and 44 for women	7.0	4.4	11.4	3.7	7.8	11.5
	July-Dec., 1917.	61 for men and 42½ for women	4.5	4.8	9.3	2.9	8.0	10.9
	Mean		5.3	6.0	11.3	3.3	7.6	10.9
Factory C— 9.2-inch shells	Aug., 1916-April, 1917	63½ for men and 44½ for women	7.0	4.8	11.8	2.8	5.1	7.9
	June-Dec., 1917.	54 for men and women	4.0	2.0	6.0	4.3	3.5	7.8

by sickness and leave; but the fraction of time lost by 'leave' (e.g., to a woman whose husband was back for a few days from the war) was very small. I obtained the lost time records every week for 17 or 18 consecutive months, and these values have been averaged and are recorded in the Table. At factory A, where 6 inch shells were made, there were 1,300 men at the beginning of the statistical period and 750 women, but by the end of the period the number of men had fallen to 700 and that of the women had increased to 1,350.

It will be seen that on an average the men lost 6.0 per cent. of their time from sickness, and the women, 6.4 per cent., but with both sexes there was a steady fall in the sickness experienced during the three six-month statistical periods investigated. This may have been to a small extent due to the fact that at first a 63-hour week was worked, both by day and by night, but from April, 1917, onwards Saturday afternoon work (of four hours' duration) was dropped, so that the average hours were 62 in the second statistical period, and 61 in the third period.

At factory B, where 9.2 inch and 15 inch shells were made, there were 1,500 men and 700 women at first, with a gradual change to 900 men and 500 women at the end of the period. The men worked a 63-61 hour week as at factory A, but the women were on a three shift system, and averaged only 45-42¾ hours a week. This difference of hours produced a corresponding effect on the time lost from sickness, for the women lost only 3.3 per cent. on an average, and the men, 5.3 per cent.

The most striking evidence of all was obtained at factory C, where 9.2 inch shells were made. Here there were 1,300 men and 400 women employed at first, with a gradual change to 900 men and 850 women at the end of the period. For the first 9 months the men averaged 63¼ hours' work per week (57 hours on day shift and 69½ hours on night shift), and the women 44¼ hours, but in the last seven months both men and women worked a 54 hour week (48 hours on day shift and 60 hours on night shift) on the same modified two shift system. We see from the Table that during the first statistical period the men lost no less than 7.0 per cent. of their time from sickness (probably because of the terribly long night shift), whilst the women lost only 2.8 per cent., or two-fifths as much. When the hours were changed, and the women did 9¾ hours' work more than before and the men 9¼ hours less, the women's lost time increased to 4.3 per cent., whilst the men's lost time decreased to 4.0 per cent.

Grouping the results of all three factories together and averaging them when the hours worked were the same, we

J

observe the following close parallel between hours of work and time lost from sickness.

		63¼	62	54
Men	Hours of work	63¼	62	54
	% time lost from sickness...	7.0	5.7	4.0
Women	Hours of work	62	54	44
	% time lost from sickness...	6.4	4.3	3.1

Though the *average* results show a striking correspondence between hours of work and sickness, great variations are observed from month to month, and even from half year to half year, as can be seen from the Table (*e.g.*, at Factory B). The time lost from avoidable causes showed no sort of parallel to that lost unavoidably, except for the men at Factory C. In their case the avoidable lost time was more than twice as great in the 63¼ hour period as in the 54 hour period, and probably a portion of this time was really lost unavoidably, owing to fatigue. At the other factories, and in the women at Factory C, the avoidable lost time generally varied *inversely* with the unavoidable time. This suggests that the lost time assigned to sickness was over-estimated, rather than under-estimated as in Loveday's data, but probably many industrial workers, and especially the women, get into the habit of taking an occasional day off from work whether they are sick or not. Thus we see from the Table that at each of the three factories the women lost almost the same amount of *total* time during each of the two or three statistical periods, in spite of the considerable variations of avoidable and unavoidable time.

Other evidence of the influence of fatigue on lost time was obtained at Factory C, where the time keeping of groups of women on specific operations was determined.[1] It was not possible to separate the time lost avoidably and unavoidably, but from the total times recorded in the Table it will be seen that the women on the rather light operation of boring the shells lost only two-thirds as much time as those on the heaviest operation (rough turn). Also the average time lost during the 54 hour week was 1.5 per cent. greater than that in the 44¼ hour week.

Shell operation.	Character of work.	Time lost during		
		44¼-hour weeks.	54-hour weeks.	Mean.
61 women boring	Rather light ...	3.7 %	4.7 %	4.2 %
26 women recessing and threading	Moderate	3.9	7.6	5.7
36 women rough turning	Rather heavier ...	6.8	6.5	6.6
Mean ...		4.8	6.3	5.5

[1] Report No. 6 of Industrial Fatigue Research Board, 1920, p. 32.

Since it is the exception for employers to differentiate between avoidable and unavoidable lost time in their records, the question arises as to the possibility of estimating sickness from the total times lost. Before describing the method I have suggested,[1] it is desirable to know something as to the times lost by the individual workers of a group. With this object I classified the time keeping of about 80 women engaged in turning fuse bodies, during 10 weeks (in Sept.-Dec., 1916), when they were on a $58\frac{1}{2}$ hour week. In all, 763 weekly hours of work were classified, and out of this number 39 per cent. amounted to $58\frac{1}{2}$-58 hours, or represented practically perfect time keeping. Another 25 per cent. came to $57\frac{3}{4}$-$50\frac{1}{4}$ hours, so on 64 per cent. of all possible occasions the women lost $8\frac{1}{4}$ hours or less of work per week. As they did $8\frac{1}{2}$ hours on Saturdays, and 10 hours on other days, it follows that on none of these occasions can a whole day's work have been lost. On the other hand, it is probable that most of the 21 per cent. of women who put in 50-$40\frac{1}{4}$ hours work did stay away for a whole day.

ANALYSIS OF TIME KEEPING

Hours worked in a $58\frac{1}{2}$ hours week.		Women turning fuse bodies (lost 15.6 % time).	Men sizing fuse bodies (lost 10.7 % time).
$58\frac{1}{2}$-58 hours	(practically perfect time keeping)	39 } 64	39 } 70
$57\frac{3}{4}$-$50\frac{1}{4}$ hours	(less than 1 whole day lost)	25	31
50-$40\frac{1}{4}$ hours	(probably 1 whole day lost)	21	20
40-$30\frac{1}{4}$ hours	(probably 2 whole days lost)	8	5.5
30-$20\frac{1}{4}$ hours	(probably 3 whole days lost)	2.5	2.5
20-$\frac{1}{4}$ hours	(probably 4 or 5 whole days lost)	2	1
0	(absent all the week)	2.5	1
		100.0	100.0

It will be seen from the Table that only small percentages of the women put in less than $40\frac{1}{4}$ hours, and that 2.5 per cent. of them were absent for the whole week. The total time lost averaged 15.6 per cent., so that it was very considerable. In a

[1] Memos. Nos. 12 and 18 of Health of Munition Workers Committee, 1916 and 1917.

group of men engaged in sizing fuse bodies the total time lost
in the 58½ hour weeks of the same statistical period averaged
10.7 per cent., and from the analysis in the Table it will be seen
that these men put in 40¼ or more hours with about the same
frequency as the women, but that they put in 40 or less hours
much less frequently, and this was the cause of their better
average time keeping.

I think it will be generally admitted that when a manual
worker stays away for a whole week it is almost always because
of sickness, and that when he (or she) stays away for less than
a whole day it is generally for other reasons than sickness.
On these assumptions we can say that 64 per cent. of the women
lost 0-8¼ hours avoidably, and 2.5 per cent. of them lost the
whole week unavoidably.   Probably most of the women who
stayed away for more than one day did so because of sickness,
whilst of those who stayed away for one day only, part were
sick and part were not.   In comparison with the women, it
appears as if the men lost rather more avoidable time, whilst
they almost certainly lost less unavoidable time.

I have applied this method of analysis of time keeping by
classifying separately what I have termed (a) broken time, (b)
short weeks, and (c) absent weeks.   If any worker put in less
than 45 hours of work out of a possible 57 hours or more (i.e.,
put in a ' short week '), I assumed that the time lost was probably because of sickness.   If he put in more than 45 hours, I
assumed that the time lost was mostly because of slackness, or
was avoidable, and I called this ' broken time.'   A classification
of the times lost under the three categories during 13 months
(from Nov., 1915, to Dec. 1916) by the workers at a fuse factory
gave the following results.[1]

ANALYSIS OF TIME KEEPING

Operatives.	Character of operation.	Mean percentage of time lost as			Total lost time.
		Broken time.	Short weeks.	Absent weeks.	
Women gauging fuse parts	Very light	4.4	2.0	2.3	8.7
Youths boring top caps	Light	4.1	3.5	1.9	9.5
Women milling fuse bodies	Light	5.9	4.4	1.8	12.1
Women turning fuse bodies	Moderate	6.2	5.4	2.6	14.2
Men sizing fuse bodies	Heavy	4.9	6.1	2.1	13.1

[1] Cf. Memo. No. 18 of Health of Munition Workers Committee, p. 12.

Taking the total lost time first, it will be seen that this corresponds closely with the character of the work done, except that the men on the heavy operation of sizing lost rather less time than the women on the moderately heavy operation of turning fuse bodies. This was probably because their usual hours of work were shorter (Cf. Chapter III). As regards the time lost from 'absent weeks,' there is very little to choose between the different groups of workers, but the time lost from 'short weeks' varies greatly. It was at a minimum of 2.0 per cent. in the women on the light sedentary operation of gauging fuse parts, and increased steadily to a maximum of 6.1 per cent. in the men on heavy work. The 'broken time' was much more steady than the short weeks, so that these results, taken as a whole, support the method of analysis adopted. It is not to be compared in value with the direct classification of lost time under avoidable and unavoidable headings, but it is better than no classification at all.

The favourable influence of a reduction in the hours of work on the time lost from sickness may continue progressively for several years after the change. This was well shown by the state of the sick benefit fund at the Engis Chemical Works, when the working day was reduced from 10 hours to $7\frac{1}{2}$ hours (Cf. Chapter IV. p. 69). During the 10-hour day period (1889 to 1892) there was so much sickness that expenditure considerably exceeded receipts, but from 1892 onwards, when the $7\frac{1}{2}$ hour day came into force, there was a gradually increasing excess of receipts over expenditure. In 1893 the excess amounted to 400 francs, in 1896 to 800 francs, in 1899 to 2,100 francs, and in 1904, to 3,300 francs. The men showed a new spirit of sobriety and self-respect. They abandoned clandestine drinking in the factory, and even outside working hours drunkenness almost entirely ceased. The men acquired the habit of invariably washing and changing their clothes before leaving the factory—signs of a new personal self-respect.[1]

The Causes of Avoidable Lost Time

SYSTEMS OF WAGE PAYMENT.—Of all the causes responsible for variations in the amount of avoidable lost time, those dependent on systems of wage payment are probably the most potent. Workers on a piece rate are apt to keep much worse time than those on a time rate, especially if the working hours are long, as they know that they can more or less make up for the hours they have lost by greater exertions in the hours during which they put in an attendance. A large body of evidence relating to piece workers and time workers was obtained at shipyards, and some of it is summarised in the Table.

[1] Cf. Goldmark. "Fatigue and Efficiency," p. 151. 1913.

PERCENTAGE OF TIME LOST BY SHIPYARD WORKERS (1915-1916)

Occupation·		Shipyard A	Shipyard B	Shipyard C	Shipyard D	Mean.	
Piece rate workers	Riveters	19	24	20	31	24	21
	Platers	18	–	16	25	20	
	Caulkers	24	25	18	24	23	
	Drillers	18	9	16	24	17	
Time rate workers	Fitters	8	–	13	13	11	11
	Joiners	9	–	5	–	7	
	Labourers	10	–	13	–	12	
	Carpenters	12	–	11	12	12	
	Electricians	–	–	10	14	12	

These data were obtained at four large yards, and they show the average time keeping during certain periods in 1915 and 1916. Data from yard A relate to the full 104 weeks, those from B to 48 weeks, from C to 23 weeks, and from D to 22 weeks. The first half of the workers recorded were on pure piece rates, and the second half on time rates. It will be seen that on an average the piece workers lost 21 per cent. of their time, and the time workers, 11 per cent., or half as much, but the comparison is not absolutely reliable, as the men were putting in a certain unknown amount of overtime. The piece rate workers were all men engaged on the iron work of the ship, and, as a group, were a good deal more exposed to the weather than the time rate workers. However, this was not the cause of their bad time keeping, as is shown by the following data, which relate to groups of men engaged on very similar work, but under different conditions of exposure.

TIME LOST BY OUTDOOR AND INDOOR WORKERS

Occupation.	Time lost by	
	Shipyard men, working out of doors.	Engine-shop men working indoors.
Platers (journeymen)	16·0 %	6·7 %
Platers (apprentices)	15·7	6·4
Fitters (journeymen)	11·2	10·7
Fitters (apprentices)	9·4	9·5

It will be seen that the shipyard platers, who were on a piece rate, lost about $2\frac{1}{2}$ times more time than the boiler platers in the engine shops at the same shipbuilding works, the reason being that these boiler platers were paid at a time rate. The fitters, however, who were on a time rate whether they worked in the shipyard or in the engine shops, lost about the same amount of time in each instance. The data relate to groups of 130 to 336 shipyard men, and of 50-400 engine-shop men, and they represent averages of two month periods in 1915, 1916, and 1918.

Time keeping is affected, not only by the system of payment, but by the scale of pay. This is shown by the graphs in Fig. 29, which record the average amount of time lost by shipyard

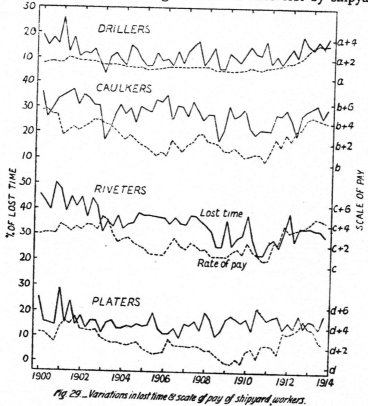

Fig 29.— Variations in lost time & scale of pay of shipyard workers.

workers in every quarter of the year from January, 1900, till December, 1913. The data in each case relate to groups of 200 to 250 men (or squads in the case of the riveters), all of whom were on piece rates. The average daily rate of pay of the men is indicated as a dotted line, and it underwent considerable variations during the 14 years. I am not at liberty to quote it in absolute figures, but it may be stated that the drillers were paid at the lowest rate, and then in order came the caulkers, the riveters and the platers. In correspondence with this rate of pay, the drillers were the best time keepers, and they lost only 13 per cent. of their time during the whole period. The better paid caulkers lost 28 per cent. of their time, and the still better paid riveters lost 34 per cent. of theirs, but the platers, who were paid most of all, formed an exception, as they lost only 16 per cent. of their time.

It will be seen from the Table of values that in all four classes of workers the scale of pay varied three to five shillings a day in extreme cases, and this variation usually caused more or less

Occupation.	Variation in daily scale of pay in shillings.
Drillers	a + .7 to a + 3.5
Caulkers	h + .3 to b + 5.3
Riveters	c + .5 to c + 4.8
Platers	d + .4 to d + 4.7

synchronous variations in the time keeping. In the drillers time keeping was poor in 1900-02, when pay was fairly good, whilst it was good from 1904-09, when pay was low. Then it gradually got worse again as pay improved, and it was specially bad in 1912-13, when pay was at its maximum. In the caulkers and riveters the time keeping and pay showed somewhat similar synchronous variations to those observed in the drillers, but in the platers there was little or no correspondence, as the time keeping was always fairly good, whatever the scale of pay. The time keeping of the riveters was remarkably bad, and in the three years 1900—1902 the men lost no less than 43 per cent. of their time, on an average. That is to say, they worked only 31 hours out of the normal 54-hour week. It is true that they put in 6.0 hours of overtime, so their total hours of work came to 37 a week, but it would obviously have been far more satisfactory if they had kept more regular hours, and had thereby reduced the need for overtime to a minimum. Irregular time keeping is specially to be deprecated in riveters, as the men usually work together in squads of four (two riveters, a holder up, and a heater). If any of the four are absent a substitute has to be found, and this inevitably causes some delay. I saw records of cases in which, owing to absenteeism, as many as 18 different men were required to keep one squad of riveters in being during a week.

SEASONAL AND WEATHER EFFECTS.—The influence of season on time keeping is usually not at all marked, even in outdoor

LOST TIME IN RELATION TO SEASON

Occupation.	Percentage of time lost (1900-18) in quarter ending				Percentage of time lost.			Mean ratio of quarters lost to days lost.
	Mar. 31	June 30	Sept. 30	Dec. 31	1901-1911	1912-1914	1915-1917	
Mostly piece rate workers { Riveters	24.9	22.4	21.9	24.7	24.0	25.5	20.7	1.6
Holders-up	28.5	24.1	25.7	28.8	27.9	25.6	23.6	1.3
Heaters and Catchers	22.2	20.0	21.8	22.7	20.4	22.3	26.9	1.3
Platers	16.2	14.4	14.3	15.6	14.4	15.7	17.9	2.3
Plater's Helpers	19.3	16.6	17.4	18.7	18.6	16.4	16.5	1.3
Caulkers	18.6	18.0	17.4	18.5	17.3	22.7	20.0	1.9
Drillers	13.7	14.3	13.2	15.2	12.7	16.0	17.4	1.3
	20.5	18.5	18.8	20.6	19.3	20.6	20.4	1.6
Time rate workers { Carpenters	7.1	6.8	6.6	7.3	5.5	6.1	11.8	1.7
Joiners	6.4	5.4	5.9	6.8	4.8	5.9	10.4	2.0
Fitters	6.9	6.2	6.1	7.1	6.1	7.3	8.1	1.7
Labourers	8.6	7.3	7.8	8.3	7.1	7.0	10.7	1.4
	7.3	6.4	6.6	7.4	5.9	6.6	10.2	1.7

workers. This is well shown by the data in the Table, which relate to groups of 150 to 600 men at a shipyard. The left half of the Table shows the average time lost in each quarter of the year from July, 1900, to June, 1918, and it will be seen that in the iron-workers, who were mostly on piece rates, the time lost in the winter quarters (October—March) was only about 2 per cent. higher than in the summer quarters. The other shipyard workers lost about 1 per cent. more time in the winter than in the summer. These men were on time rates, and on an average they lost only about a third as much time as the iron-workers (viz. 6.9 per cent. as compared with 19.6 per cent).

On the right side of the Table is recorded the time lost by the shipyard workers during three successive periods, viz., the eleven years between 1901 and 1911, the three years just before (and at the beginning of) the war, and the three full war years, 1915-1917. It will be seen that wartime had apparently no influence on the time keeping of the iron-workers, whilst it caused a considerable deterioration in that of the other shipyard workers. It is to be remembered, however, that wartime caused considerable changes in the personnel of the yards. Many of the keener and more patriotic men enlisted, and their places were often taken by inferior men. Also wages were increased, probably somewhat in excess of the usual scale of expenditure.

Since shipyard workers, and especially the riveters, often have to work without any cover whatever, they are almost inevitably affected by wet weather. I tested the effect of weather on the time keeping of the riveters at one yard during the years 1916-1917. Every day the average state of the weather was recorded, and I assigned "bad weather marks" on the following scale : showers=1 : heavy showers=2 : heavy rain=3 : continuous rain=5. The marks accruing each week were added up, and the relationship between weather and the mean number of hours worked by the riveters was found to be as follows :

Bad weather marks per week.	Number of instances.	Weekly hours worked by riveters.
0 to 1	40	43.5
2 to 5	29	42.7
6 to 9	9	42.1
10 or more	10	39.6

It will be seen that in very bad weather weeks the men worked 3.9 hours less than in good weather weeks.

THE MONDAY EFFECT.—The low output usually exhibited on the first day of the working week has been commented on in a previous Chapter. This is largely due to lack of skill from want of practice, but in addition there is a disinclination for work of any kind, and this is shown in the bad time keeping often exhibited on Mondays. The Table shows the percentage of time lost by shipyard workers during four odd weeks, selected at random during 1916, and it will be seen that it was always greater on Monday than on other days, both in piece workers and time workers.

PERCENTAGE OF TIME LOST

	Occupation.	On Mondays.	On the other week days.
Piece-rate workers	Riveters	38	28
	Caulkers	29	21
	Drillers	30	20
	Platers	26	20
Time-rate workers	Shipwrights	14	11
	Fitters	17	13
	Joiners	8	6
	Labourers	22	19

In coal miners the Monday effect appears to be more marked than in shipyard workers. The following data show approximately the number of absent underground colliers in the South Wales coal area during each of two weeks in June, 1918, when the average time keeping was good, and during each of two weeks in August, when it was bad. In both instances the absenteeism was at a maximum on Monday, and dwindled down to a minimum, which was about half the Monday value, on Friday.

Day of Week.	Absentees in June.	Absentees in August.
Monday	10,300	19,700
Tuesday	8,300	15,700
Wednesday	7,300	13,200
Thursday	6,700	11,600
Friday	5,400	10,500
Saturday	7,100	12,600
Average	7,500	13,900

It is evident that this absenteeism is not due to the strenuous nature of the miner's work. If the labour is so considerable that the men are not capable of putting in more than five days of good work per week, they ought to take their holiday in the middle of the week and not on Monday, when they are invigorated by their week-end rest.

The disinclination for work experienced by most men on Monday morning can be to some extent combated by making a later start than on other days. On a two-break system, for instance, the early 'quarter' (*i.e.*, from 6 a.m. to 8 or 9 a.m.) is sometimes omitted altogether, and work is begun after breakfast, at 8.30 to 9.30 a.m. On a one-break system, work may be begun an hour later than usual.

TWO-BREAK AND ONE-BREAK SYSTEMS

The influence of two-break and one-break systems on output has been discussed in a previous Chapter. In the two-break system the workers generally start at 6 a.m., and put in about two hours' work before they get a half-hour breakfast interval. Hence there is a considerable temptation for them to miss this unsatisfactory before-breakfast work altogether, or miss a 'quarter,' and come on to work for the chief morning spell at 8.30 to 9.30 a.m. In the last column of a previous Table (p. 153) is recorded the ratio of the number of quarters lost by shipyard workers to whole days lost during an 18-year period, and it will be seen that the average ratio was 1.6 or 1.7 to 1. In other words, for each three whole days the men stopped away from work, they stopped away five additional quarters. Different groups of men showed very different ratios. The platers head the list with a ratio of 2.3 to 1, but this high value was due, not to their stopping away for more quarters than the other iron workers, but to their absence for fewer whole days. It would have been a good thing if their system of missing quarters but of attending regularly for the rest of the working day had been more generally imitated.

The influence of two-break and one-break systems on time-keeping has been studied by Loveday,[1] and he found that a change to the latter system produced a distinct improvement. At two textile factories, when a $49\frac{1}{4}$-hour week on the one-break system was substituted for a $55\frac{1}{4}$-hour week on the two-break system, the lost time fell from 4.8 per cent. and 6.8 per cent. to 3.8 per cent. and 5.2 per cent. respectively. At an engineering works, where a 51-hour week on the one-break system was substituted for a $51\frac{1}{2}$-hour week on the two-break system, the

[1] Interim Report of Health of Munition Workers Committee, 1917, p. 58.

amount of avoidable lost time fell from 6 per cent. to 1.1 per cent. At another engineering works the time lost by bad time keeping during the two-break period was as much as 10 per cent. of possible hours, but when a one-break system was substituted the loss was reduced to 2.5 per cent.

On the one-break system the workers start at from 7 to 8 a.m., after (presumably) having had a substantial breakfast, and they work on till their dinner hour. Hence if they are late they are liable to be shut out and to miss 4 or 5 hours of work, whilst unpunctuality on the two-break system usually means the possible loss of only two hours' work. The change of system may therefore mean a great improvement in punctuality. For instance, a firm manufacturing textile machinery in 1918 reduced their hours from 53 to 48, and went on to the one-break system. They found, in consequence, that only $1-1\frac{1}{4}$ per cent. of the men arrived late, and $1-1\frac{1}{2}$ per cent. of the women, whereas under the two-break system 14-17 per cent. of the men, and 17-25 per cent. of the women were late.[1]

The advantages of the one-break system are so great that no case is reported of an engineering establishment, once they have adopted it, reverting to the old two-break system.[2] In Scotland the one-break system is now almost universal in hosiery, woollen, spinning and weaving factories, but a few textile factories in other parts of the country have reverted to the two-break system after some months' trial of the alternative scheme. The reasons appear to be that the workers, especially the women, do not feel equal to making a very substantial breakfast before starting work, and they find the usual $4\frac{1}{2}$ hour morning spell too long for them. It is to be remembered that even on the one-break system work is sometimes started at 7.30 a.m., and even if it is started at 8 a.m. some of the workers may have half-an-hour to an hour's journey from their home to the factory. Hence there may be a $5\frac{1}{2}$ hour interval between breakfast and dinner. This objection can be overcome by providing such of the operatives as desire it with breakfast at the factory canteen immediately before they start work, and by giving all of them a ten minute break in the middle of the $4\frac{1}{2}$ hour spell, during which they can get a cup of tea and light refreshment. If this short break were fixed at about 10.15 a.m., and its brief duration were insisted upon, few if any of the operatives would try to convert it into their real breakfast interval : *i.e.*, they would have taken a good meal before starting work, and would avoid the unsatisfactory before-breakfast work of the two-break system.

[1] Report of Chief Inspector of Factories, 1918, p. 3.
[2] Report of Chief Inspector of Factories, 1918, p. 3.

The improved time-keeping observed under the one-break system may be due in some part to the reduction in the total weekly hours of work, but it is probably due chiefly to the abolition of before-breakfast work. This is well shown by the experience of a firm of steam packing manufacturers.[1] They formerly adopted a 60-hour week on the two-break system, and working hours ran from 6—8.30 a.m., 9—12.30 p.m., and 1.30—6 p.m. Then a 54-hour week was followed, work being on the two-break system, but starting at 7 a.m. instead of 6 a.m. This plan was retained for three years, but it led to no improvement of time keeping, or of anything else, so a 49-hour week on the one-break system was adopted.   Work spells ran from 8—12.30 and 1.30—6, and it was found that output was maintained, whilst the time keeping and health of the workers so much improved that on these grounds alone the firm would not go back to the old hours.

TIME KEEPING OF NIGHT SHIFTS AND DAY SHIFTS

In that night work tends to act adversely on health, one would naturally expect night shift workers to keep worse time than day-shift workers, and, other conditions equal, this is actually the case. For instance, Greenwood[2] investigated the time keeping of about 500 men employed in munition work on a permanent night shift for 47 weeks, and he found that they lost 5.7 per cent. of their shifts, whilst the 1,500 men on permanent day shift lost only 4.0 per cent. of their shifts. Again, I found that at a 3 inch shell factory 50 men on permanent night shift lost 5.0 per cent. of their time, whilst 83 men employed by day on the same work lost 4.4 per cent. of their time.

When the operatives work alternate weeks or fortnights of day and night shift their time keeping is usually better by night.   Loveday records[3] the following percentages of time

Number of men		% time lost by day shift			% time lost by night shift.		
By day.	By night	Unavoid-able.	Avoid-able.	Total.	Unavoid-able.	Avoid-able.	Total.
5,500	2,700	5.5	11.0	16.5	2.1	6.3	8.4
8,600	4,400	5.2	10.0	15.2	2.2	8.1	10.3

[1] Report of Chief Inspector of Factories, 1918, p. 9.
[2] Interim Report of Health of Munition Workers Committee, 1917.
[3] Interim Report of Health of Munition Workers Committee, 1917, p. 48.

lost by large bodies of men at an engineering works. The first set of data relate to skilled men, and the second to unskilled men, and it will be seen that the men lost 5 to 8 per cent. more time by day than by night. This was chiefly owing to the time lost before breakfast in the morning.

However, even on the one-break system workers tend to keep better time by night than by day, as the night shift have no inclination to oversleep themselves or stop in bed like the day shift. This is shown by some observations which I made on a group of 700 women and girls engaged in the light sedentary occupation of gauging and assembling fuse parts.[1] These operatives put in a 63½ hour week by day and a 56½-62½ hour week by night, and during an eleven week period the women on permanent day shift lost 10.6 per cent. of their time, whilst those on alternate weeks of day and night shift lost only 7.3 per cent. The corresponding figures for the girls (aged 19 or 20) were 12.3 per cent. and 8.7 per cent.

The intrinsically harmful effect of night work is seen in the time keeping of operatives working alternate fortnights of day and night shift. The following data relate to women engaged for a three month period on the same light sedentary work of gauging and assembling fuse parts. It will be seen that on an average the day shift lost 1.3 per cent. more time than the night shift, but a study of the times lost in the individual weeks of the monthly cycle shows that both the women and the girls lost distinctly more time in the second week of their night shift fortnight than in the first week, and distinctly *less* time in the second week of their day shift fort-

	Percentage of time lost during			
	Night Shift.		Day Shift.	
	1st week.	2nd week.	1st week.	2nd week.
221 women aged 21 or more	5.8	6.4	8.2	7.5
89 girls aged 19 or 20 ...	6.3	7.9	8.8	7.3
Average ...	6.6		7.9	

night than in the first week. The effect of the night work on time keeping is cumulative, just as it was observed to be on output,[2] and the adverse effect persists into the first week of the day shift fortnight.

[1] Interim Report of Health of Munition Workers Committee, 1917, p. 35.
[2] Cf. Chapter V., p. 94.

GENERAL CONCLUSIONS

The data above described, though far from complete, are sufficient to show that it is well worth the while of employers to tabulate regularly the time keeping of their employees, and to determine how far the lost time is avoidable, and how far unavoidable. Systematic study of such time keeping records will often reveal the reasons of the absenteeism, and suggest remedies. Bad time keeping has a much more adverse effect on the output of most factories than is indicated by the loss of a certain proportion of working hours. The absence of a single man engaged on a key operation may put back a dozen dependent workers. Again, when a man sees that several of his mates are absent, he imagines that they are enjoying themselves on a holiday, and his own dormant inclination to slackness is encouraged to awake. Though it is impossible to prove it statistically, it is probable that an increase of the time lost by the workers at a factory by e.g. 5 per cent., may often lead to 10 per cent. reduction of output. Hence every reasonable precaution ought to be taken to encourage the workers to keep as perfect time as possible.

The total time lost ought not to rise much above 5 per cent., and if it is regularly over 10 per cent. there can be very little doubt that some of the conditions of work need revision. For instance, the fact above noted that shipyard workers usually lost about 20 per cent. of their time indicated most significantly that the hours of work needed alteration. Since much of this lost time was due to lost 'quarters,' the abandonment of work before breakfast, and the reduction of the working week from 54 hours to 48 hours or less, was clearly indicated. The figures likewise suggest that no man ought to be allowed extra pay for overtime work unless he has put in almost a full week of normal working hours. It borders on the ridiculous that while the riveters at one yard in 1900-1902 lost 43 per cent. of their normal working time, they were allowed to put in 6 hours overtime work at increased rates of pay.

The importance of systematically investigating the time lost by sickness is so obvious as to need no comment. It should be the regular business of a medical man officially attached to the staff to examine the sickness records, with a view to taking remedial measures whenever and wherever possible. When, in course of time, a large body of sickness records is accumulated from all kinds of factories and works in all kinds of industries, it will be possible for the authorities at individual factories to determine whether the state of health of their workers is above or below that observed elsewhere, and to adopt remedial measures if necessary.

CHAPTER IX

SICKNESS AND MORTALITY

CONTENTS

Introduction—Physique in relation to Industry—Sickness in relation to Industry—Mortality in relation to Industry —The Influence of Fatigue on Sickness—The Influence of Fatigue on Mortality.

INTRODUCTION

The crucial test as to whether the fatigue of industry falls within physiological limits, or exceeds them and becomes pathological, is found in its effects on the health of the worker. So long as a man manages to remain in good health, he has not much ground for complaint about the fatigue of his work. Supposing that he has occasional short periods of sickness, as is almost inevitable, he likewise has not much ground for complaint if his sickness does not exceed the average experienced in the healthiest trades. Even when it does exceed them, as is usually the case, it by no means follows that the excess of sickness is in any way due to the fatigue induced by industrial work. In fact we know that in many occupations, such as those of the potter, stone quarrier and file maker, the abnormal sickness and mortality experienced are due very largely to the inhalation of dust. In other occupations, such as those of lead and arsenic workers, they are due to the poisonous action of the substances handled, and in others, such as those of sorting wool and hides, they are due to bacterial infection. Hence it is a matter of great difficulty to determine how far, if at all, the sickness and mortality experienced by industrial workers are due to fatigue, and how far to other causes. There can be little doubt that in many cases fatigue is a predisposing cause of sickness, even if it is not the direct and immediate cause. Fatigue may impair digestion, and thereby interfere with the adequate nutrition of the body. Vitality is lowered, and the system becomes more liable to bacterial infection. Prof. Irving Fisher, when discussing the effect of the long working day on the health of workmen, says ' A typical succession of events is, first fatigue, then colds, then tuberculosis, then death."[1] Again,

[1] Bulletin of the Committee of One Hundred on National Health, No. 30, p. 45, 1909.

K

sickness may be due to poor factory conditions, such as bad lighting (which may cause eye strain and headaches), inadequate heating (which may induce colds), and so on. More frequently, it is due to poor conditions of home life, such as inadequate food and housing, or to lack of reasonable precautions in avoiding chills and other disabilities, or to alcoholism. Still again, it may be due to the inheritance of a poor physique, accompanied by neglect or absence of healthy conditions of life during childhood. But so important is the determination of the part played by fatigue in the production of sickness and increased mortality that, in spite of the inexactness of most of our information, it is desirable to discuss it at some length, and to point out the directions in which it may be extended and rendered more accurate. Only by analysis and discussion, coupled with the collection of fresh information, can we hope to determine to what extent sickness and mortality are due to one or other of the following causes :

(a) directly to fatigue.

(b) indirectly to fatigue.

(c) factory conditions such as lighting, heating and ventilation.

(d) occupational conditions such as the presence of dust and poisons.

(e) conditions of life outside the factory.

(f) heredity.

PHYSIQUE IN RELATION TO INDUSTRY

Industrial life has undoubtedly exerted a profound influence on the physique of the nation. It was stated in 1875[1] that 'The factory population appear to have become a distinct race, that was known at a glance, so defined had the effect of overwork and unhealthy dwellings become upon the physical appearance and condition of the people.' Again,[2] Competition. . . had in half a century produced a race of pale, stunted and emaciated creatures.' These statements hold very largely at the present day, as was revealed by the examination of men for military service during the war. The Ministry of National Service have published a detailed report[3] dealing with a portion of their statistical information, and their principal conclusions are very instructive. They afford food for much serious thought, which, it is hoped, will provoke decisive remedial action.

[1] British Sessional Papers, Vol. 16, p. 23, 1875.

[2] Mrs Sidney Webb. " The Case for the Factory Acts," London, 1901, p. 46.

[3] Report Vol I. of Ministry of National Service on Physical Examination of Men of Military Age, London, 1920.

Between November, 1917, and November, 1918, the Medical Service Boards under the control of the Ministry made 2,425,184 medical examinations, a small proportion of which were re-examinations. These were usually the lower grade men, so that the proportion of such men is thereby rather exaggerated.

The men were placed in one of the following four grades :

Grade I.   Those who attain full normal standard of health and strength and are capable of enduring physical exertion suitable to their age.

Grade II.   Those who are of moderate muscular development, and able to undergo a considerable degree of physical exertion of a nature not involving severe strain. They have fair hearing and vision, and do not suffer from progressive organic disease.

Grade III. Those who present marked physical disabilities, such as severe flat foot. They are not fit to undergo much physical exertion.

Grade IV. All those who are totally and permanently unfit for any form of military service.

As the result of the examinations, 36 per cent. of the men were placed in Grade I, 22-23 per cent. in Grade II, 31-32 per cent. in Grade III, and 10 per cent. in Grade IV ; or roughly speaking, out of every 9 men of military age in Great Britain, 3 were perfectly fit and healthy, whilst 2 were considered by the Committee who drew up the Report to be upon a definitely infirm plane of health and strength, 3 were incapable of undergoing more than a very moderate degree of physical exertion and could almost be described as physical wrecks, and the remaining man was a chronic invalid with a precarious hold on life.

Men engaged in different occupations showed very different gradings, as is seen in the following data, which relate to Yorkshire men aged 18 to 25.

GRADING OF YORKSHIRE MEN AGED 18-25

Occupation.	Grade I.	Grade II.	Grade III.	Grade IV.
Miners	72.7	12.2	11.0	4.1
Agriculturists	69.6	17.2	9.9	3.3
Engineers	60.9	23.9	13.4	1.8
Iron and steel workers ...	60.2	25.6	11.2	3.0
Woollen trade	46.1	21.3	25.5	7.1
Lace workers	45.0	26.9	22.7	5.4
Tailors	33.9	21.4	33.5	11.2

It will be seen that whilst nearly 73 per cent. of the miners, and 70 per cent. of the agriculturists, were classed as Grade I, factory workers showed a very much poorer physique, and only 34 per cent. of the tailors attained this standard. In fact, no less than 45 per cent. of the tailors fell in Grades III. or IV. Arguing from the figures in this Table, the Committee came to the following conclusion :—

"It can hardly be doubted that the gradual fall in the index of fitness shown in this Table is a true criterion of the effects of the various occupations upon the physical welfare of the workers. They correspond to what we know of the conditions of life in the several trades and their accepted effect on health too closely to be explained by the hypothesis that the agriculturist is an agriculturist because he is healthy, and the tailor a tailor because he is unhealthy. This may be true to a certain very limited extent of certain trades and industries."

The Committee have no evidence whatever to offer in support of the sweeping statement made in the first sentence of this paragraph, and the final sentence quoted shows that they themselves were a little doubtful of its validity. Such evidence as we have indicates that the index of fitness is due very largely to other causes than the occupation of the workers. For instance, the measurements of Liverpool school children made by Dr. Arkle[1] at the request of the Liverpool Education Committee showed remarkable differences of stature and weight at schools of different grades. From the Table it will be seen that four groups of schools were examined. The boys at the higher grade schools were, at the age of 7, 2.1 to 3.4 inches taller than the boys at the Council Schools, and at the ages of 11 and 14 they were progressively taller. In fact, boys of 14 were no less than 6.5 inches taller than the sons of the poorest class of parents, who were almost entirely unemployed or casual labourers.

Coupling the observations at the various grades of Council Schools with those made at the Higher Grade Schools, it is evident that there is a close parallel between stature and the general conditions of life surrounding the boys during childhood. It is more than likely that the differences observed are due in some part to heredity, and that the children of the well-to-do parents were of better physique at the time of birth, but of this we have no evidence. Such evidence is almost unobtainable, and the only way to get it would be to take a large sample of the offspring of unemployed and casual labourers, and transfer them, from the time of their birth onwards, to the con-

[1] Cf. Leverhulme. "The Six-Hour Day," p. 171. London, 1918.

ditions under which the higher grade boys are brought up. Their average stature, as compared with that of the children left in their native surroundings, would then afford a direct measure of the influence of environment.

STATURE OF LIVERPOOL SCHOOL BOYS

Class of School.	Height in inches of boys aged			Difference in height from boys of higher grade schools.		
	7	11	14	7	11	14
Higher Grade Schools: Sons of wealthy citizens	47.4	55.5	61.7	–	–	–
Council Schools: Sons of well-to-do citizens	45.3	53.1	58.2	2.1	2.4	3.5
Council Schools: Sons of labouring classes	44.8	51.8	56.2	2.6	3.7	5.5
Council Schools: Sons of unemployed or casual labourers	44.0	49.7	55.2	3.4	5.8	6.5

The weight of the boys corresponded with their differences of stature. For instance, boys of 14 at the higher grade schools weighed 94.5 lbs., or 23.4 lbs. more than the sons of the casual labourers. There can be little doubt that these substantial differences of stature and weight are accompanied by considerable differences in capacity to endure physical exertion, and that when the boys at these schools grew to military age, they would be found to show very different gradings, quite apart from any effects of occupation. The only way to determine the genuine effect of occupation upon physique would be to take large samples of youths who were just going to start on such trades as mining and tailoring, and transpose them. A medical examination from year to year coupled with a corresponding examination of untransposed men, would show what effect, if any, the industry had upon their health and physique. It is probable that, at the outset, many of the would-be tailors would find themselves physically incapable of following the miner's calling. The miners are proverbially a hardy race, the sons and grandsons of miners, and though I can quote no direct evidence, I have no doubt whatever that their children are of better physique than the children of tailors.

Again, it is well known that the strongest men are often selected for the heaviest trades, such as that of iron and steel manufacture, as it is found that men of poor physique are very little use, and, if they attempt the work, they soon have to be discharged as incompetent.   Hence it follows that the differences of grading recorded by the Ministry of National Service afford no proof whatever of the direct effects of industry upon physique, though they suggest that *a part* of the differences are due to this cause.   How large that part is we cannot say, but it is evidently of great importance that attempts should be made to determine it.

SICKNESS IN RELATION TO INDUSTRY

There is a well marked seasonal variation in the sickness experienced by industrial workers.   In Fig. 30 is represented the relative number of members of a large Trade Union who

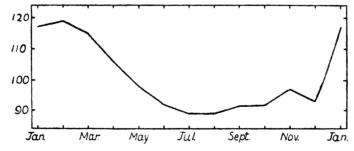

Fig. 30. _ Seasonal variation in sickness.

were on sick benefit each month during the years 1910 to 1915.[1] Taking the average amount of sickness as 100, it will be seen that in February it rose to a maximum of 119, and then fell gradually till in July and August it reached a minimum of 89. Probably a small part of this low value was due to holidays, but in any case the sickness was considerably smaller in the summer months than in the winter and spring.

The amount of sickness varies greatly in different occupations.   This is well shown by the statistics collected by a sick benefit society at Leipsig, during the years 1887 to 1904.[2]   In 1902 there were 141,000 members, so the data are reliable for the time at which they were collected.   It will be seen that the men in the heavy industries of iron and steel manufacture and of iron founding lost about 12 days a year from sickness, whilst those engaged in work such as book-keeping and accounting, which involved no physical strain, lost only 5 days a year. However, it cannot be said that the data, taken as a whole, show a

[1] Cf. Interim Report of Health of Munition Workers Committee, 1917, p. 51.
[2] Kober and Hanson. " Diseases of Occupation and Vocational Hygiene," p. 749.

close parallel between the amount of sickness and the physical fatigue of the occupations. For instance, compositors and type setters lost twice as much time as weaving mill operatives.

Occupation.	Days of sickness per year.	
	Males.	Females.
Iron and steel workers	12.6	—
Iron founders and machinists ...	11.9	16.7
Compositors and type-setters ...	11.5	—
Agricultural labourers	10.2	11.6
Textile mill workers	8.8	12.3
Printers and lithographers	8.5	11.3
Boot and shoe makers	6.4	9.3
Weaving mill operatives	5.6	—
Book-keepers and accountants ...	5.1	5.6

The women invariably lost more time than men employed in the same industry, and this excess of sickness on the part of the women has been observed in many other instances.[1] In Swiss cotton spinning mills it was found that the women experienced 28 per cent. more sickness than the men, whilst in the weaving sheds they experienced 39 per cent. more. Again, the sickness recorded by German insurance societies in the years 1888 to 1907 was usually, though not invariably, greater for women than for men. The men and women were not employed in the same trades, but presumably the character of the occupations was in each case suited to the sex of the workers.

Year.	Days of sickness lost per year by	
	Men.	Women.
1888	5.6	5.1
1892	6.3	5.7
1903	7.0	7.2
1904	7.6	8.2
1905	7.8	9.3
1906	7.3	8.0
1907	7.9	8.3

The number of cases of sickness was always less among the women than among the men, but the duration of sickness per

[1] Cf. Goldmark. "Fatigue and Efficiency," 1913, p. 40.

case was greater. It averaged 21.7 days for the women and 18.0 days for the men in these insurance societies.

A very extensive body of evidence relating to the sickness of its members was put on record by the Manchester Unity of Odd-fellows Friendly Society. The data concern two main groups of men—(a) about 500,000 agricultural and outdoor workers; (b) about 30,000 men engaged in the iron and steel industry, and to a small extent in quarries and chemical works. From the average results recorded in the Table it will be seen that at each age group these latter workers experienced much more sickness than the former, men of 20-44 losing about half as much time again.

SICKNESS IN RELATION TO OCCUPATION

Age Group.	Weeks of sickness per year experienced by		Excess of sickness experienced by iron and steel workers.
	Agriculturists.	Iron & steel workers	
20—24	.82	1.20	46 %
25—34	.92	1.37	49
35—44	1.28	1.88	47
45—54	2.14	2.83	32
55—64	4.61	6.27	36

The influence of the weekly hours of work of munition workers, and the severity of their occupation, on the time lost by sickness, have been discussed in the previous Chapter. Other information bearing on the health of munition workers was obtained by Agnew,[1] who visited eight factories and subjected about 3,000 men and boys to a careful medical examination. Only men aged 41 or more, and boys aged 18 or less, were examined, and Agnew found that 78 per cent. of the men, and 91 per cent. of the boys, were in normal health; 17 per cent. and 8 per cent. respectively were slightly below normal; 5 per cent. and 1 per cent. were much below normal, and 0.4 per cent. and 0.2 per cent. were in a bad state of health. Of course, men who were really sick would escape examination altogether, but amongst the men who were well enough to turn up at the factories there was a distinct relationship between health and duration of weekly hours of work. It will be seen from the Table that in every instance a larger proportion of the men and boys working the longer hours showed subnormal health than of those working the shorter hours.

[1] Interim Report of Health of Munition Workers Committee, p. 86.

HEALTH OF MUNITION WORKERS IN RELATION TO WEEKLY HOURS OF WORK

	Weekly hours of work.	Very heavy or heavy labour.		Medium or light labour.	
		Number of workers in group.	Percentage with subnormal health.	Number of workers in group.	Percentage with subnormal health.
Men aged 41 or more	Under 70	190	21	203	23
Ditto	Over 70	147	31	82	33
Boys aged 18 or less	Under 60	165	5	162	8
Ditto	Over 60	62	11	1010	10

The health of the 2,509 female munition workers examined by Miss Campbell[1] did not appear to be so good as that of the men, for only 58 per cent. of them were in good health, 35 per cent. showed some signs of fatigue or ill-health, and 7 per cent. showed marked fatigue or ill-health.

Sickness in industrial workers is often of a neurasthenic type. The great nerve strain of certain occupations such as telephone operating has been commented on in a previous Chapter, but in some countries nervous overstrain appears to be rife in many industries. It is found that in German insurance sanatoria, other than those devoted to tuberculosis cases, the most common diseases observed in the patients are nervous disorders springing from industrial overstrain.[2] Two physicians in the Berlin State Insurance Sanatorium at Beelitz state that neurasthenia is steadily increasing in frequency and in severity. Of the 1815 male patients discharged in 1909 nearly 70 per cent. were nervous cases, and of the total number of 54,234 working days lost by the men at the Sanatorium, no less than 44,965 days were due to nervous disorders. Of the 34,244 days lost by the women, 25,075 days were due to these disorders. This astonishing excess of nervous cases is due partly to the physicians describing many cases of heart trouble, indigestion, and other illnesses as neurasthenic, but doubtless they had good grounds for their diagnosis.

A good deal of evidence of industrial overstrain comes from America. A physician at the St. Louis Jewish Dispensary stated that of the 7,000 government workers who applied for relief during the period of ten years studied by him, 20 per cent.

[1] Final Report of Health of Munition Workers Committee, p. 147.
[2] Goldmark. "Fatigue and Efficiency," p. 103.

to 30 per cent. were the subjects of neurasthenia.[1] He considered that two of the most important factors in the causation of this condition were irregularity of employment and piece-work. Again, the U.S. Public Health Service, in a report[2] dealing with tuberculosis among industrial workers in Cincinnati, ascribed the prevalence of that disease in the boot and shoe industry to speeding-up more than to dust inhalation. They consider that "high-pressure work. . . is one of the most important causes of the lowered physical vitality noticed among these workers, as the constant strain of work at top speed, week after week, must tell in the end." Other evidence of over-speeding in the boot and shoe industry has been adduced by the U.S. Bureau of Labour, and by labour unions.[3]

In this country there was undoubtedly a great deal of industrial overstrain during the first years of the war, but in peace times it is probably not so extensive as it appears to be in Germany and the United States. It is specially liable to occur in women such as dressmakers who are overworked at certain seasons of the year, and of other women, such as laundresses, who are liable to be overworked during the middle days of the week. In such intermittent occupations much can be done by a little forethought on the part of employers to reduce the intermittency, whilst the recent and very general movement in favour of shorter working hours will do still more to reduce chronic overstrain.

MORTALITY IN RELATION TO INDUSTRY

The mortality of different classes of industrial workers is subjected to a detailed investigation by the Registrar-General for a triennial period at ten year intervals,[4] and his statistics reveal very striking differences in different industries. A small sample of his figures is recorded in the Table, and it will be seen that in most of the industries quoted the mortality is less than the average observed in all the male population of the Kingdom. In agriculture, the mortality of men aged 35-45 is only about half as great as the average of all males, and in coal mining, three-fourths as great. In the iron, steel, nail and chain industries, however, the mortality is greater than the average in all the age groups recorded.

It will be seen that the relative mortality differs considerably at different ages. In textile workers, for instance, it is greater than the average between the ages of 20 and 25, and again from 45 upwards, but between the ages of 25 and 45 it is well

[1] *Op. cit.*, p. 110.
[2] U.S. Public Health Bulletin, No. 73, 1916.
[3] Cf. Report No. 7 of National Industrial Conference Board, 1918, p. 59.
[4] Cf. Registrar General's Annual Report, 65, Suppl. II., 1908.

below the average. In order to compare the mortality of the workers as a whole in the different industries, the Registrar-General calculates a ' comparative mortality figure ' for the workers aged 25 to 65. Men below 25 are ignored, as they

RELATIVE MORTALITY (1900-1902).

Occupation.	Age Group.				
	20-25	25-35	35-45	45-55	55-65
All males (occupied and retired) ...	100	100	100	100	100
Agriculturists (farmers, graziers, gardeners, agricultural labourers)	74	66	55	57	62
Builders	75	79	94	97	96
Coal miners	100	81	73	81	107
Engine & machine makers and fitters	98	79	81	87	100
Metal workers	95	92	96	103	111
Textile workers	102	90	89	106	122
Iron, steel, nail & chain manufacturers	104	110	113	123	122

often shift from one occupation to another, whilst the men over 65 often drop out of their occupation altogether. The comparative figure depends on the mortality in the various age groups and on the relative numbers of men falling in them, and from the Table it will be seen that the differences observed in the industries recorded are even more pronounced than in those previously quoted. From the 1900-1902 data it will be seen that in the two healthiest industries the men had a comparative mortality figure of about 600, whilst in the least healthy industry, that of the potter, the figure was 1,420, or nearly two-and-half times greater.

DIMINUTION IN MORTALITY

Occupation.	Comparative mortality figure.		Percentage decrease.
	1890-1892.	1900-1902.	
Railway engine driver, stoker ...	934	582	38
Brick and tile maker	857	622	27
Platelayer, railway labourer	1221	707	42
Shipbuilder	836	735	12
Machine maker and fitter	1256	848	32
Bricklayer, mason, builder	1157	862	25
Bookbinder	1225	889	27
Printer	1267	935	26
Textile dyer and bleacher	1585	1066	33
Dock labourer, wharf labourer ...	2114	1374	35
Lead manufacturer, leaden goods maker	2061	1385	33
Potter, earthenware manufacturer ...	1970	1420	28

A comparison with the mortality observed ten years pre-viously shows a great improvement in almost all cases, and in platelayers and railway labourers the mortality fell 42 per cent. There is some doubt as to whether the data for the two periods are strictly comparable, for the system of classification is not always identical. For instance, it was found that in a few groups of industrial workers, such as shop-keepers and general labourers, there was apparently an increase of mortality during the decennial period, but this was probably due in part to a more accurate statement of occupation in 1900-02.

The mortality figures for the 1910-12 census have not yet been published, but information received privately from the Registrar General shows that the mortality continued to decrease, though not at so great a rate as in the previous decennium. For instance, the mortality of railway engine drivers and stokers was 8 per cent. less than in 1900-02, that of dock and wharf labourers was 18 per cent. less, and that of potters and earthenware manufacturers, 16 per cent. less. These last two groups of workers showed comparative mortality figures of 1,127 and 1,196 respectively, so that their death rate was half as great again as that of all occupied and retired males, who had a figure of 790, and two-and-a-half times that of men such as gardeners, nurserymen and seedsmen, who had a figure of 457.

The great differences of mortality shown by these figures may be due in part to fatigue incident to the various occupations, but we have no information to that effect. All we know is that in some occupations the excessive mortality is largely due to special disabilities not related to fatigue at all. For instance, the high mortality observed in potters is due in large part to the inhalation of dust. A comparison of the mortality of the potters and other males in six Staffordshire pottery towns by Dr. R. Reid[1] gave the following comparative figures :

COMPARATIVE MORTALITY IN POTTERY TOWNS IN 1900-1902

Occupation.	Phthisis.	Respiratory Diseases.	Other causes	All causes.
Potters	318	637	771	1726
Artizans	144	286	587	1017
Other occupied males ...	124	209	730	1063
All males, England and Wales	186	174	640	1000

[1] Report of Departmental Committee on Lead, Vol. II., p. 71, 1910.

It will be seen that whilst the mortality of the potters from other than lung diseases was about the same as that observed in the rest of the male population of the pottery towns, the deaths from phthisis were 2½ times as numerous, and from other respiratory diseases three times as numerous. Dr. Reid calculated that, compared with the other industrial workers in the six towns investigated, about 60 extra men and women died every year from phthisis, and 90 from other respiratory diseases. This was almost entirely the result of inhaling pottery dust, for only 4 of the deaths were due to lead poisoning.

In addition to its direct effect on mortality, industry may exert a considerable indirect effect through its influence on the second generation. Women workers in some industries not only bear fewer children than the average, but the infants suffer a higher mortality, and it is probable that the physique of such as survive is impaired. For instance, the Medical Officer of Health at Kearsley, a Lancashire town of about 10,000 inhabitants, found that whilst the general death rate remained stationary between 1885 and 1904, the infant death rate rose from 143 to 229. During the same period the birth rate fell from 39 to 27 per 1,000. These striking figures were attributed to the fact that the town had developed into a manufacturing district of many mills, where large numbers of women are employed.[1] Again, Sir George Newman[2] showed that the infant mortality rate in eight typical textile towns in 1896-1905 was considerably higher than in eight typical non-textile (but industrial) towns, the average values being 182 and 150 respectively. Probably this difference was chiefly dependent on the fact that no less than 43 per cent. of the industrial women in the textile towns were married or widowed, as against 3 per cent. of the industrial women in the non-textile towns.

The effect of industry on birth rate is strikingly shown by figures relating to 172,365 Italian working women. Prof. Broggi states that between the ages of 15 and 54 their fertility was only about a third as great as that shown by Italian women in general, the average child-bearing coefficient being 45 per 1,000 as compared with 120 per 1,000.[3]

THE INFLUENCE OF FATIGUE ON SICKNESS

None of the evidence quoted above definitely shows the influence of fatigue on mortality, and but little of it indicates its influence on sickness, though some lost time data recorded in the last chapter showed a very definite effect. Mr. E. A.

[1] Cf. Goldmark. "Fatigue and Efficiency," p. 94.
[2] G. Newman. "Infant Mortality," 1907, p. 105.
[3] Cf. Goldmark. "Fatigue and Efficiency," p. 96.

Rusher and I have recently[1] tried to obtain other information
on the subject in some branches of the iron and steel
industry. For this purpose we tabulated the sickness and
mortality data of about 22,000 iron and steel workers for the
years 1913-1918. These data had accrued under the National
Health Insurance Act, for under this Act all industrial workers
receive sickness benefit for illnesses of over three days' duration,
and the cause and length of these illnesses are accurately
recorded. We divided causes of sickness into four categories,
of which (a) included rheumatism, sciatica and allied disorders :
(b) included pneumonia, bronchitis, influenza, pleurisy, coughs,
colds, and other diseases of the respiratory tract (except
phthisis) : (c) included injuries incurred when following employment, and (d) included sickness due to all other causes, and
injuries incurred when not following employment. The intention
of this scheme of classification was to separate off the classes
of sickness which are generally supposed to be incurred by men
who undertake hot and heavy work, causing vigorous perspiration. Such men, if they do not speedily change into dry
clothing, are thought to be specially liable to suffer from
rheumatism, and from respiratory diseases.

In the Table is shown the number of days of sickness
experienced per year. It averaged 6.5 working days for the
whole body of steel workers, and of this time 2.0 days were due

DAYS OF SICKNESS PER YEAR EXPERIENCED BY STEEL
WORKERS AGED 16 TO 70

Occupation.	Days of sickness per year.					Percentage variation from the average of all workers combined.				
	Rheumatism.	Respiratory diseases.	Injuries.	Other causes.	All causes.	Rheumatism.	Respiratory diseases.	Injuries.	Other causes.	All causes.
Steel melters, teemers and pitmen	1.3	2.2	1.2	3.3	8.0	+44	+10	+71	+14	+23
Puddlers ...	1.6	2.7	.7	2.8	7.8	+78	+35	0	—3	+20
Tinplate millmen ...	.9	2.1	.8	3.5	7.3	0	+5	+14	+21	+12
Rolling mill men, soaker men, hot bank men	.9	2.0	.9	3.2	7.0	0	0	+29	+10	+8
Engine men, crane men, locomotive men	.6	2.2	.4	2.8	6.0	—33	+10	—43	—3	—8
All other workers (largely labourers)	.8	1.9	.5	2.7	5.9	—11	—5	—29	—7	—9
All workers combined	.9	2.0	.7	2.9	6.5	0	0	0	0	

[1] Report No. 5 of Industrial Fatigue Research Board, 1920.

to respiratory diseases, and .9 day to rheumatism. The steel melters and pitmen showed 23 per cent. more sickness than the average, the puddlers 20 per cent. more, the tinplate millmen 12 per cent. more, and the rolling mill men 8 per cent. more. All of these groups of men, and especially the first three groups mentioned, are employed on heavy work carried out at high temperatures, whilst the remaining two groups of men recorded in the Table, viz., the engine and crane men, and the " other workers," who are to a large extent general labourers, are for the most part employed on lighter work, carried out under normal conditions of temperature. These two groups showed 8 to 9 per cent. less sickness than the average, so that at first sight it looks as if there were a clear relationship of cause and effect, but an analysis of the time lost under the various categories of sickness does not altogether bear out the clarity of the relationship. The excess of sickness experienced by the puddlers was due entirely to rheumatism and respiratory diseases, and this excess is presumably owing to the custom followed by many puddlers of alternating periods of extremely hard work, generally of about 20 minutes' duration, with periods of similar length in which they rest or do light work. Thereby they incur great risk of chills. The steel melters owed some of their excess of sickness to rheumatism and respiratory diseases, but even more of it to injuries and to " other causes." Since their heavy work comes in occasional bursts, when it is excessively severe, alternating with long periods of comparative rest, and in that some of the men put on a dry shirt after a bout of heavy work, it is probable that they do not run so much risk of rheumatism and respiratory diseases as the puddlers, but the excess of sickness from " other causes " suggests that their heavy work causes a lessened resistance to disease in general. It suggests, in fact, that their excess of sickness is to some extent due to the direct influence of the fatigue of their calling.

The tinplate millmen did not lose any more time from rheumatism and respiratory diseases than did all the workers combined, and this is probably due to the fact that they remain almost continuously at their hot and heavy work throughout their shift. I kept some of these millmen under close observation for several days, and found that they seldom took rest pauses of more than four minutes' duration, and never took more than nine minutes. Such short periods would not, as a rule, be sufficient to induce chills. Almost all of the excess of sickness experienced by the millmen was due to " other causes," so it looks as if the fatigue of their work lowered their resistance to disease in general, as it appeared to do in the steel melters. The group of blast furnace men investigated were found to show one or two days more sickness per year in the younger men, and four days more in the older men, than that experienced by the steel workers. Practically none of these blast furnace men are employed at high temperatures, but most of them have to work in the open, at fairly heavy occupations, in all kinds of weather. Hence it would seem that work under exposed conditions is a more potent cause of sickness than the fatigue incident to hot and heavy work carried out under cover. The effects of exposure were well shown by the sickness from rheumatism, for amongst the older men this was twice as great as in the steel workers.

THE INFLUENCE OF FATIGUE ON MORTALITY

The mortality of the iron and steel workers was investigated for the 1913-18 period in addition to their sickness, and the mortality rates were compared against the average values recorded by the Registrar General for all occupied and retired

TOTAL DEATHS COMPARED WITH THOSE OF ALL MALES (OCCUPIED AND RETIRED).

Occupation.	Respiratory diseases.			Tuberculosis.			All causes combined.		
	Actual.	Expected.	Percentage.	Actual.	Expected.	Percentage.	Actual.	Expected.	Percentage.
Steel melters, teemers, and pitmen	35	16.0	+119	15	20.1	—25	125	104.5	+20
Puddlers ...	30	11.6	+159	7	11.2	—38	66	73.1	—10
Tinplate millmen ...	22	14.8	+49	7	21.0	—67	69	99.3	—31
Rolling mill men, soaker men, hot bank men	36	16.7	+116	11	24.0	—54	114	112.9	+1
Engine men, crane men, locomotive men	22	13.0	+69	10	17.3	—42	77	86.5	—11
All other workers ...	165	81.2	+103	55	110.3	—50	513	541.6	—5
All workers combined	310	153.3	+102	105	203.7	—48	964	1018	—5

males, in the period 1910-12. The Table shows a portion of the comparative results obtained, and from the final column it will be seen that there were actually 964 deaths altogether, as compared with the expected number of 1,018 deaths. That is to say, the mortality of the steel workers was 5 per cent. less than that of all males. It does not follow that the steel industry is a healthy one, because "occupied and retired males" include many weaklings who are unfit for any trade, or only for light work, whilst most steel workers have necessarily to be healthy men of good physique. Again, there is a continuous weeding out of the less healthy and vigorous men in most trades, especially the heavy ones, whereby the death rate of the men remaining in the trade is lowered. But the data in the Table are roughly comparable amongst themselves, and we see that the steel melters head the list with a mortality 20 per cent. above the average of all males, or 26 per cent. above the average of the whole group of steel workers. It is distinctly probable that this excess of mortality was due to the direct effects of fatigue, for it was found that in each category of disease tabulated these melters showed a death rate above the average. The puddlers and tinplate millmen, however, showed a lower mortality than the average, so presumably the fatigue of their heavy work did them no permanent harm.

Every one of the groups of steel workers investigated showed a much greater mortality from respiratory diseases than that experienced by all males, the average excess being 102 per cent. ; i.e., 310 deaths were experienced instead of the expected number of 153.3 deaths. The puddlers headed the list, just as they did in respect of sickness from respiratory disease, and showed an excess of no less than 159 per cent. Presumably this was owing to their custom of intermittent work, for the tinplate millmen showed a smaller excess of deaths from respiratory disease than any other group of men. From tuberculosis (mostly phthisis) all the groups of men suffered considerably less than all males, the average deficiency being 48 per cent. Probably this was due partly to retirement of many of the tuberculous men from their occupation before death, and partly to the fact that most of the men, owing to their being at work under sheds or in the open air, reduce their risk of phthisis, though they incur more risk of acquiring other respiratory diseases.

The blast furnace men showed a considerably greater mortality than the steel workers. Between the ages of 16 and 33 their death rate was .8 per cent. per year, that of occupied and retired males being .4 per cent. : between 34 and 48 the rates were 1.3 per cent. and .9 per cent. respectively : between 49 and 58, 2.7 per cent. and 2.0 per cent., and between 59 and 69, 5.8 per cent. and 4.4 per cent. This excess of mortality, just like the excess of sickness, was presumably due to exposure to weather rather than to the fatigue of the industry.

To sum up, therefore, the data adduced appear to indicate that in a heavy trade such as the iron and steel industry fatigue

L

has comparatively little direct effect in increasing either sickness or mortality.   The steel melters, who have occasional bursts of excessively exhausting work, may afford an exception to this dictum, but otherwise it appears that the effects of exposure to the weather, and of resting from work when in a state of perspiration, are more potent causes of sickness and death than the fatigue incident to hot and heavy work.

CHAPTER X

INDUSTRIAL ACCIDENTS AND THEIR CAUSATION

CONTENTS

The Frequency of Accidents—The Causation of Accidents—Does Fatigue cause the Rise of Accidents during Work Spells?—The Dependence of Accidents on Speed of Production and on the Psychical State of the Workers—Other Evidence of the Effect of Speed of Production—The Influence of Alcohol Consumption—The Influence of Inexperience—The Influence of Lighting—The Influence of Temperature.

THE FREQUENCY OF ACCIDENTS

Industrial accidents are much more numerous than is generally supposed, and it is of great importance that their number should be reduced to the lowest level possible, not only on humanitarian grounds, but because they constitute a direct tax on the economic efficiency of industry. It is stated[1] that 4,554 workers were killed in 1914, and 222,000 injured, by accidents in British factories, mines and means of transport. The greatest mortality is experienced in mines and quarries, and the last report of the Chief Inspector of Mines[2] records that in 1918 no less than 1,487 men were killed in these industries, or in one case as many as 1.55 per 1,000 workers employed. For every million tons

FATAL ACCIDENTS IN MINES AND QUARRIES

Men employed in	Total in		Number per 1,000 employed in	
	1917	1918	1917	1918
Coal mines	1370	1401	1.34	1.39
Metalliferous mines ...	25	19	1.22	.91
Quarries	56	67	1.28	1.55
Total	1451	1487	—	—

[1] Labour Year Book, 1916, p. 233.
[2] Report for 1918 [Cmd. 339.]

of coal raised 5.86 miners were killed, and this terrible mortality should impress on all of us the need for strict economy in the use of coal.

The Annual Reports of the Chief Inspector of Factories and Workshops record all the accidents which are reported to them under the Notification of Accidents Act, *i.e.,* accidents which are sufficiently serious to necessitate absence from work for seven days, or, in certain cases, for one day. These records show that over 1,000 workers are killed every year and between one and two hundred thousand are injured, but these latter numbers are admittedly too small, owing to defective notification. It will be seen from the Table[1] that between 1907 and 1912 the number of accidents increased considerably. Doubtless they increased more rapidly still during the war, but the only data available are those recorded for 1918 and 1919, when

Year.	Fatal Accidents.		Non-Fatal Accidents.	
	Total number.	Relative percentage.	Total number.	Relative percentage.
1907	1179	100.0	123,146	100.0
1908	1042	88.4	121,112	98.3
1909	946	80.2	116,554	94.6
1910	1080	91.6	128,470	104.3
1911	1182	100.3	147,763	120.0
1912	1260	106.9	154,972	125.8
1918	1579	133.9	162,154	131.7
1919	1385	117.5	124,632	101.2

the mortality was respectively 42 and 24 per cent. greater than that in 1907-12.

These figures tell nothing as to the actual number of accidents occurring. In my own experience, which is limited to munition factories, minor and unreported accidents occur about thirty times more frequently than the notified and compensated accidents. Though it is probable that in most industries the ratio of minor to major accidents is not so great as this, it would be safe to say that the total number of accidents is at least ten times greater than the figures quoted in the Table. It is true that many of the minor accidents are quite trivial, and involve the loss of only the few minutes required for their dressing and re-dressing ; but a considerable number of them mean the loss

[1] Cf. Annual Report of Chief Inspector of Factories and Workshops for 1912. [Cd. 6852.]

of several days' work, and others cause such pain or discomfort during work as materially to reduce the efficiency of the worker.[1]

In America the accident roll is considerably heavier than in this country, even after making due allowance for the larger industrial population. Tolman and Kendall,[2] in their book on 'Safety,' state that in 1907 there were 35,000 fatal accidents and 2,000,000 cases of injury in the United States, and they even go so far as to say that 'in the wasted lives of our people we have been making ourselves ridiculous in the eyes of the World Powers.' They quote a criticism to the effect that 'everywhere in America, in the railways, factories and building trades, we see how little regard is paid to human life,' and they state that 'it is the general opinion of the engineering profession that one-half of the accidents in the United States are preventable.' The correctness of this opinion may be realised before many years, for Evans[3] states that between 1913 and 1917 the number of fatal accidents in industry fell from 25,000 to 22,000, an improvement of 12 per cent. The number of serious accidents fell from 700,000 to 500,000, and the accidents severe enough to keep a man from work six weeks or more fell from 300,000 to 226,000. This improvement was due to education both of employer and employee, and the use of safer types of machinery.

The accompanying Table shows the mortality of certain groups of industrial workers from accidents in the United States in 1913, and in England and Wales during the years 1900-1902.[4] If the same comparison years had been taken it is probable that

MORTALITY FROM ACCIDENTS PER 100,000 MEN EMPLOYED

Industry.	United States, 1913.	England and Wales, 1900-1902.
Coal miners	350	172
Railway employees ...	240	120 to 189
Quarrymen	170	124
Agriculturists	35	33 to 77

the differences would have been even greater than those recorded, but taking the figures as they stand, we see that the coal miners in America experienced twice the mortality of our miners. Of the various railway employees in this country, the

[1] Cf. Article by the author in the " Quarterly Review," Oct., 1919, p. 382.
[2] " Safety," by W. H. Tolman and L. B. Kendall, New York, 1913.
[3] W. A. Evans. Journal of Industrial Hygiene, Vol. I., p. 397, 1919.
[4] U.S. Department of Labour, Bulletin No. 157, 1915.

engine drivers had a mortality of 120, and guards and porters, one of 189. Of the agriculturists, the gardeners had a mortality of 33, and the farm labourers, one of 77. Hence the mortality in these industries does not appear to differ very much in this country and in the States, but the figures must be accepted with caution, as the groups of workers compared are not absolutely the same.

THE CAUSATION OF ACCIDENTS

Before attempting to suggest remedial measures for reducing the number of accidents, it is desirable to discuss accident causation somewhat fully. A few accidents, such as those due to defective machinery, show a clear relation between cause and effect, but they are exceptional. Of the 162,154 accidents reported to the Home Office in 1918, only 53,491, or a third of the whole, were due to machinery, and not more than 35 per cent. of these machinery accidents were due to absence of guards. Even the absence of a guard is only a contributory cause of accident, and other factors such as carelessness and want of thought play a considerable part, which it is important for us to investigate when considering remedies.

Evidence throwing light on accident causation can be obtained by tabulating the times of occurrence of accidents during the course of the working day, but such evidence is of very doubtful significance unless it is amplified by collateral information on output and the conditions of production. However, a very large amount of evidence concerning the hourly incidence of accidents has been collected in America and in other countries, so that it is desirable to discuss this evidence briefly. Much of it has been recorded in detail by a Committee of the British Association,[1] who have illustrated their report with numerous charts. Nearly all their records show that during the course of the morning spell of work the number of accidents per hour rapidly increases, till it reaches a maximum in the penultimate hour, which is often two to four times greater than that shown in the first hour of the spell. In the last hour there is generally some diminution of accidents, though occasionally the absolute maximum is reached in this last hour. In the afternoon spell of work the accidents usually vary in the same way as in the morning spell, since they are infrequent in the first hour, and gradually increase, but the maximum is sometimes reached earlier in the spell. The accident data were obtained in many different industries, such as textiles, engineering, metal working, building, mining, and agriculture, and were fairly consistent

[1] British Association Reports, 1915, p. 283.

in their general relationships, though the rate of increase of
accident incidence during the spells was very variable.   Some
of the data obtained by the Massachusetts Accident Board[1] are
reproduced in Fig. 31.   In all the industries referred to, the
work spells ran from 6.30 to 12.0, and from 1 to 5.30.

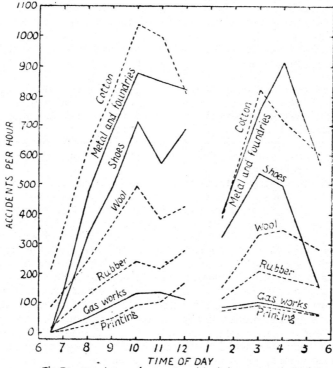

Fig 31.— Hourly incidence of accidents in various industries.

In no instance was output determined at the same time as
accident frequency, but the Committee pointed out that in such
occupations as they had been able to record the hourly output,
this output usually rose and fell during each spell somewhat like
accident frequency, though the maximum output was usually
reached in the second hour of the spell, instead of the penultimate hour.   Since output tends to diminish with fatigue,
whilst accident frequency tends to increase, they suggest that
the gradual fall of output and increase of accidents noted in the
latter part of the work spells "may well be measuring an

[1] First Report of Industrial Accident Board, Massachusetts, 1912-13.

increase of fatigue." They think that the small output observed in the first hour is due to lack of practice-efficiency, whilst the reduction of accident frequency observed in the last hour of the spells is due to the excitement which accompanies the anticipation of the meal break, with its rest from work.

The importance of fatigue in the causation of accidents is emphasized by many other investigators. Bogardus[1] stated that 82 per cent. of the 2,678 accidents studied by him involved fatigue as a casual factor. He considers that fatigue induces loss of muscular accuracy with a consequent increase of accident frequency. Imbert[2] states that innumerable instances can be adduced to prove that accidents result from the physical or mental fatigue of the workers, and in proof of his contention he records the rapid increase in the accidents experienced by the workmen in the district of Hérault during the last two hours of their morning and afternoon spells of work. Le Roy[3] considers that the increasing frequency of accidents during the course of the work spells brings us necessarily to a consideration of fatigue as one of the chief causes of accidents.

Everyone will agree that considerable fatigue is a contributory cause of accidents. Striking evidence to this effect is sometimes adduced in explanation of railway accidents. For instance, a signalman or engine driver may have made some fatal mistake because he was over-fatigued from excessive hours of work. It was pointed out to the United States Congress[4] that the signalmen, who usually work regular terms of twelve hours each, sometimes take each other's places in case of sickness or an unexpected call of a man away from his home, and thus remain on duty thirty-six hours at a time. Such prolonged hours of work must inevitably tend to diminution of mental and muscular control, but it does not by any means follow that the considerable rise of accident frequency which is almost invariably shown during the course of work spells is due wholly or even partly to the onset of fatigue.

DOES FATIGUE CAUSE THE RISE OF ACCIDENTS DURING WORK SPELLS?

A simple method of determining whether the hourly variations of accident frequency are due to fatigue is to compare the accident rate during the afternoon and morning spells of work. If a man

[1] Bogardus. American Journal of Sociology, 1911, pp. 17, 206, 351.

[2] Imbert. Revue Scientifique, June, 1904, p. 715. Imbert and Mestre. Revue Scientifique, Sept., 1904, and October, 1905, p. 521.

[3] Le Roy. Bulletin de l'Inspection du Travail et de l'Hygiéne Industrielle. Paris, 1906, No. 3-4.

[4] Nineteenth Annual Report of Interstate Commerce Commission, No. 195, 1905-1906.

is really fatigued by his work, he will certainly be in a greater state of fatigue during the afternoon spell than during the morning spell, and in such a case one would expect an excess of accidents, unless other factors come into operation which neutralise the tendency to accident increase. In order to test this hypothesis, I have calculated the ratios between the hourly rate of accidents in the afternoon and morning spells observed in all the suitable series of data recorded by the British Association Committee. These ratios are arranged in order, according to the weekly hours of work in the industry, and it will be seen that in the first half, where the hours averaged 57.1 a week, the ratio of after-

Industry.	Weekly hours of work.	Ratio of afternoon to morning accidents.
Textiles	60 or more	.94
Building	60 or more	.89
Paper	60	.92
Tannery	55–59	1.01
Coach-building	54–60	.86
Cotton	56	.88
Wool	56	.90
Motor cars	55	1.17
Motor cars	55	1.05
Pottery and glass	50–60	.94
Means ...	57.1	.96
Automatic machines	54	1.21
Shoes	54	.93
Metal and foundries	54	1.15
Chains and engineering	50	1.07
Gas works	48	1.02
Electric supply	48	.98
Building	44–48	1.03
Printing and publishing	42–48	1.25
Means ...	49.9	1.08

noon to morning accidents is .96 to 1. In the second half, where the hours averaged 49.9 a week, the ratio is 1.08 to 1, whilst the average ratio for the whole set of data is 1.01 to 1. That is to say, the accident frequency was practically no greater in the afternoon than in the morning, and it showed no indications of being larger when hours of work were long than when they were short.

We saw in Chapter II. that hourly output was practically as great in the afternoon spell as in the morning spell, unless the work was very heavy and the hours very long, but it was pointed out that the morning output was reduced by lack of practice-efficiency. Hence it followed that the extra fatigue suffered during the afternoon spell lowered output to about the same degree that lack of practice-efficiency lowered it in the morning spell. How would lack of practice-efficiency affect accident frequency? It would tend to increase it rather than diminish it, for the unpracticed neuro-muscular mechanisms of the body would be more clumsy at performing their tasks, and therefore more liable to induce accidents, than when they were practiced, but judging by the minimal number of accidents experienced in the first hour of work, lack of practice cannot be an important contributory cause. There are other factors, such as those of psychological origin, which might tend to increase morning accidents more than afternoon accidents. They will be discussed later on, but it may be said that they do not appear to be of much weight, so we must conclude that in ordinary industries, under normal hours of work, there is no good evidence that the rise of accidents observed during the work spells is due to fatigue.

Direct evidence in support of my argument is afforded by the accident frequencies observed when the workers were undoubtedly suffering from fatigue. Data in point were obtained at the fuse factory which has been mentioned in previous Chapters.[1] I tabulated all the accidents treated at the factory dressing station for a three month period (Nov. 2, 1915—Jan. 31, 1916), when the workers were on a 12-hour day and a 75-hour week, and for the subsequent $22\frac{1}{2}$ months when they were on a 10-hour day and a $64\frac{1}{2}$ to $54\frac{1}{2}$-hour week. The ratios between accident frequency during the three month 'fatigue period,' and the subsequent 14 months, are recorded in the Table, and it will be seen that in the men the accidents of various types were always, with one exception, more numerous in the fatigue period than subsequently, the average ratio being 1.20 to 1. This excess was due to the longer hours worked (12 per day instead of 10), and if due allowance be made for these hours, the excess is practically *nil*. The women, however, showed a very different record. They always experienced more than twice as many accidents in the fatigue period as in the subsequent 14 months, their average ratio being 2.87 to 1. Correcting for the longer hours worked, one may say that the women's accidents were about $2\frac{1}{4}$ times more numerous in the fatigue period. Sprains were affected no less than cuts and burns, so fatigue must have induced such extra

[1] Cf. Memo. No. 21 of Health of Munition Workers Committee, 1918. [Cd. 9046.]

RELATIONSHIP BETWEEN ACCIDENTS IN FATIGUE PERIOD AND
IN SUBSEQUENT PERIOD

Type of Accident.	Total cases occurring in fatigue period.		Ratio of accident-frequency in fatigue period to that in subsequent 14 months.		Ratio of afternoon accidents to morning accidents.			
					In fatigue period.		In subsequent 14 months.	
	Men.	Women	Men.	Women	Men.	Women	Men.	Women
Cuts ...	660	1,145	1.14	2.73	1.07	1.45	1.08	1.17
Foreign bodies in eye	68	76	0.65	2.09	0.90	1.51	0.98	1.67
Burns ...	83	136	1.16	3.50	1.31	1.29	0.76	1.12
Sprains ...	87	363	1.27	2.95	0.92	0.72	0.63	0.80
Previous injuries	338	779	1.43	3.01	—	—	—	—
Weighted mean	—	—	1.20	2.87	1.06	1.29	1.00	1.11

slackness of muscles, tendons and joints, coupled with carelessness in putting strains on them, as to lead to this unexpected
result. The previous injuries referred to were cases (mostly
septic cuts) which were dressed for the first time one or more
days after they had been incurred.

The right half of the Table records the ratios between afternoon and morning accidents. It will be seen that in the fatigue
period the men showed a ratio slightly above unity, whilst the
women showed a ratio of 1.29 to 1. In the subsequent period
the men's ratio dropped to 1.00, whilst the women's ratio was
1.11, so it is probable, for this and other reasons subsequently
referred to, that this excess of afternoon accidents in women was
the genuine result of fatigue, whilst the considerable excess
observed in the fatigue period was undoubtedly the result of
fatigue. In the men, however, there is little if any indication
that fatigue was sufficient to increase the accident frequency
either in the fatigue period, or subsequent to it.

Another proof of the great fatigue of the women during the
12-hour day period was afforded by certain of the medical data
tabulated. The women were treated at the ambulance room for
faintness nine times more frequently than the men, whilst in the
subsequent 10-hour day period they were treated only three times
more frequently. Again, the women were given sal-volatile,
almost always as a restorative, 23 times more frequently
than the men during the 12-hour day period, but only three

times more frequently during the subsequent 10-hour day period.

Further proof of the influence of hours of work on accidents in men and women was obtained at the 9.2 inch shell factory previously mentioned. During the first ten months investigated the men were working 57 hours by day and 69½ hours by night in alternate weeks, and the women 47 hours by day and 48¼ hours by night. On an average, the women experienced about 10 per cent. more accidents per hour than the men, both in day shifts and night shifts. In the next three months the men and women worked the same hours, the men now putting in 9 hours less by day and 9½ hours less by night than before, whilst the women put in 1 hour more by day and 11¾ hours more by night. In consequence of these changes, the ratio of women's accidents to men's accidents rose to 1.32 for the day shift, and to 1.74 for the night shift. That is to say, the accidents of the women on night

RATIO OF WOMEN'S ACCIDENTS TO MEN'S ACCIDENTS

Type of accident.	Day Shift.		Night Shift.	
	Men working 57 hours and women 47 hours.	Men and women working 48 hours.	Men working 69½ hours and women 48¼ hours.	Men and women working 60 hours.
Cuts ...	1.12	1.05	0.94	1.46
Foreign bodies in eye...	0.98	1.19	1.29	1.41
Burns ...	2.11	3.19	2.71	5.69
Sprains ...	1.64	2.00	1.43	1.89
Previous injuries ...	1.11	3.05	1.36	2.05
Weighted mean ...	1.11	1.32	1.09	1.74

shift increased 60 per cent., and those of the women on day shift increased 19 per cent.; but these increments were the result of very marked alterations in the hours of work, and presumably of the fatigue induced, especially as regards the women. The doubling and quadrupling of accident frequency usually observed during the course of work spells is so excessive, in comparison with these moderate increments, that for this reason alone one would be disinclined to attribute it to fatigue. Coupled with the other arguments already adduced, this evidence clearly negatives the hypothesis that fatigue is the chief factor in accident causation.

The Dependence of Accidents on Speed of Production and on the Psychical State of the Workers

To what cause or causes is the rise of accidents observed during work spells attributable, if fatigue is but little responsible? We shall see that the psychical state of the workers, with its influence on carelessness and inattention, is probably the most important cause of all, whilst speed of production is likewise an important cause.

Before endeavouring to prove the correctness of these contentions, it is desirable to offer a few criticisms on the methods employed in collecting accident data. The usual plan is to tabulate the number of accidents occurring during each hour of the working day, oblivious of the fact, already pointed out in relation to output investigation, that practically no operative starts work at the nominal starting time, whilst most operatives knock off work some minutes before nominal finishing time in order to clean up machinery, and make preparations for departure. Again, even when an operative, such as an engineer, starts work, he may spend some minutes in collecting tools and material, and this is less risky work than manipulating his machine, with its sharp cutting tools. Hence the number of accidents recorded in the first and last hours of each work spell is generally too low, in comparison with those in the middle hours. It is impossible to determine, in any given case, the extent to which the recorded information is erroneous, but the results shown in the subjoined Table (p. 191) will give an idea of what it was at a fuse factory. The accidents occurring in the first and last half or quarter hours of each work spell were enumerated separately, and it will be seen that as a rule they were abnormally low in comparison with those enumerated in the intermediate hours of full work. Hence, in considering accident incidence, it is best to ignore altogether the accidents occurring in these brief initial and final periods, and consider only the accidents in the intermediate hours.

What degree of reliability can be placed on the tabulated times of accident occurrence? In some factories the reputed time of occurrence of each accident is noted, and at other factories, only the time at which it is treated at the ambulance station. This was the plan followed at the munition factories where I collected my data, so I assumed that a short time ($5\frac{1}{4}$ minutes) must have elapsed between the time of treatment and the time of occurrence, but I found that the times of treatment of some classes of accident are quite unreliable as an index of the times of occurrence. Muscular sprains and strains in particular are more often than not treated some hours after they are incurred. I found that the operatives preferred to come for treatment at certain hours, and disliked other hours. On tabulating the hours at which previous injuries (incurred one or more days before treatment) were dressed for the first time, I found that the women treated at the fuse factory were nearly three times more numerous between 9.30 and 10.30 a.m. than between 7.30 and 8.30 a.m. The night shift women, on the other hand, came most frequently between 7 and 8 p.m., and were only two-thirds as numerous between 9 and 10 p.m., and a sixth as numerous between 4 and 6 a.m.

Accidents such as cuts, which are specially frequent in lathe and drill work, are almost always treated soon after they are incurred, because they bleed and become a nuisance. Workers who get foreign bodies in the eye likewise come for treatment at once, so I have placed chief reliance on these two classes of accident. Many investigators tabulate only those accidents which are sufficient to prevent work for the remainder of the day, for a week, or for as long as 15 days[1], and one may be fairly confident that accidents of such severity are treated very soon after they are incurred. Even then there is another source of error. For instance, an accident occurring within a few minutes of, e.g., 10 o'clock, is usually recorded as occurring at 10.0 a.m., and if the accident incidence is subsequently tabulated between the hours of 10.1 and 11.0, 11.1 and 12.0, etc., it will differ appreciably from that tabulated between the hours of 10.0 and 10.59, 11.0 and 11.59, etc. Severe accidents are, of course, much less frequent than trivial accidents, and it is much more troublesome to collect them in sufficient numbers to yield a reliable basis for discussion, but trivial accidents afford valuable material for elucidating accident causation. Nobody incurs even a trivial accident wilfully, and frequently it is a mere matter of chance whether an error of neuro-muscular co-ordination or of judgment results in a trivial accident or a severe one.

In order to compare accident incidence with output, I determined output by means of hourly power load observations.[2] These observations were made for three to five days and nights on three separate occasions (spread over 15 months) at the fuse factory, in respect of the sections where over two-thirds of the lathe and drill workers were employed, and as the mean results show a close correspondence, they may be accepted as a reliable index of output for the whole statistical period investigated. The means of the day shift and night shift values for 1917 are recorded in the Table, and are reproduced at the bottom of Fig. 32. The hourly incidence of cuts and of eye accidents is likewise

[1] Cf. Bogardus. American Journal of Sociology, Nov., 1911.
[2] Cf. Memo. No. 21 of Health of Munition Workers Committee, 1918.

ACCIDENTS PER 10,000 LATHE WORKERS PER WEEK.

	Day Shift.						Night Shift.				
Time of day.	Men: cuts		Women: cuts		Men and Women: eye accidents	Output of lathe sections in 1917	Time of night.	Men: cuts	Women: cuts	Men and Women: eye accidents	Output of lathe sections in 1917
	1915	1916 and 1917	1915	1916 and 1917							
7.0 to 7.30	9	16	2	6	3.0	56.2	6.30 to 7.0	35	16	6.7	53.5
7.30 to 8.30	24	29	17	13	4.5	101.7	7.0 to 8.0	60	31	7.1	99.0
8.30 to 9.30	33	47	26	25	5.4	105.4	8.0 to 9.0	53	33	6.8	103.6
9.30 to 10.30	64	54	72	43	6.1	110.4	9.0 to 10.0	50	32	5.1	108.5
10.30 to 11.30	54	65	90	44	6.0	110.8	10.0 to 10.30	44	33	5.0	101.6
11.30 to 12.0	36	55	57	36	4 5	100.4					
1.0 to 1.30	67	43	63	24	6.0	86.9	11.30 to 11.45	32	20	9.5	70.9
1.30 to 2.30	50	56	80	37	6.6	110.0	11.45 to 12.45	40	29	8.0	112.9
2.30 to 3.30	46	54	72	36	5.9	103.3	12.45 to 1.45	43	27	7.0	108.9
3.30 to 4.30	48	52	80	38	6.7	104.7	1.45 to 2.45	37	30	9.5	109.5
4.30 to 5.30	44	49	63	31	6.4	105.4	2.45 to 3.0	23	24	3.5	98.8
5.30 to 6.0	39	50	52	36	5.9	53.0					
6.15 to 6.30	39	—	52	—	—	—	3.30 to 3.45	33	19	3.7	79.7
6.30 to 7.15	42	—	52	—	—	—	3.45 to 4.30	36	22	7.4	115.2
7.15 to 8.0	36	—	48	—	—	—	4.30 to 5.15	34	21	8.4	111.8
8.0 to 8.30	14	—	47	—	—	—	5.15 to 6.0	36	26	5.2	103.1
							6.0 to 6.30	37	26	4.8	89.6
Actual number of accidents in statistical period	660	3687	1145	3933	969	—		1972	1904	803	—

recorded in the Table, and reproduced in the Figure. It will be seen that during the 1915 fatigue period (the 12-hour day) the women were treated for cuts at the rate of 17 in the first full hour of work (reckoned per 10,000 lathe workers per week). In subsequent hours the frequency rose rapidly, till it was 5.3 times greater in the last hour of full work of the morning spell. In the afternoon spell the cuts were numerous at first, and then they gradually fell away. This was especially the case in the short evening spell of work (6.15 to 8.30 p.m.), but this was largely because the women were so tired that they sat about, doing no work, and thereby avoided the risk of accident. During the subsequent 22½ months (1916 and 1917) the women's cuts showed similar though less marked hourly variations. They were only 3.4 times more numerous in the last hour of the morning spell than in the first hour, and this less rapid rate of increase was almost certainly due to the smaller fatigue induced by the 10-hour day than by the 12-hour

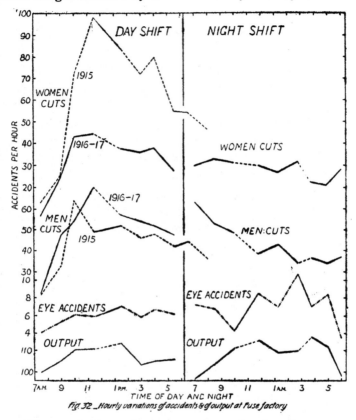

Fig. 32 _Hourly variations of accidents & of output at Fuse factory

day. The much lower frequency of cuts in the afternoon spell of the 1916-1917 period than in 1915 is even more striking testimony of the reduction in fatigue.

The men, in contradistinction to the women, showed no more rapid increase of cuts in 1916-17 than in 1915, and no greater frequency during the afternoon spell of work. In 1915, the frequency was 2.4 times greater in the last hour (or hours) of work of the morning spell than in the first hour, and in 1916-1917 it was 2.2 times greater. On comparing the general contour of the cuts curves with that of the output curve, it will be seen that there is a considerable qualitative resemblance, though not a quantitative one. The output rose only 9 per cent.

during the morning spell, and fell 5 to 7 per cent. during the afternoon spell; *i.e.*, it did not show a tenth the variations of accident frequency.   However, it is probable that a small increase in output may lead to a large increase of accidents, because in most of the small lathe operations performed at a fuse factory the speeding up has to be done mainly by quickening the rate at which the cutting tools (generally on a capstan) are changed and brought into contact with the metal object. Not much quickening of the actual cutting operations is permissible, so a given speeding up of output means a relatively much greater speeding up of the movements made at times when the workers are specially liable to knock their hands against the cutting tools. It will be seen that the eye accidents, which have been averaged for men and women, are very much steadier than the cuts.   In the morning spell they increased only from 4.5 to 6.1, and in the afternoon they were still more steady.   Since these accidents are due to small particles of metal and emery flying from the metal objects turned or from the tools sharpened, one would naturally expect them to show a closer quantitative resemblance to speed of production than the cuts.

The accident data of the night shift differ greatly from those of the day shift.   The shifts worked were of $10\frac{1}{2}$ hours' duration, and they were split into three work spells.   The data tabulated relate to the $22\frac{1}{2}$ month period in 1916 and 1917, and it will be seen that the cuts incurred, so far from starting at a minimum and increasing during the first work spell, tended to vary in the reverse direction.   In the men they were 20 per cent. more numerous in the first hour of work than in the third hour, and they fell considerably on passing from the first spell to the second spell.   In the women they likewise fell between the first and second spells, but they were nearly constant during the first spell.   There was none of the pronounced rise observed during the first spell of the day shift.

The hourly output varied somewhat in the same manner as the day shift output, though it is not possible to compare it exactly, owing to the different system of spells and breaks. Still, it undoubtedly rose considerably between 7 p.m. and 12.45 a.m., at the time when the accident frequency was diminishing rather than increasing.   Hence it may be thought that speed of production can have played no part in the causation of the night shift accidents.   Probably it did play a part, but its influence was overpowered by the psychical factor, dependent on the habits of the munition workers.   When on night shift, these workers usually got up three or four hours before they were due at the factory, and spent these hours in

M

household work, in shopping, or amusements, and in having substantial meals. Hence they came on to work in a lively and sometimes an excited state, but they gradually calmed down during the course of the night, since they had only an unexhilarating breakfast and bed to look forward to. The day shift, on the other hand, got up as late as possible, almost always by artificial light, and after a hurried breakfast, arrived at the factory in a lethargic and depressed condition. They brightened up gradually in the course of the morning, as they generally had some tea at about 9 a.m., and had their dinner break to look forward to. In consequence, their inattention and carelessness increased, and accidents multiplied accordingly.

It appears, therefore, that the psychical state of the munition workers had a more important influence on the frequency with which they incurred cuts from their lathe and drill tools than the speed of production factor. Upon eye accidents, however, speed of production played a greater part, for these accidents were frequent in the second spell of night work and the first $1\frac{1}{2}$ hours of the third spell, when output was large, and were distinctly less frequent in the first spell and last hour of the last spell, when it was smaller.

In the manufacture of big shells it is not possible to speed up during the actual operations so much as in the smaller work connected with fuse production, and consequently the speed of production factor plays a relatively smaller part in accident causation. At a 6 inch shell factory, for instance, it was found that the accidents fell off much more rapidly during the course of the night than at the fuse factory, whilst they showed a much smaller increase during the course of the day. Presumably this was because the speed of production factor did little to accelerate day shift output, and did little to prevent the fall of night shift output induced by the changing psychical condition of the workers.

The United States Public Health Service[1] investigated the question af accident causation in considerable detail. Their investigators collected accident statistics for three months at a motor car factory, and for two years at a fuse factory, and they tabulated 46,000 accidents altogether. In order to determine the relationship of accidents to output, they express their hourly accident rates in the form of accidents per unit of output. They accept the validity of my suggestion that in lathe work and similar machine operations given variations of output may induce relatively greater variations of accident rate. Taking the number of accidents in the first hour of the working day as 100, they calculated the expected number in the subsequent

[1] Public Health Bulletin No. 106, 1920.

hours on the hypothesis that the accidents increased four times more rapidly than output : *e.g.*, a 5 per cent. increase of output caused a 20 per cent. increase of accidents.   They found that the variations of accident rate during the morning spell of work at the motor car factory (*i.e.*, the 8-hour plant) corresponded closely with this hypothesis, and the same correspondence held for operatives engaged on machine work at the fuse factory (the 10-hour plant).   In the afternoon spells, however, the accident rate was in all cases greater than the theoretical.   At the fuse factory the ratio of actual accidents to theoretical accidents (taken as unity) was .9, 1.2, 1.2, 1.0 and 3.3 in the successive hours of the spell.   On splitting up the work at the fuse factory into different categories, it was found that the accidents incurred by the operatives engaged in muscular work were almost always greater than the theoretical, and especially so in the afternoon spell, whilst those incurred by operatives engaged in dexterous work and machine work showed a smaller excess.

These observations were considered to prove that the excess of accidents over the theoretical number was due to fatigue. Unfortunately the psychical factor, on which I lay so much stress, was entirely ignored by the writers of the report, and they fail to record the evidence in its favour which was at their disposal.   Fortunately A. H. Ryan, who was one of the numerous investigators engaged in collecting the information on which the report is founded, has independently described the hourly incidence of the night shift accidents at the fuse factory.[1] In the first spell of work, which lasted six hours, the accidents were at a maximum in the first full hour of work, and then they gradually dwindled, but admittedly some of these accidents were due to dayshift workers engaged on overtime work.   From the fourth hour onwards, however, all the day shift workers had departed, and we find that whilst the accidents suffered by the night shift in the fourth and fifth hours of work of the first spell amounted to 112 and 114, those in the five full hours of work of the second spell amounted to 88, 93, 91, 82, and 89 respec-tively ; *i.e.*, they were considerably less numerous, in spite of the terribly long hours of work.   Even when calculated per unit of output they showed similar relationships, except that in the last full hour of work there was a considerable rise (44 per cent.). This was probably a genuine fatigue effect, but the rest of the figures agree with my own night shift data and show a very different incidence from that exhibited by the day shift, which was of the usual type.

The influence of the psychical state of the workers on

[1] Ryan. " Journal of Industrial Hygiene," Vol. 2, p. 466. 1921.

accidents is suggested by comparing the accident frequency during day work and night work. At each of the four munition factories investigated, the number of accidents (per hour) was distinctly smaller by night than by day, both in the men and the women. As can be seen from the Table, the results are very consistent, and on an average it was found that the night shift accidents were 16 per cent. less numerous than those of the day shift. Presumably this was because the night workers, though they came on in an excited condition, speedily settled down into a calm mental state, with its accompanying concentration on the work in hand. The day workers, on the other hand, though sleepy at first, soon became lively and somewhat inattentive, and remained so through the day.

PERCENTAGE FREQUENCY OF NIGHT SHIFT ACCIDENTS ON DAY SHIFT ACCIDENTS

Character of munition factory.	Accidents in men.	Accidents in women.
Fuse factory ...	93 per cent.	87 per cent.
6 inch shell factory ...	78	83
9·2 inch shell factory ...	82	80
9·2 and 15 inch shell factory...	81	82
	83	83

In the iron and steel industry it has generally been found that accident frequency is greater by night than by day, and sometimes it is 50 per cent. higher.[1] In one large steel plant accidents were 16 per cent. more numerous by night during the years 1905-1910.[2] The difference was most marked in the yards, where night shift accidents were 128 per cent. in excess, and in the mechanical department, where they were 118 per cent. in excess. Probably this was chiefly because of defective lighting, and less rigorous supervision of the men. It was found that at one works the night shift men had disciplinary action taken against them six times more frequently than the day shift.[3] This was attributed to the men taking alcohol just before coming on to work, and to their smuggling it into the works in larger quantities by night than by day. However, at one large steel works the accidents were 3 per cent. more numerous by day than by night, so it is evident that the excess

[1] Bulletin No. 216 of U.S. Department of Labour, 1917, p. 12.
[2] Cf. Lee. "The Human Machine in Industry," 1918, p. 69.
[3] Bulletin No. 234 of U.S. Department of Labour, 1918, p. 153.

of night accidents can be remedied. At all the munition works above mentioned both lighting and supervision were good.

OTHER EVIDENCE ON THE EFFECT OF SPEED OF PRODUCTION

Other evidence on the effect of speed of production on accidents is afforded by comparing variations of output and accident frequency over daily and monthly intervals.   In a previous Chapter it was pointed out that output generally starts at a minimum on the first day of the working week, works up to a maximum in the middle of the week, and falls off towards the end of it. Accident frequency, however, usually shows the reverse relationship, and is at a minimum in the middle of the week. The British Association Committee[1] recorded a large number of accident data, collected in many different industries, and a classification of the days of the week on which accidents reached their maximum and their minimum gave the following results :

	Monday.	Tuesday.	Wednesday	Thursday.	Friday.
Maximum number of accidents occurred	11	4	3	3	8
Minimum number of accidents occurred	3	5	9	8	4

It will be seen that maximum frequency was generally observed on Monday and Friday, and minimum frequency on Wednesday and Thursday. Saturday results were ignored, as they are usually upset by the half-holiday.

The excess of accidents at week ends is probably due partly to the psychical state of the workers, which is less steady than in the middle of the week, owing to the excitements attending the week end relaxation from work ; but it may also be due to lack of practice-efficiency at the beginning of the week, and to cumulative fatigue at the end of it. In my own observations at the fuse factory I tabulated separately the 11,894 cuts recorded, and the 1850 eye accidents,[2] and these results are plotted out in Fig. 33, along with the power load observations. It will be seen that the frequency of the cuts remained fairly steady both by day and by night, except that on Sunday night they were rather less frequent than usual, chiefly because this Sunday work was occasionally omitted. The eye accidents, on the other hand, show a very marked diurnal variation, which

[1] British Association Reports, 1915, p. 283.
[2] Cf. Memo. No. 21 of Health of Munition Workers Committee.

synchronises well with the variations of output. The day shift accidents rose from a minimum of 74 on Monday to a maximum of 120 on Wednesday, and then fell to 85 on Saturday, whilst the night shift accidents rose from 75 on Sunday to 110.5 on

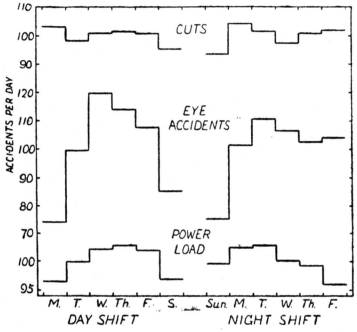

Fig. 33. — Diurnal variations of accidents and of output

Tuesday and then fell away. Hence these results support the conclusion, previously arrived at, that eye accidents afford a better measure of the influence of speed of production than any other class of accident.

The influence of speed of production is likewise exhibited when the records are analysed over longer statistical periods. The output per hour of certain typical products of the fuse factory is recorded in the Table for three or four month periods in 1916 and 1917, and it will be seen that it rose gradually both in men and women. Presumably, therefore, the speed of production gradually increased with the majority of the factory workers, and in agreement therewith it will be seen that the number of accidents increased considerably in the men, and to a smaller extent in the women. The data quoted are the means of the cuts suffered by the day and the night shifts.

Statistical period.	Average hourly output.		Cuts per 10,000 workers per week.	
	Men.	Women.	Men.	Women.
Feb. 1 to May 1 1916.	113	113	358	260
May 2 to Aug. 21	124	124	379	291
Aug 22 to Dec. 18	130	134	418	287
Dec. 19 to April 1 1917.	137	—	477	307
April 2 to Aug. 4	140	—	573	309
Aug. 12 to Dec. 15	147	—	489	344

The only data known to me, other than those already quoted, in which output and accidents have been determined for the same operatives, relate to the 'press hands' employed on stamping machines at a metal working factory.[1] The data adduced show that the output was nearly steady, but it reached a maximum in the last hour of both work spells. The accidents, however, reached a maximum in the second hour of the morning spell, and the third hour of the afternoon spell.

	Morning Spell.				Afternoon Spell.			
	1st hour.	2nd hour.	3rd hour.	4th hour.	1st hour.	2nd hour.	3rd hour.	4th hour.
Total pieces produced	38,700	40,030	40,260	41,275	39,870	40,925	40,815	41,190
Accidents incurred	195	233	211	145	175	205	222	165

THE INFLUENCE OF ALCOHOL CONSUMPTION

The psychical state of the workers with its accompanying influence on accident liability is apt to be affected by the consumption of alcohol. This was especially the case in the night shift workers investigated by me, for if they took alcohol at all, they were bound to consume it shortly before going on to work, as they had no chance of getting it during the course of the night. Hence any alcohol effect, if it did exist, would be most marked during the first spell of work, and least marked during the last spell. Owing to the increasing restrictions on the sale of alcoholic liquors during the war, the general sobriety

[1] Bulletin No. 234 of the U.S. Department of Labour, 1918, p. 154.

of the nation greatly increased. From 1915 onwards the convictions for drunkenness in both sexes gradually fell, till in 1917 they were only a third to a fourth their 1914 value.

The actual quantity of alcohol consumed in the early part of 1917 had fallen to 74 per cent. its pre-war amount, but from April onwards it was suddenly reduced to 29-39 per cent. of this amount. Presumably the 9,000 workers at the fuse factory where the accidents were tabulated must, as a group, have been affected by these restrictions in more or less the same way as the nation at large, so that one would expect to observe some effect on accidents.

The night shift accidents (cuts) have been grouped in the Table in three statistical periods, and in each instance the hourly number of cuts in the third spell of work is taken as the basis of comparison, and is regarded as unity. We see that in the men, the cuts in the first work spell were at a maximum of 1.9 in the first statistical period, and they fell to 1.5 and 1.4 in the subsequent periods. That is to say, they dwindled as the average consumption of alcohol dwindled. In the women the excess of accidents in the first spell over those in the third spell was not as great as in the men, and this fact is in accordance with their relatively greater sobriety. The women likewise showed some diminution of accidents between the first and subsequent statistical periods, though it was smaller than in the men.

RATIO OF ACCIDENTS IN THE THREE SPELLS OF THE NIGHT SHIFT

Statistical period.	Men.			Women.		
	1st spell.	2nd spell.	3rd spell.	1st spell.	2nd spell.	3rd spell.
Feb.—July, 1916 ...	1.9	1.0	1.0	1.6	1.2	1.0
Aug., 1916—Mar., 1917..	1.5	1.5	1.0	1.4	1.3	1.0
April—October, 1917 ...	1.4	1.0	1.0	1.4	1.2	1.0
Mean ...	1.6	1.2	1.0	1.5	1.2	1.0

The day shift workers would not as a rule be affected by alcohol so much as the night shifts, for such of them as took it would usually wait till the day's work was over. In the 1915 12-hour day period, however, the workers were kept at the factory till 8.30 p.m., so they had not much opportunity, and probably not much inclination, for drinking after work was finished. On Saturdays they stopped work at 5.45 p.m., and on Sundays they stopped at 5 p.m., and as they were paid their wages on Friday afternoon there was a considerable temptation to indulge themselves at the week ends. Certainly the accidents showed a marked weekly cycle both in the men and the women. The cuts treated were at a maximum on Monday, and they sank gradually during the course of the week to a minimum value on Friday which was 32 per cent. lower than the maximum in the men, and 27 per cent. lower in the women (Cf. Fig. 34). Then

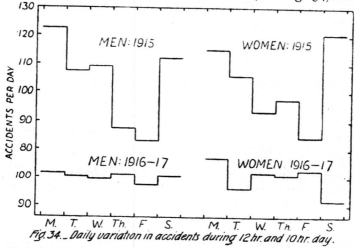

Fig. 34. _ Daily variation in accidents during 12 hr. and 10 hr. day.

on Saturday they shot up again to their Monday maximum. During the subsequent ten-hour day period, however, when work stopped at 6 p.m., the cuts remained nearly steady throughout the week in the men, and somewhat less so in the women, so presumably the alcohol was now consumed in moderate quantities spread evenly over the week.

THE INFLUENCE OF INEXPERIENCE

Inexperience is by no means an infrequent cause of accidents. Striking evidence was obtained by Chaney and Hanna[1] concerning workers employed in metal trades. The data adduced relate to men and women working stamping presses, and engaged in other occupations, and the number of accidents *per day* is recorded over certain periods during the first year for which they were working in the industry. It will be seen that on an average accidents were five times more numerous

[1] Bulletin No. 234 of U.S. Department of Labour, 1918, pp. 131 and 161.

during the first day's work than in the next five days, and subsequently they dwindled so rapidly that in the last six months of the year they were 255 times less frequent than they had been on the first day.

FREQUENCY OF ACCIDENTS

Occupation.	1st day.	2nd day to end of week.	2nd week to end of month.	2nd month to end of 6 months.	7th month to end of year.
Men on stamping presses	77	13	3	.8	.2
Women on stamping presses	252	33	4	.7	.3
Men on other occupations	89	25	8	3.0	1.0
Women on other occupations	42	12	2	.7	.3
Total ...	460	83	17	5.2	1.8

The minimum liability was by no means reached even in a year, for the following data, obtained at a large steel works, show that the workers required 15 years' experience to attain full accident immunity. The accidents tabulated were sufficient to cause absence from work on one or more days after that on which the accident was incurred.

Length of service.	Number of full-time workers.	Cases of accident.	Accident frequency.
6 months and under ...	512	57	111
6 months to 1 year ...	278	29	104
1 to 3 years ...	357	31	87
3 to 5 years ...	637	27	42
5 to 10 years ...	814	16	20
10 to 15 years ...	470	4	8.5
Over 15 years ...	459	0	0
	3527	164	

It is evident that if the fresh workers could be guaranteed against accidents even for their first week, there would be a great reduction in the total number experienced. In the above-mentioned metal works, for instance, no less than 36 per cent. of the total accidents would have been eliminated. Hence a preliminary training of fresh workers on fool-proof and dummy machines would probably be worth while, even from the economic point of view, and the dictates of humanity should afford a still stronger argument for adopting this policy, whenever it is possible. In some works a special effort is made to train and caution new men against accidents,[1] but as far as I am aware these precautions are exceptional.

It was shown by Greenwood and Woods[2] that certain individuals (in munition works) were much more liable than others to suffer from accidents. Apparently they possessed an innate clumsiness or carelessness. The output of these susceptible workers was not below the average, but it is a question whether, in such of them as happened to be employed in a dangerous occupation (e.g., manufacture of explosives), where an accident might cause frightful disaster, it would not be advisable to divert their energies into some less risky channel.

It has been found that in America, where a considerable proportion of the industrial population is foreign-born, the accident rate is considerably higher in the workers who cannot speak English. The following data were obtained at iron and steel works, over an eight year period.[3]

Nationality.	Number of workers.	Accident frequency.
American born ...	12,600	91
Foreign born, but speaking English...	18,700	99
Foreign born, but not speaking English	22,900	213

THE INFLUENCE OF LIGHTING

The influence of artificial lighting on the frequency of accidents was investigated at some length by a Departmental Committee of the Home Office.[4] The method adopted was an indirect one, and depended on a comparison of accident frequency in the winter months, when some of the early morning and late afternoon work is done by artificial light, with that observed in the summer months, when the whole of it is done by natural light. It was assumed that artificial lighting was in force from half-an-hour before sunset till half-an-hour after sunrise, and the accident rate during daylight and artificial light was computed for about 165,000 accidents on this assumption. From the Table it will be seen that, on an average, there was

[1] *Op. cit.,* p. 143.
[2] Report No. 4 of Industrial Fatigue Research Board, 1919.
[3] *Op. cit.,* p. 145.
[4] First Report of Committee on Lighting in Factories and Workshops, 1915. Cd. 8000.

an excess of 25 per cent. in accidents during artificial light.
Dock workers were the most affected, as they showed a 51 per
cent. excess of accidents, whilst textile workers showed a 46
per cent. excess.

Industry.	Per cent. increase during artificial lighting.	
	All accidents.	Accidents due to persons falling.
Textile ...	46	76
Founding metals ...	6	99
Shipbuilding ...	22	99
Drink ...	35	52
Docks ...	51	102
Building ...	—17	12
Engineering ...	32	93
Other industries ...	26	56
	25	74

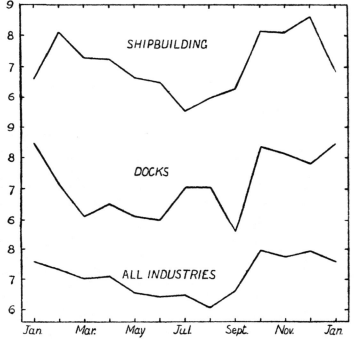

Fig. 35.—Seasonal variation in accidents due to persons falling.

On sorting out the accidents according to their causation, it was found that accidents due to machinery, and to the workers being struck by falling bodies, were about as numerous as the average, but accidents due to 'persons falling' were very much more frequent, as can be judged from the data recorded in the Table. Workers in docks, shipyards and metal foundries, which are often very badly illuminated, experienced twice as many accidents from this cause during hours of artificial lighting. The monthly variations in accidents from 'persons falling' are shown in Fig. 35, and it will be seen that the seasonal change is much greater in shipyards and docks than in all industries put together. The accident data relate to the period of January, 1913, to February, 1914, so the duplicated data for January and February have been averaged. There were 25,795 accidents in all.

We shall see, in the next section, that low temperature has a very marked influence on accident frequency, hence it follows that part of the excess of accidents noted during winter months is due to this cause, rather than to artificial lighting. Support to this conclusion is afforded by the curve in Fig. 36, which

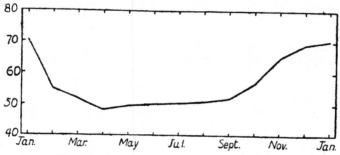

Fig. 36.— Seasonal variation in fatal accidents.

records the seasonal distribution of the 2,100 deaths observed during a three year period in 80,000 works and factories in America.[1] It will be seen that these deaths reached a maximum in January, which is the coldest month of the year, and not in December, which is the darkest month. However, the accidents recorded in Fig. 35 show a maximum in the months of October to December, which are neither the three darkest or the three coldest months, so the evidence is rather contradictory.

The above-mentioned indirect method employed by the Lighting Committee was applied directly to the statistics col-

[1] Curve constructed from diagram given by Tolman and Kendall in " Safety," 1913, p. 80.

lected by me at munition factories, and I calculated the number of accidents occurring at the fuse factory (a) during the hours (7-8.30 a.m., and 3.30-6 p.m.) in which the lighting was almost entirely artificial in the darkest months of the year, but entirely natural in the lightest months, and (b) during the intermediate hours, in which the lighting was for the most part natural even in the darkest months. I found that the frequency of accidents (cuts) during the a hours was always considerably smaller than during the b hours, and they averaged only 73 per cent. as many during the two year period investigated. This was because the workers wasted a good deal of time in starting and stopping work, and had a low speed of production, with its accompanying infrequency of accidents, in the early hours of the morning shift. These factors, which reduced the accidents so much in a munition factory, must have been operating more or less in the industries investigated by the Lighting Committee; hence it follows that the excess of accidents recorded by them during hours of artificial lighting does not correctly represent the full liability to accident during times of actual work.

The ratio of accidents during the a hours to accidents during the b hours was averaged over two month periods, but it did not show any distinct seasonal variation as regards liability to cuts, either in the men or the women. Accidents due to foreign bodies in the eye showed some correspondence to artificial illumination in the men, but not in the women, but the best proof of the relationship of eye accidents to illumination was obtained by comparing the accident frequency during night shift and day shift. At the fuse factory the men suffered 39

Factory.	Condition of Lighting.	Percentage of eye-accidents shown by night shift on those of day shift.		
		Men.	Women.	Mean.
6 inch shell factory ...	Good	77	111	94
9.2 inch shell factory ...	Good	89	109	99
9.2 & 15 inch shell factory	Moderately good	109	98	103
Fuse factory ...	Fairly good	139	144	141

per cent. more eye accidents by night than by day, and the women 44 per cent. more accidents, whilst, as already mentioned in a previous section, they suffered 7 to 13 per cent. less accidents by night, when accidents from all causes were grouped together. At the shell factories the eye accidents were practically as numerous by night as by day, though the whole of the accidents, taken as a group, were 17 per cent. less numerous. The frequency of the eye accidents was evidently affected by the lighting, for at the fuse factory this was only fairly good, in that the lights, moderate in strength, were fixed at 10 ft. above floor level, and not over the work. At the shell factories the lighting was distinctly better. At the 6 inch shell factory very bright lights were fixed 10 ft. above floor level, and usually over the work, whilst at the 9.2 inch factory bright lights were fixed 5 or 6 ft. above floor level, and directly over the work, but about half of them had shades which did not properly protect the workers' eyes from direct beams of light.

The reason why eye accidents proved to be more affected by artificial illumination than other types of accident is probably that, in the dimmer light, the workers bent nearer to their work. They would, in consequence, get more particles of metal and emery flying into their eyes.

It is probable that even at the fuse factory the lighting was better (and perhaps much better) than the average met with in the factories, works and yards investigated by the Lighting Committee, so that their results and mine are not irreconcileable.

THE INFLUENCE OF TEMPERATURE

Since the fingers tend to get numbed at low temperatures, and manual dexterity diminished, we should expect to find that accidents are more numerous than at medium or high temperatures. We should imagine that the effects of cold would be specially great in engineering shops, where the hands are constantly in contact with cold metal tools and other metal objects, and are frequently wetted the whole day through by the stream of soapy water in which many metal articles are turned. In order to obtain numerical evidence on the subject, I estimated, as best I could, the average temperature at the fuse factory over a six month period. A thermograph was installed near the centre of one of the large shops in the factory, 200 ft. × 200 ft., and by its means the temperature was registered automatically. In the largest shop of all, about 400 × 180 ft., thermometers were placed near each end and near the middle, and it was found that their average variations of temperature corresponded well with those of the thermograph. From the thermograph charts the temperature was determined during each work spell according as it fell between 60° and 64.9° F., 65° and 69.9°, and so on. The cuts treated in the spell were counted, and the relative numbers per hour during each spell were averaged for each temperature interval, with the following result :

Factory temperature.	Relative number of cuts treated.
59° or less	1.08
60° to 64°	1.03
65° to 69°	1.00
70° to 74°	1.21
75° or more	1.30

The artificial heating of the factory was so good that the temperature never fell below 53°, but at temperatures between this level and 60° the accidents proved to be slightly more numerous than at 65°—69°. This was the *optimum* temperature as regards accident immunity, but it is somewhat too high for the attainment of maximum output, and as the accidents at 60°—64° were only slightly greater than at 65°—69°, this is probably the best temperature range to aim at. Temperatures of 70° and upwards induced a considerable increase in accident rate.

Observations at lower temperatures were made at the three shell factories previously mentioned. No records of the factory temperatures were obtained, but the daily variations of *external* temperature were ascertained from a meteorological station in the neighbourhood. The shell factories were not efficiently warmed, and two of them had big doors at one end of their main shops, which were often opened to admit trucks of material. The temperature of the whole shop was thereby temporarily reduced to a level not much above that outside. The winter of 1916-1917, when the observations were made, was a very cold one, and the workers felt it keenly. On passing from autumn to winter, the number of cuts experienced gradually mounted up, till at the 6 inch shell factory they were twice as numerous in the women. Then, with the advent of spring, they fell back again. The relationship between the average number of cuts treated in each work spell, and the actual temperature at the time, is shown in the Table.

It will be seen that on the coldest days, when the external temperature was at or below freezing point, the women at the 6 inch shell factory experienced nearly two-and-a-half times more accidents than on the warmest days, when it was at or above 48°, whilst the men experienced twice as many accidents. At intermediate temperatures the accidents were intermediate in number, and there was evidently a close relationship between

ACCIDENT FREQUENCY IN RELATION TO EXTERNAL TEMPERATURE

Factory.	Sex of workers.	External temperature.					Extreme variation.
		32° or less.	33°–37°	38°–42°	43°–47°	48° or more.	
6 inch shell factory	Female	2.84	2.12	1.96	1.55	1.17	1 to 2.43
9.2 inch shell factory	Female	1.72	1.53	1.38	1.28	1.16	1 to 1.48
6 inch shell factory	Male	3.77	2.88	2.64	2.44	1.76	1 to 2.14
9.2 inch shell factory	Male	4.16	3.64	3.00	3.33	2.99	1 to 1.39

temperature and accident liability. A similar phenomenon was observed at the 9.2 inch shell factory, though it was not so marked, and it was seen also at the third shell factory. In every instance the women proved distinctly more susceptible than the men. Probably this was due in part to their lower powers of resistance, and in part to the fact that they were doing less active work than most of the men.

These data, though they relate only to munition factories, indicate that temperature must be an important contributory cause of accidents in most industries. It is a cause which can be and ought to be avoided in practically all indoor industries, but there is plenty of room for amendment. Glaring instances of extremes of temperature are frequently noted by factory inspectors. We read[1] of a clothing factory with a temperature of 39°, of a large provender mill with one of 28°, and of the carding room at a flax mill with one of 35.5°. In the reverse direction, we read of temperatures of 109° and 113° in cotton mills, and of 106° and 111° in print works.

[1] Annual Report of Chief Inspector of Factories, 1912, pp. 81 and 124.

CHAPTER XI

THE PREVENTION OF INDUSTRIAL ACCIDENTS

CONTENTS

Introduction—The Safety Habit of Mind—Accident Prevention
by Mechanical Means—The Effect of Safety Organisation—Accident Frequency and Accident Severity—
The Use of the Comparative Method.

INTRODUCTION

We saw in the last Chapter that three principal factors have
always to be considered in accident causation. First and foremost, as a rule, comes the psychical state of the worker. Less
important is his neuro-muscular co-ordination in its relationship to speed of production, whilst his condition of fatigue,
though liable to be of outstanding importance in some cases,
usually plays a comparatively small part. How are the conclusions arrived at concerning these three factors to be applied
to what was the main object of their study, viz., the prevention
of accidents? There is no difficulty so far as concerns the
fatigue factor. It is obvious that the hours of work and the
severity of the work ought to be reduced, so far as possible,
to such a level that they no longer exert more than a very
small influence on accident causation. The speed of production
factor can be countered to some extent by checking over-speeding, but it is partly a mechanical problem, bound up with the
installation of safeguards and safety devices, and reference to
this mechanical side will be made later on.

There remains the most important factor of all, that relating
to the psychology of the worker. What can be done to
diminish carelessness and thoughtlessness, to train the worker
to concentrate his attention on his work, and on its ever present
risks and possibilities of accident? Much can be done by means
of ' safety first ' methods, which have been discussed so widely
within recent years. These methods naturally fall into two
groups. Those of one group aim at the cultivation of a ' safety
habit of mind,' and those of the second group seek to establish
a ' safety condition of body,' by the installation of mechanical
guards.

The Safety Habit of Mind

In order to cultivate a safety habit of mind, it is necessary to impress upon the worker at all times, in season and out of season, the importance of taking every precaution he reasonably can take to avoid the risk of accident. The simplest and most obvious method to this end is the posting of suitable notices where they are bound to catch his eye. Notices should be placed at danger spots such as railway crossings, near hoists, cranes, etc., and to be of value they must arrest attention.[1] A simple but useful type consists merely of the words:

STOP   LOOK   LISTEN

Other more elaborate signs, which are taken from the report of an address by Lord Leverhulme to the students of Sheffield University, are of this form:[1]

THINK SAFETY and PRACTISE IT.	DANGER. DANGER SIGNS ARE FIXED FOR YOUR SAFETY. DO NOT DISREGARD THEM.	BETTER BE SAFE THAN SORRY.
READ THE SAFETY NOTICES.	READ THE SAFETY NOTICES.	READ THE SAFETY NOTICES.

These and other notices should be posted near the entrance of the works and shops, and in the shops themselves. In America they sometimes erect Bulletin Boards in conspicuous places, and on these boards are posted miscellaneous information such as a monthly report of accident records in the various departments of the works, an analysis of the accidents, showing causes, copies of suggestions for accident prevention made by workmen's committees, and newspaper clippings of accidents. Interest is stimulated by illustrated posters, and by pictures of injured men with stories of the accidents, and all these notices are changed at frequent intervals, so as to maintain the interest of the workers. In America, again, an organisation has been running for some years which supplies fresh bulletins every week to subscribers, and in this country a British Industrial ' Safety First ' Association was founded in 1918 in order to stimulate the adoption of safety methods in factories, workshops and mines. Official approval of this Association is shown by the fact that the Chief Inspectors of Factories and Mines are represented on it.

[1] Cf. Annual Report of Chief Inspector of Factories, 1918, p. 18.

The direct human appeal can be made by such means as exhibiting goggles fractured by a spattering of molten metal or flying metal turnings, or by a partly burnt boot, if these relics are accompanied by a description of the accident, with personal details. However, even these appeals are not much use unless one can convince the workers that precautions against accidents are really worth taking a little trouble about. Again, it is sometimes necessary to convince them that foolhardiness in neglecting safety methods is not a real sign of bravery.

Probably every kind of warning notice and accident bulletin would lose its efficacy in course of time unless an interest in accident prevention is stimulated by the existence of ' Safety Committees.' For instance, in 1906 the United States Steel Corporation formed a chief committee which inspected the works with reference to the best methods of preventing accidents. They selected inspectors to examine the conditions at the various works belonging to the Corporation, and suggested means for preventing accidents and protecting the workmen. Subsequently ' plant committees ' were formed, made up of superintendents, master mechanics, and safety inspectors. Every week they met to discuss proposed safety devices, and accidents which had occurred since their last meeting. There were also committees of foremen and of workmen, which made regular inspections to see that all safety devices were installed and all safety regulations enforced.[1]

As a rule the scheme of Safety Committees is not so elaborate as that mentioned, and in this country the workmen usually take a larger share in control than they appear to do in America. At one large factory Accident Enquiry Committees were established composed of a certain number of employees nominated by the firm, and of an equal number elected by the workpeople themselves.[2] The chief duties of the committees were (i) to enquire into and report on all accidents that occurred in their departments, and (ii) to nominate quarterly two members to make regular inspections of the departments along with the department manager and a foreman. The workers' representatives retired after six months' service, and were not eligible for re-election for a period of twelve months. In this way a large number of workers in each department were trained in methods of accident prevention, and acquired a safety habit of mind.

Subsequently a Safety Inspector was appointed to supervise all the accident prevention measures, and notices and warn-

---

[1] Cf. Tolman and Kendall. " Safety," New York, 1913, p. 130.
[2] Leaflet published by the Home Office on " Safety Committees in Factories and Workshops." London, 1917.

ings—which were varied from time to time—were posted throughout the sections, and especially in dangerous places. As a result, the number of accidents was reduced by more than 50 per cent. in the first year, and by a further 12 per cent. in the subsequent year.

The Chief Inspector of Factories[1] points out that in forming a Committee it is of the highest importance for an employer to make it evident to all concerned that he is really in earnest in his desire to reduce accidents. He must inspire energy both amongst those who represent the management on the Committee and those who represent the workers. Before launching his scheme he should consult the officials of the Trade Unions to which the workers belong, and obtain their assistance and support in the formation of the Committee. The essential feature of the constitution of the Committee is that there shall be joint representation of the management and of the workers. It is advantageous to make the representation equal, for questions before the Committee can then be decided by a majority vote, whereas without it decisions can only be reached by agreement. The Committee should meet not less frequently than once a fortnight, and their principal function should be to enquire into each accident (other than those of a trivial nature, such as small cuts with lathe tools, etc.), to inspect the site of the accident, to investigate the circumstances of the case, and to make recommendations, where possible, to prevent a recurrence of similar accidents. The Committee should publish an account of each accident investigated, and of the causes which led to it, for experience shows that the publicity so obtained is of immense educational value, and has a marked effect on the workers whose accidents have resulted from carelessness and negligence. It is probably the most efficacious method of all for developing and maintaining the safety habit of mind.

Again, the Committee, after regular inspections of the plant along with the departmental manager or foreman, should forward to the employers recommendations as to effective guarding of machinery, the provision of safety appliances, lighting, ventilation, first aid provision and other means for securing safer working conditions. It is a good plan to encourage suggestions from the workers themselves by means of a *suggestion box*. The value of suggestions by the employees is attested by the following instance.[2] "In the case of a machine operated by women serious accidents were continually occurring, and all attempts to adequately prevent them failed. A suggestion of a safety

[1] Cf. Annual Report for 1918, p. 17.
[2] Leverhulme. "The Six-Hour Day," 1918, p. 187.

appliance to be fixed to the machine was made by one of the employees.   It was so applied, and no accident has since occurred."

The appointment of safety inspectors is much to be desired, more particularly in large works.   They are generally made responsible for seeing, not only that the machinery is protected, but that all the requirements of the Factory Acts are duly observed.   The practical value of such an officer is well shown by the report of a Home Office Inspector.[1]

"In one large iron mill where they have had their own safety inspector for some time, it was necessary to withdraw him during the latter part of the war owing to the scarcity of men.   The result of doing so showed the value of his work, for when an inspection was made of the works, only a few months after he had given up, the fencing was found to be in a most unsatisfactory state, guards having been removed, in many cases totally destroyed, and in others lying damaged and useless, while the machinery was running in a most dangerous state."

Evidently there was great need in this iron mill, not only for a safety inspector, but for a thorough safety campaign in order to stimulate a safety habit of mind in the workers. Indifference and inertia are the chief checks to the success of the movement, and they can only be combated by continuous and active effort.   To quote an American manager, who was asked how he achieved such success in his campaign : " I made a noise, and I kept right on making a noise until every man in the shop got to thinking about safety."

ACCIDENT PREVENTION BY MECHANICAL MEANS

The mechanical side of accident prevention is of much greater importance than could be deduced from most of the accident statistics published.   Such statistics indicate that preventable accidents, due to unguarded machinery, lack of safety devices, and mechanical defects, are comparatively infrequent.   For instance, an inspector concluded[2] that out of 12,600 machinery accidents reported to the certifying surgeon in one division of the country, a remedy of any kind, mechanical or otherwise, could be suggested only in 700 cases. Again, of 1,311 accidents recorded in 1911 by the North German Iron and Steel Association, for which compensation was paid, only 46 were attributed to lack of safety appliances and warning notices, while 37 were

[1] Cf. Annual Report of Chief Inspector of Factories for 1918, p. 21.
[2] Annual Report of Inspector of Factories for 1912, p. 17.

the result of the men not using the safety appliances installed, and of disobeying notices.

The importance of mechanically preventable accidents depends chiefly on their severity. Though relatively infrequent, they are much more often of a severe or fatal character than accidents of other types. This is specially the case in certain heavy trades, such as the iron and steel trade. Chaney and Hanna[1] state that the serious and fatal accidents occurring in this trade in America are primarily due to fundamental engineering or structural defects in which the workman has no part. On analysing 372 cases of fatal injury, it was concluded that no less than 57 per cent. of them could have been prevented by some engineering revision. Reductions in rates of death and severe injury during past years are due chiefly to improvements in engineering structure and practice, not only in respect of mechanical safeguards, but in design of building, adequate lighting, and removal of hazardous conditions. Thus in blast furnaces severe and fatal accidents were often caused by the furnace breaking out at the base, owing to insufficient strength in the walls, but from 1910 onwards this class of accident disappeared owing to structural improvements. Again, many accidents were due to poisoning by carbon monoxide gas, which leaked from defective pipes and junctions, but since 1910 this cause of accident has likewise been greatly reduced by mechanical improvements.

In this country the Factory Department has always given a large amount of attention to the fencing of machinery, and to the provision of safeguards against accidents. Under the Factory Acts the inspectors are entitled to prosecute employers who employ defective and insufficiently guarded machinery. They do not hesitate to take action when necessary, though it is found in practice that a warning is usually sufficient to induce offenders to observe the requisite precautions. A marked advance in the protection of machinery has been made in several industries by means of trade agreements. In 1912 such agreements were made between representatives of employers, operatives and factory inspectors in regard to cotton-spinning, cotton-weaving, woollen and worsted mills.[2] Other agreements have been made in bleaching and dyeing and in the tin-plate trade. A clear understanding was reached as to what parts of each machine were to be considered dangerous, and in some cases the actual form of the guard was standardised. In the building trade a special sub-committee of the Industrial Council (formed under the Whitley scheme) is con-

[1] Bulletin No. 234 of U.S Department of Labour, 1918.
[2] Annual Report of Inspector of Factories for 1912, pp. 75 and 94.

sidering the fencing of wood-working machinery. It is to be hoped that the Councils in other industries will similarly take the question of fencing of machinery into consideration. As the Chief Factory Inspector points out,[1] a great work would be accomplished if, trade by trade, the fencing of machinery could be standardised. The hands of the inspectors would be strengthened enormously thereby.

The effect of safeguards in reducing accidents is well shown by data relating to stamping presses.[2] In one of two factories using nearly the same number of presses and producing the same kind of work 13.3 per cent. of the 150 women employed suffered accidents during the year, but in the other factory, where a safety device was used, only 3.2 per cent of the 187 women employed suffered injury. Again, in the hardware industry[2] one of the two factories compared showed dangerous conditions in respect of unprotected belts, revolving parts of machines and stamping presses, and the 1,006 men employed by the firm had an accident rate of 17.5 per cent, and the 138 women one of 17.4 per cent. At a similar factory, where the buildings were better and more attention was paid to safety devices, the 2,488 men employed had an accident rate of 3.2 per cent., and the 500 women, one of 1.4 per cent. It was found that where men and women are working on presses under practically the same conditions, the accident rate for the women is almost always higher than for the men. In 18 factories the women averaged almost a third more accidents than the men. Though the women are less given than the men to removing the safeguards provided, they take more risks in cleaning and adjusting machinery in motion, and in disregarding orders.

A large number of safeguards and safety devices are described and illustrated by Tolman and Kendall in their book on ' Safety,' and a few of these may be briefly referred to. Some are used to protect emery wheels, which are employed for grinding tools in almost all workshops where sharp tools are used. Not infrequently the wheels burst as the result of centrifugal force, and at all times particles of steel and emery are apt to fly off, so that accidents from these wheels are common. Yet these accidents can easily be diminished or prevented by means of metal guards, a safety collar, and a plate glass eye shield, whilst the belting which drives the wheel can likewise be enclosed.[3] Again, drill-presses can be fitted with gear shields, shields over the feed mechanism and belt drive, safety chains, and other protective mechanisms. Lifts can be fitted with a

[1] Report for 1918, p. 15.
[2] Cf. Tolman and Kendall. " Safety," p. 65.
[3] Op. cit., p. 76.

device for illuminating the threshold as they approach each floor, for it is found that the great majority of lift accidents are incurred when stepping on or off the lift. The hooks of hoists can be made of such a form as to exclude the possibility of squeezing the fingers when inserting the hook, whilst crane hooks can be furnished with a safety rim.

One of the most frequent sources of accident is the neglect of employees to replace the guards on machinery after cleaning and oiling. To prevent this, it is desirable to have notices, printed in red, fixed in such a way that they are visible only when the guard is removed, so that as long as the guard is not replaced there is a constant reminder of the fact.

Other safeguards and safety devices relate to the person rather than to the machinery. In many occupations it is important that the eyes be protected by safety goggles. It has been estimated that in normal times over 5 per cent. of all industrial accidents must be ascribed to eye injuries, and in munition work they probably amount to 7 per cent., and occasionally may reach 20 per cent.[1] It was found by Newell[2] that of the fatal accidents in the United States which he enquired into (representing a third of all the fatal accidents incurred), 8.3 per cent. were eye accidents, whilst of 2,000,000 non-fatal accidents approximately 10 per cent. related to the eyes. At the present time there are 15,000 persons in the United States who are blind as the result of such accidents.

The Health of Munition Workers Committee[3] describe suitable forms of goggles, and point out that as no foreign bodies are likely to enter from above, the upper part of the goggle may be left open so as to allow of ventilation.

In most occupations it is desirable that special clothing be worn, especially by the women. Women should wear an overall dress for general purposes, but for very dirty work and outdoor work a trouser suit with tunic was found very advantageous.[4] For protection against wet, oil, and acids, an impervious apron and bib should be worn in addition to the overall or trouser suit. A cap should be worn for protection against dust and dirt, and for safeguarding the hair from dangerous machinery, and accessories such as gloves, clogs, veils and respirators are necessary in certain processes. Loose clothing should be studiously avoided, both by men and women.

It is usually much easier to understand the principle of a safety device and appreciate its merits by visual inspection

---

[1] Memo. No. 15 of Health of Munition Workers Committee, 1916.
[2] Bull. New York State Industrial Commission, February, 1919, p. 86.
[3] *Op. cit.*
[4] Final Report of Health of Munition Workers Committee, 1918, p. 97.

than by means of a written description or an illustration, and in order that employers of industry, factory inspectors, employees and others may have an opportunity of familiarising themselves with the safety devices which have been adopted in different industries, a number of 'Safety Museums' have been established. The first of these museums was formed in Holland in 1893, and ten years later another was established in Berlin. Within the next few years a number of other countries followed suit, and in 1913 there were 23 museums and institutes for the study of industrial hygiene.[1] They are situated in Paris, Brussels, Copenhagen, Dresden, Frankfort, Milan, Montreal, Munich, New York, Stockholm, Vienna, Zurich, and other industrial centres. A museum was in course of erection in London at the time of outbreak of the war, but it has not yet been opened.

The New York museum contains two groups of exhibits in the department of accident prevention, (i) General exhibits, relating to boilers, power-machines, hoists, electricity, fire prevention, etc., and (ii) Particular exhibits, relating to individual industries such as mining, metal-working, textiles, building and agriculture. There is a department of industrial hygiene which has exhibits relating to ventilation, lighting, baths, clothing, infectious diseases, and samples of substances detrimental to health. A library has been formed containing more especially the literature relating to accident prevention, whilst lectures on the subject are given from time to time, to audiences ranging up to 2,100 men.

In addition to devices for preventing accidents, numerous devices exist for minimising the effects of accidents after they have been incurred. All large factories should have a well-appointed surgery, with one or more nurses in attendance, where injuries can be properly dressed, whilst smaller factories should have first-aid boxes of surgical dressings and requisites in each workshop, under the control of someone who has undergone a course of training in ambulance work. If no such aids are available, small cuts and other wounds frequently become septic, and may lead to serious blood poisoning. The Home Office Inspectors[2] point out again and again the frequency with which septic poisoning follows on trivial accidents : and one of them states that ' not many months pass without an inquest on some workman who has died from blood poisoning following on a slight wound which, under proper care and immediate treatment, would probably have healed.' The reverse picture is well illustrated by the report of an inspector to the effect that ' the

[1] Tolman and Kendall. " Safety," p. 395.
[2] Annual Report of Inspector of Factories for 1912, p. 6.

manager of an engineering firm informed me that the number of days of absence from work by injured men had decreased, on an average, by about 70 per cent. since the provision of " first aid " (*i.e.*, a first aid outfit).'

A Home Office order issued in 1916 requires that in blast furnaces, copper mills, iron mills, foundries and metal works first-aid boxes should be provided in the proportion of at least one to every 150 persons, and an ambulance room wherever 500 or more persons are employed. This order has recently been extended to woodwork, and it would evidently be a simple matter to extend it to other industries.

In some industries it is necessary to organise special methods for minimising the effects of accidents. In coal mining, for instance, it is vitally important to provide artificial breathing apparatus, and to train men in its use, and in rescue work. Again, men in charge of electric power houses, where they are liable to be struck senseless by electric shocks, should know how to attempt to resuscitate one another by performing artificial respiration.

THE EFFECT OF SAFETY ORGANISATION

The effect of the introduction of safety methods is shown by statistics drawn from many different industries. The following data, recorded by the U.S. Department of Labour,[1] were obtained at a steel works with about 6,000 employees. It will be seen that with well-developed safety organisation the number of accidents fell to about a third.

Year.	Condition of safety organisation.	Accident frequency rate
1900 1901 1902 1903 1904	Not yet developed : improvement due partly to re-construction and improved methods	370 350 340 350 330
1905 1906	Organisation begins	300 214
1907 1908 1909 1910 1911 1912 1913	Organisation well developed	189 150 174 134 112 153 115

[1] Bulletin No. 234, p. 201, 1918.

In some industries the improvement has been still more rapid. In 1911 the Pennsylvania Railway Company reduced their accidents to 37 per cent. of their number in the previous 12 months, whilst the Chicago and North Western Railway Company, as the result of 20 months' safety work, obtained the following results[1] :

51.6 per cent. less trainmen killed, and 42.5 per cent. less injured.

29.9 per cent. less employees of all classes killed, and 31.4 per cent. less injured.

36.6 per cent. less passengers killed, and 16.0 per cent. less injured.

As the result of more prolonged experience, the Chicago Company obtained a reduction of 66 per cent. in their fatal accidents, and of 40 per cent. in non-fatal accidents. Some Companies exceeded this figure, for the Southern Pacific Company obtained a reduction of 86 per cent. in fatal accidents and 70 per cent. in non-fatal accidents. Of organisations dealing with other industries, the Kodak Company obtained a reduction of 78 per cent. in all accidents, and the Pullman Corporation one of 41 per cent.

In this country the safety movement has not hitherto been adopted so widely as in America, and but few statistics of its effects are available. A safety inspector states that at the factory to which he was appointed the accidents reported to the Home Office in the first six months of 1916 were 116, whilst in the first six months of 1917 they had fallen to 41. At the soap factory, Port

		Degree of injury.				Total acci-dents.	% on total employees
		Fatal.	Severe.	Moderate-ly severe.	Slight.		
1916	Males	1	1	4	146	152	6.0
	Females	0	1	0	48	49	1.7
	Total ...	1	2	4	194	201	3.7
1917	Males	0	1	1	66	68	2.6
	Females	0	1	0	32	33	.9
	Total ...	0	2	1	98	101	1.6

[1] Tolman and Kendall. " Safety," p. 141.

Sunlight, the safety first campaign came into operation in the middle of 1916, and from the Table it will be seen that in 1917 the accidents, per employee, had fallen to less than half, both in respect of severe and slight accidents.[1]

The adoption of safety methods by the London General Omnibus Company caused a gradual reduction of bus accidents from 35 (per 100,000 miles covered) in 1913 to 14 in 1918.[2] The fatal accidents, however, showed no improvement, probably because of the increased speed of the omnibuses. Again, the safety first campaign on a British railway resulted in the reduction of accidents to employees by 16 per cent. in 1915 and 17 per cent. in 1916.[3]

Only time and experience can show whether the reductions of accidents recorded are capable of extension to other industries. It is to be remembered that a great reduction of accidents may be due in part to the occurrence of a high accident rate before the adoption of safety methods, owing to excessive carelessness and neglect of precautions. Conversely a small accident reduction may be due to the previous attainment of a high level of accident prevention. Hence the real efficacy of safety methods at any given factory can be estimated only by comparing the accident rate with that observed at other factories in the same industry, which have admittedly adopted a complete scheme of safety organisation.

Standardised information relating to accidents in the Iron and Steel Industry (in America) has been furnished by Chaney and

Department.	Number of full-time workers.	Accident frequency per 1000 workers.	Accident severity rate.	Percentage of severity rate on frequency.
Erecting structural steel	2,157	365	129	35.3
Blast furnaces ...	124,636	187	29	15.5
Steel works—Bessemer...	28,101	269	25	9.3
Steel works—open hearth	71,293	225	24	10.7
Mechanical ...	97,162	188	14	7.4
Foundries ...	95,917	191	13	6.8
Heavy rolling mills ...	67,663	138	13	9.4
Fabricating shops ...	108,538	240	12	5.0
Sheet mills ...	128,423	153	9	5.9
Wire drawing ...	59,481	197	9	4.6
Total, and mean for these and other departments	1,310,911	177	15.1	8.5

[1] Cf. Leverhulme. "The Six-Hour Day," p. 189.
[2] "The Organiser," January, 1920, p. 57.
[3] "The Organiser," June, 1919, p. 612.

Hanna.[1] The data here quoted relate to over a million workers for the years 1910-1914, and the accident rates may be regarded as a fair average of past experience against which employers in other works can match their rates. A rate above these averages is one which ought to be reduced with all expedition. It will be seen that the accident rate is quoted per 1,000 ' full time workers,' and by this is meant men who put in at least 300 days' work a year, at an average of 10 hours per day. It will be seen that the rate varied from a maximum of 365 in the men engaged upon the erection of steel structures, to a minimum of 138 in those working the rolling mills. The ' severity rate,' which represents the number of days lost from accident per full time worker per year, varied much more widely, for it ranged from 129 days in the structural steel men to 9 days in the men engaged in wire drawing. Even when expressed as a percentage on the frequency rate it varied as 35.3 to 4.6, or as 8 to 1. The method of estimating severity rates is described in the next section.

ACCIDENT FREQUENCY AND ACCIDENT SEVERITY

More important than a numerical measure of the total accidents incurred is an estimate of their severity, and of the consequent amount of working time lost to the community. Everyone would agree that a severe accident, resulting in the loss of a limb, is more to be deplored than a hundred trivial accidents which cause no permanent injury, but from the purely economic point of view it may not be so serious, as it may not mean so much loss of working time and capacity to the community. In any case, it is very desirable to obtain some measure of the economic effects of accidents of different degrees of severity, for only by this means can the accidents incurred in various occupations and industries be compared. Mere number is often an entirely fallacious guide. In coal mining, for instance, the number of accidents may be much smaller than in light metal work such as machining small metal objects, but the accidents are frequently of a severe or fatal character, whilst those incurred in light lathe work are very seldom of this class. In America the economic effects of accidents have recently been estimated by calculating ' accident severity rates.'

The accident severity rate is calculated on the basis of the scale of pay given by insurance agencies in compensation for injury. Since these scales are not uniform or stereotyped, no definite agreement has yet been reached as to the best method of calculating severity rates. Chaney and Hanna,[2] representing the

[1] Bulletin No. 234 of U.S. Department of Labour, 1918.
[2] Bulletins Nos. 216 and 234 of U.S. Department of Labour, 1917 and 1918.

U.S. Bureau of Labour, assume that when a man suffers a fatal accident, 30 years of industrial life are lost to the community, and as each man averages about 300 days of full time work per year, 30 × 300 = 9,000 days of industrial life are lost. The International Association of Industrial Accidents Boards and Commissions considers that a fatal accident represents the loss of 20 years of industrial life, or of 6,000 days, and I think that in most industries this is a more suitable figure. Again, Chaney and Hanna assume that if a man is totally disabled by an accident, he represents a greater loss to the economic condition of the community than if he is killed, so they assess his accident as equivalent to the loss of 10,500 days. The International Association, however, assess it at 6,000 days, and here again I think they adopt a more appropriate figure, as it is very seldom that a man is so disabled that he can do no work at all. Even a blind man can learn a trade. The loss of limbs is in most instances rated at a higher level by the Association than by Chaney and Hanna, the scales adopted for the more frequent accidents being as follows :

Disability.	U.S. Bureau of Labour.	International Association.
Death ...	9,000 days	6,000 days
Permanent total disability	10,500	6,000
Loss of arm ...	2,808	4,500-3,600
Loss of leg ...	2,592	4,500-3,000
Loss of hand ...	2,196	3,000
Loss of foot ...	1,845	2,400
Loss of eye ...	1,152	1,800
Loss of thumb ...	540	600
Loss of first finger ...	414	300

The method of calculating the severity rate may be illustrated by a concrete instance. In a certain steel works the 1,400 full time workers in one year suffered 324 accidents, which included 1 death, the loss of 2 arms, 1 foot, 5 thumbs, and 25 first fingers. These disabilities correspond to the loss of 29,511 days, whilst 2,790 days were lost from temporary disabilities, or 32,301 days in all. This represents 23 days per full time worker, and this figure is termed the accident severity rate. The accident frequency rate per 1,000 full time workers is $324 \times \frac{1000}{1400} = 231$.

The Table quoted in the previous section showed how variable the frequency rates and severity rates were in different departments of the iron and steel trade, though as a rule the two rates showed a considerable correspondence. If different industries are compared, however, the rates are sometimes found to vary in opposite directions. For instance, 116,000 workers in the machine building industry had a frequency rate of 118 and a severity rate of 5.6 days, but the 7,600 workers in a steel works had a frequency rate of 114 and a severity rate of 21.2 days ; *i.e.,* nearly four times the severity rate, but a smaller frequency rate.

The importance of determining the severity rate is indicated by the accompanying data, which show the effect of the safety movement on the accidents experienced by about 80,000 iron and steel workers. Between 1912 and 1917 the frequency fell from 192 to 81, or by 58 per cent., but the severity rate fell only from 13.8 to 10.2, or by 26 per cent., so that the ratio of severity to frequency, which may conveniently be expressed as a percentage of the one value on the other, rose from 7.2 to 12.6.

ACCIDENTS TO IRON AND STEEL WORKERS

Year.	Full-time steel workers.	Frequency rate.	Severity rate.	Percentage of severity on frequency.
1910	79,000	184	17.1	9.3
1911	80,000	174	13.5	7.8
1912	94,000	192	13.8	7.2
1913	91,000	156	15.1	9.7
1914	77,000	113	10.9	9.6
1915	79,000	111	10.3	9.3
1916	109,000	101	10.7	10.6
1917	87,000	81	10.2	12.6

More striking still are the comparisons of frequency rate and severity rate at two groups of iron and steel works,[1] in one of which a bonus was offered to the foremen in proportion to the degree the accident rate was brought down below the average experience of past years, and in the other of which no bonus was offered. It will be seen that in the subsidised works the frequency rate was reduced from 180 to 36 in five years, whilst in the non-subsidised works the rate was reduced only from 186 to 90. The severity rate, however, went up rather than down at the

	1912.	1913.	1914.	1915.	1916.	1917.
Frequency rate in bonus works	180	103	37	45	36	36
Frequency rate in non-bonus works	186	173	108	98	130	90
Severity rate in bonus works	8.1	4.9	7.2	7.3	9.2	7.6
Severity rate in non-bonus works	16.5	14.9	12.4	12.7	14.3	12.6

[1] U.S. Dept. of Labour. Monthly Labour Review, Vol. 9, p. 272, 1919.

subsidised works, though it showed some reduction at the unsubsidised works. It is true that the rate was always bigger at the latter works than at the former, but this was because the plant was inferior.

It looks as if the foremen at the subsidised works concentrated their energies on the number of the accidents incurred, rather than on their quality, and in so doing they missed the chief aim and object of the safety movement, viz., the diminution of the sum total of suffering and lost time produced by accidents.

THE USE OF THE COMPARATIVE METHOD

The value of the comparative method for ascertaining in what directions preventive measures should be specially attempted has been briefly mentioned already. The Table of frequency and severity rates recorded on page 221 indicated that severe accidents were specially numerous in certain occupations, and suggested that more vigorous efforts ought to be made to reduce them. The appalling severity rate experienced by men engaged in erecting steel structures needs no comment.

The comparative method can, however, be applied in many other directions, a few of which will now be pointed out. A simple plan is to compare the accident frequency in men and women at the same factory. The Table records the ratio of women's accidents to men's accidents, taken as unity, at the various munition factories investigated by me.[1]

RATIO OF WOMEN'S ACCIDENTS TO MEN'S ACCIDENTS

Type of accident.	Fuse factory.		6 inch shell factory.		9.2 inch shell factory.		9.2 & 15 inch shell factory.		Mean of shell factories.
	Day shift.	Night shift.	Day shift.	Night shift.	Day shift.	Night shift.	Day shift.	Night shift.	
Cuts ...	.7	.6	1.2	1.4	1.3	1.2	1.0	1.0	1.2
Eye accidents	.3	.3	1.7	2.6	1.1	1.3	1.8	1.6	1.7
Burns ...	.5	.3	2.9	4.3	2.7	4.2	4.9	4.8	4.0
Sprains ...	1.7	1.7	2.1	1.9	1.8	1.7	2.1	2.1	1.9

It will be seen that at the fuse factory the women suffered only a third to two-thirds as many cuts, eye accidents and burns as the men (for their light lathe and drill work was less risky than the tool setting, metal casting, etc., done by the men), but nearly twice as many sprains. These sprains were chiefly wrist sprains, incurred by the women in pushing home the clamping lever of the lathes. The levers were designed for the stronger

[1] Memo. No. 21 of Health of Munition Workers Committee, 1918, p. 41.

O

wrists of men, but it would be an easy matter, by lengthening or otherwise altering them, to render them more suitable for the weaker wrists of the women. It is true that the women at the shell factories likewise experienced nearly twice as many sprains as the men, but compared with the frequency of cuts—which formed by far the larger proportion of accidents—the sprains were not so numerous as at the fuse factory.

At the shell factories the women suffered 20 per cent. more cuts than the men, and 70 per cent. more eye accidents, and they experienced no less than four times as many burns. These burns were chiefly on the hands, and they were due to the large and hot metal turnings jumping out from the shells during turning. They did much more damage than the light turnings met with in fuse manufacture, and the increase in the proportion of eye accidents was likewise due to these turnings. It is obvious, however, that the eye accidents could have been prevented by goggles, and the burns by the use of gloves.

The effect of the large shell turnings in causing eye accidents and burns can be still better realised by comparing the accident frequency at the shell and the fuse factories. From the Table it will be seen that the women at the 9.2 and 15 inch shell factory experienced 2.3 to 3.6 times more eye accidents than the fuse factory women, and 7.2 to 8.4 times more burns, though the cuts and sprains were almost the same. The men, on the other hand, experienced no more eye accidents and burns at the one factory than at the other, for they were not, for the most part, employed in the actual turning of the shells.

ACCIDENTS PER 10,000 WORKERS PER WEEK

Type of accident.		Day Shift.			Night Shift.		
		Fuse factory.	Big shell factory.	Ratio.	Fuse factory.	Big shell factory.	Ratio.
Men	Cuts	481	469	1.0	441	355	.8
	Eye accidents	86	70	.8	122	76	.6
	Burns	18	24	1.3	28	21	.8
	Sprains	17	27	1.6	18	21	1.2
Women	Cuts	313	329	1.1	282	262	.9
	Eye accidents	25	90	3.6	39	88	2.3
	Burns	10	84	8.4	10	72	7.2
	Sprains	28	40	1.4	30	32	1.1

A comparison between the day shift and night shift accidents at these munition factories was made in the previous chapter, and it likewise suggested measures for accident prevention.

CHAPTER XII

FACTORY CONDITIONS

CONTENTS

Introduction — Lighting — Ventilation and Heating (Impure Atmosphere, Suitability of Humidity and Ventilation, The Optimum Temperature)—Seasonal Variation of Output—Seating Accommodation—Washing Facilities —Industrial Canteens.

INTRODUCTION

It is now well recognised that factory conditions exert a powerful influence on the efficiency of the worker. They act both directly and indirectly. The direct effect of good lighting and suitable heating can easily be recognised, but the indirect effect may be equally important. Bad factory conditions may cause a lowering of health and well-being, a slackness and depression of spirits, which react on the productivity of the worker. In course of time they may induce chronic ill-health, and seriously reduce the duration of his industrial life. Hence bad factory conditions are economically unsound, as well as morally reprehensible.

Dr. Arthur Shadwell,[1] who has inspected a large number of factories in America and Germany as well as in this country, considers that on the whole a higher standard is maintained in Germany than with us, though we outstrip America. But if the best factories alone be taken no superiority can be claimed for Germany. He states that he has seen nothing anywhere so well built and well equipped as the great mills in the Bradford district, but the earlier development of manufacturing industries in England and the traditional practice of workmen starting factories for themselves on a small scale with small means has produced a larger number of antiquated, cramped and dilapidated premises.

LIGHTING

It would be thought that nowadays everyone would recognise the importance of good lighting for industrial work, yet it is by no means the case, if practice rather than theory be accepted as

---

[1] " Industrial Efficiency," London, 1913, p. 321, *et seq.*

the criterion. For instance, Shadwell states that the file-cutting and cutlery industries are often carried on under conditions so inferior that it is difficult to understand how the work is done at all. He continues, " I have seen, even in a superior factory, men grinding hollow-ground razors—a delicate operation requiring the nicest manipulation—in a light so bad that they must have been guided more by sense of touch than by sight."[1] He is of the opinion that good lighting is better secured in Germany than in England and better in England than in America. The German factory law alone mentions ' sufficient light ' as one of the conditions to which attention must be paid, and Shadwell has not seen a single ill-lighted room or workshop in the country.

The general effects of bad illumination are summarised in the evidence of an expert witness before the Health of Munition Workers Committee.[2] (a) The quality of the work and output both suffer if the illumination is inadequate. (b) Inadequate illumination increases the nervous strain on operators, and reacts on their physical condition. (c) The risk of accident and of machinery breakdowns is increased. (d) It is generally recognised that operators work more cheerfully in well-lighted rooms : bad lighting has a depressing effect on the spirits, and thus affects the operator's capacity for work.

The Departmental Committee on Lighting in Factories state[3] that complaints as to eyestrain and headaches, attributed to insufficient light, are common. Numerous references are also made to discomfort and injury to the eyes caused by glare from light sources. They quote specific instances showing the effect of lighting on output. Thus in one case output was diminished 12 to 20 per cent. during the hours of artificial lighting, and in another the earnings of the workers increased 11.4 per cent. after the installation of a better system of lighting. Again, Tarbell states[4] that in an American steel plant the adoption of an efficient lighting system resulted in an increase of over 10 per cent. in the output of the night shift. The provision of indirect lighting, with spot lamps at special places, has been found beneficial to the employee in the linotype rooms of many printing houses, and to his output.[5]

A series of experiments has recently been carried out by the Commonwealth Edison Company, Chicago, in which various

[1] Op. cit., p. 322.
[2] Final Report of Health of Munition Workers Committee, 1918, p. 88.
[3] Cf. First Report, 1915, p xii. [Cd. 8000].
[4] Tarbell. " New Ideals in Business," 1916, p. 328.
[5] Cf. Bulletin No. 15 of Advisory Council of Science and Industry (Australia), 1919, p. 26.

factories were run for successive months first with the existing lighting, next with greatly improved lighting, and then under the old conditions again. Full records of output were kept, and it was found in one factory that output in several operations increased 8 to 27 per cent. It was estimated that by an increased expenditure on lighting which did not amount to more than 5 per cent. of the pay-roll, an average increase in production of 15 per cent. could be secured.[1]

Another series of experiments has been made at an engineering works in this country.[2] In the machine shop for finishing pulleys the old equipment consisted of 60-watt vacuum lamps, which were either bare, or were equipped with ordinary iron shades. There was a great deal of glare, as well as tremendous variations in intensity of illumination. This system was replaced by units consisting of 200-watt gas-filled lamps in scientifically designed reflectors, whereby the average illumination was increased nearly twenty-five times. Engineers made an exact comparison of output before and after the change, and they found the production to be increased by 20 to 35 per cent., at a total extra cost of 5.5 per cent. of the wages bill. Similar tests carried out in the soft metal bearing machine shop showed a 15 per cent. increase of production. In the heavy machine shop the increase amounted to 10 per cent., and in the assembling shop, to 12 per cent., though the additional cost of the improved installation represented only 0.9 to 1.2 per cent. of the wages bill.

Observations made by Elton[3] at a silk factory showed that the amount of cloth produced by the weavers gradually increased between December and March. On investigating the output from hour to hour of the working day, it was found that between 9.45 a.m. and 3.15 p.m. the average improvement amounted to 2 per cent., but during the first and last hours of the working day it came to 11 per cent. This was due to the fact that artificial lighting (quite good of its kind) was required at these times during the earlier weeks of the period investigated, but not during the later weeks.

The study of factory lighting, and the attainment of adequate illumination, received a great impetus in this country by the publication of the previously mentioned report of the Departmental Committee. The Committee laid down the following conditions of good factory lighting :

(1) Adequacy (*i.e.*, sufficient for the proper carrying out of the the health, comfort and safety of workers).

[1] L. Gaster in " The Organiser," August, 1919, p. 181.
[2] H. E. Goody in " The Organiser," August, 1920, p. 149.
[3] Report No. 9 of Industrial Fatigue Research Board, 1920.

(2) A reasonable condition of constancy and uniformity of illumination over the necessary area of work.

(3) The placing or shading of lamps so that light from them does not fall directly on the eyes of an operator when engaged on his work, or when looking horizontally across the work room.

(4) The placing of lights so as to avoid the casting of extraneous shadows on the work.

The Committee recommend that ' adequate and suitable lighting ' be required to be added to the Factory Acts by a statutory provision, and that this provision should include the observance of the last three conditions, whilst special emphasis should be placed on the avoidance of glare, excessive contrast and flickering lights. In order to delimit ' adequate lighting ' in numerical terms, the Committee made a number of direct measurements of the lighting of factories in terms of the ' foot-candle.' One foot-candle may be defined as the illumination produced by a light source of one standard candle at a point of a surface one foot from the source and so placed that the light rays strike the surface at right angles. Thus if a source of one candle be placed one foot above a horizontal table, the illumination at a point on the table vertically below the source is one foot-candle. Similarly, with a source of 50 candles at a

ARTIFICIAL LIGHTING IN FACTORIES

Class of factory.	Level at which illumination was measured.	Mid-point of obser-vations (in foot-candles).	Percentage of observations lying below the following values of illumination (in foot-candles).			
			0.25	0.5	1.0	1.5
Weaving sheds	Floor	0.4	28	66	93	100
Ditto	Loom	2.0	0	3	18	36
Spinning mills	Floor	0.6	22	45	69	84
Ditto	Machine	0.6	23	40	64	79
Lace factories	Floor	0.35	32	73	100	—
Clothing workshops	Floor	0.85	10	25	59	85
Ditto	Where coloured materials were being sewn	3.6	0	1	6.5	13
General engineering (excluding foundries)	Floor	0.6	14	41	76	91
Ditto	Machine	1.6	4	16	36	48
Foundries	Floor	0.4	36	63	85	93

distance of one foot, the illumination is 50 foot-candles, whilst if the distance is increased to 10 feet, since the illumination is inversely proportional to the square of the distance from the source, the illumination will be 50 ÷ 100, or 0.5 foot-candle.

The Committee usually measured the artificial light at floor level and at the working level, and some of their results are summarised in the Table. A large number of observations were made at different factories in each industry investigated, and the 'mid-point' recorded shows the point above and below which equal numbers of observations lie. For instance, equal numbers of the weaving shed floors investigated had an illumination above and below 0.4 foot-candle, whilst equal numbers of the looms had an illumination above and below 2.0 foot-candles. The proportions of the factories investigated which, at floor level, had a poor light of less than 0.25 foot-candle power, a moderate light of 0.5 foot-candle power, and a good light of 1.0 or more foot-candle power, are shown on the right side of the Table. It will be seen that no less than 28 per cent. of the weaving shed floors, 32 per cent. of the lace factory floors, and 36 per cent. of the metal foundries had the poor light mentioned, and the Committee recommended that a statutory provision be made to the effect that the illumination of the floor be not less than 0.25 foot-candle in workshops, and not less than 0.4 foot-candle in foundries. In passages and stairways, however, where good illumination is not so necessary, they recommended a minimum value of 0.1 foot-candle, and in open yards and approaches, one of 0.05 foot-candle.

The Committee made numerous investigations on the natural lighting of factories, and they estimated the percentage of daylight which reached the factory floors from the outside. In roof-lit factories (and foundries) it amounted to 2 per cent. or more in 49 per cent. of all cases, but in factories lit by combined roof and side lighting it reached this figure only in 29 per cent. of all cases, and in factories lit exclusively by side lighting it reached it only in 2 per cent. of all cases. In fact, 71 per cent. of the side-lit factories allowed less than 0.5 per cent. of the external daylight to reach their floors, and 48 per cent. of them, less than 0.25 per cent.

Though these figures illustrate very clearly the advantages of roof-lighting, it is the modern custom to build factories with a number of floors, which can only be side lit. Nevertheless a good illumination is often attained, for almost the whole of the walls may be made up of windows. In many American factories 50 to 80 per cent. of the total wall space is utilised in this way.[1]

[1] Bulletin No. 15 of Advisory Council of Science and Industry (Australia), 1919, p. 26.

It is true that the middle of a wide work room is liable to get comparatively little light, but this defect is partially overcome by having the adjacent walls whitewashed, and by using ribbed glass or prisms in the windows. Experiments have shown that ribbed glass throws from three to fifteen times as much light into the middle of the room as plain glass, whilst prisms may increase the effective lighting up to fifty-fold.[1]

The Committee comment on a very common defect in factories, the dirtiness of the windows. Not only is a large proportion of daylight prevented thereby from entering the room, but the daylight period of work is considerably shortened and needless expense is incurred by the necessity for lighting up earlier. The Committee accordingly recommend the adoption of a general provision to the effect that "all external windows of every workroom shall be kept clean, on both the inner and outer surfaces."

It has been pointed out[2] that though most factory managers provide enough light for the worker, this lighting is usually not distributed properly. There is too much glare and reflection, especially from highly polished machinery. The glare from nickel plated machinery, be it a large factory machine or a typewriter, may cause fatigue which would be eliminated by painting the machine dull black. As this would render it inconspicuous it might, in some instances. be safer to paint it white.

VENTILATION AND HEATING

Next to adequate lighting the most important factory condition is a good supply of fresh air of suitable temperature. This fact is recognised in the Factory Acts, which provide that (a) In every room in any factory or workshop sufficient means of ventilation shall be provided and sufficient ventilation shall be maintained : (b) In every factory and workshop adequate measures must be taken for securing and maintaining a reasonable temperature in each room in which any person is employed, but the measures so taken must not interfere with the purity of the air in any room in which any person is employed.

In past years it was usual to lay great stress on the purity of the air, especially in regard to its content of carbonic acid, but it is now realised that the carbonic acid itself is quite harmless in the quantities present even in most vitiated air, though it is often a useful index of the adequacy of the ventilation. However, even a low carbonic acid value is not necessarily an indication of

---

[1] Clewell. "Metal Worker, Plumber and Steam Fitter," 1918, p. 9.
[2] F. B. Gilbreth and L. M. Gilbreth. "Fatigue Study," London, 1917, p. 78.

suitable ventilation, for such values may be experienced in shops which provide a large cubic air space per worker, but in which the air is nearly stagnant owing to defective ventilation. Thanks largely to the investigations and writings of Dr. L. E. Hill, we now realise that the essential condition of good ventilation is *moving air*. Stagnant air, however pure, is depressing and relaxing, and fails entirely to provide the stimulating effect of cool air in gentle motion which is provocative of the best physical and mental exertion. The exhilarating influence of atmosphere depends essentially on the cooling of the skin by moving air. Cool air is more stimulating than warm, and more conducive to physical effort.' Direct experimentation in the laboratory teaches us that a desirable atmosphere should be :

(a) Cool rather than hot.

(b) Dry rather than damp.

(c) Moving rather than still.

(d) Somewhat variable in temperature rather than uniform and monotonous.

IMPURE ATMOSPHERE.—The only easily measurable impurity which is added to the air inside the workshop is carbonic acid. This gas is usually present in external air to the extent of 2 to 4 volumes per 10,000, but in crowded buildings it may rise to over 40 per 10,000. A Departmental Committee of the Home Office recommended in 1902 that in all classes of factories and workshops (other than those specially dealt with) the ventilation should be sufficient to keep down the carbonic acid to 12 volumes per 10,000 during daylight, or after dark when only electric light is used, but when gas or oil is used for lighting the proportion shall not exceed 20 volumes. This standard of purity may appear rather low, but it is probably better than that usually met with in public halls or theatres, and in the homes of the workers. Thus an examination of the air of a large public hall at different times and at different points during the course of an evening showed the presence of 14.2 to 44.4 volumes of carbonic acid per 10,000. The innocuousness of the carbonic acid expired by human beings is shown by an experiment[2] in which eight men were shut up in an air-tight chamber of about 106 cubic feet internal volume. After 44 minutes the carbonic acid present had risen to 5.26 per cent. (*i.e.*, 526 volumes per 10,000) and the wet bulb temperature to 83°F. Everyone felt great discomfort, but when the still air was thoroughly stirred by putting on electric fans relief was immediate and very great. No headaches or after

[1] Final Report of Health of Munition Workers Committee, 1918, p. 85.
[2] L. Hill, R. A. Rowlands, and H. B. Walker. " Journal of Physiology," Vol. 41, Proc., p. iii., 1910.

effects were produced by this high percentage of carbonic acid, and in another experiment the emptying of a bag of carbonic acid into the chamber, whereby the amount present in the air was raised to 2 per cent., had no influence whatever on the comfort of the two occupants.

The carbonic acid present in workshop air is usually a fair index of the amount of various ill-defined volatile substances which arise from the skin of human beings, especially when personal cleanliness is defective. These substances are probably harmless in themselves, but they excite a feeling of discomfort or even of disgust. Of greater practical importance are the bacteria of human origin. There is no doubt that colds and sore throats are for the most part spread from an infected individual to his neighbours by organisms which are carried in the expired air, especially during coughing and sneezing. These " colds " are often regarded as trivial in character, but it appears likely that if any correct estimate of lost time and diminished output owing to colds could be obtained, they would prove to be the most important infectious source of reduced industrial efficiency. Of diseases more serious in regard to life as well as health, tuberculosis of the lung is undoubtedly often disseminated in a like manner.[1]

In addition to these impurities of human origin, many others are produced in the course of the industries themselves. Some of them, such as the fumes arising from hot oil and from varnishes, are merely unpleasant. Others are directly harmful, e.g., the fumes of lead, brass, and of substances used more especially in munition and aeroplane manufacture (tri-nitro-toluol, tetryl, nitrous fumes, tetra-chlorethane).[2] The influence on mortality of dust-producing occupations such as are found in the manufacture of pottery, files and cutlery, cotton and woollen goods, etc., has been referred to in a previous chapter.

SUITABILITY OF HUMIDITY AND VENTILATION.—The suitability of the factory air for physical labour, and for the comfort of the workers, depends on its temperature, its humidity, and on the degree of ventilation. All these qualities can be investigated by means of thermometers. Though ordinary dry bulb thermometer readings are very useful under most circumstances, they tell one nothing about the humidity of the air, and if the temperature is at all high it is most desirable to take wet-bulb thermometer readings, as they afford a valuable index of comfort. So long as the wet-bulb temperature is below a certain level, sufficient evaporation can take place from the skin to keep the temperature

[1] Memo. No. 9 of Health of Munition Workers Committee, 1916, p. 4.
[2] Memo. No. 8 of Health of Munition Workers Committee, 1916. Final Report, p. 75.

of the body normal, even if the dry-bulb temperature be very high. An instance of this is seen in persons who succeed in living healthily in the tropics for weeks at a temperature well above the normal body temperature. Haldane[1] takes the wet-bulb temperature as the measure of endurance, and as the result of observations on Cornish tin miners and others he considers the endurable limit for men resting and lightly clad to be 88°F., or 93° if in a wind with a velocity of 170 ft. per minute. If active work is being done it is impossible to stand these high temperatures. For instance, a man climbing 13 ft. per minute in still air can only just endure a wet-bulb temperature of 78°, and if the air is moving 135 ft. per minute, one of 85°F. At a a temperature of 80° the work done by a miner begins to fall off, and at 85° hard work is scarcely possible. Haldane fixes a wet-bulb temperature of 75° as the permissible maximum for the temperature of the weaving sheds and spinning mills of textile factories, and regards 70° as the desirable maximum.

The wet-bulb temperature is considered by J. L. Bruce[2] as a misleading index of comfort, and he prefers the dew-point, *i.e.*, the temperature at which the air becomes supersaturated with moisture. He states that with a dew-point in the neighbourhood of 62°F. work can be carried on without inconvenience even if the wet and dry-bulb temperatures are very high. For instance, with a dry-bulb temperature of 111° and a wet-bulb of 82° hard work was done without discomfort, as the dew-point was fairly low (viz. 66°) : but with a dry-bulb of 90°, a wet-bulb of 81°, and a dew-point of 74.5°, efficient mental or physical work was practically impossible. Hence Bruce maintains that comfortable and invigorating conditions are indicated better by the dew-point than by wet or dry-bulb temperatures, or by the difference between the two temperatures. Hill agrees with this view, so far as it concerns relatively calm air, but he contends that readings of the *kata-thermometer,* an instrument invented by himself, form the best indicator of comfort.

The kata-thermometer[3] consists of an alcohol thermometer with a cylindrical bulb about 4 cm. long and 2 cm. diameter, and a stem 20 cm. in length. The instrument is heated in hot water to above 100°F., the bulb is dried, and the instrument is suspended in the atmosphere under investigation. The rate of cooling of the thermometer is measured by taking the time in seconds which the meniscus takes to fall from 100°F. to 95°F.

[1] J. S. Haldane. Report on Health of Cornish Miners, 1914, p. 93.

[2] J. L. Bruce. Public Health Section, Royal Society of N.S. Wales, November, 1916.

[3] For this and other references see Reports Nos. 32 and 52 of the Medical Research Council on "The Science of Ventilation and Open-Air Treatment," by L. E. Hill, 1919 and 1920.

This gives the dry-bulb reading, and shows the rate of cooling due to radiation and convection. By dividing the time into a factor (determined for each kata-thermometer), the rate of cooling at body temperature (*i.e.*, 98.4°F.) is calculated in milli-calories per square centimetre per second. A wet-bulb reading of the instrument is taken by surrounding the bulb with a wet muslin glove, and this gives the rate of cooling by evaporation as well as by radiation and convection. The difference between the wet and dry kata values affords a measure of the rate of loss of heat by evaporation only. This loss was shown by Hill to be dependent on the difference between the absolute humidity of the air and the humidity of the air saturated at 36.5°C., and on the velocity of the air current. Hence the kata-thermometer shows the influence of the movement of air on evaporation, which wet and dry-bulb determinations, and the dew-point cal-culated therefrom, fail to do.

The capacity of the kata-thermometer to afford an index of air velocity and of the vaporisation effected thereby is illustrated by the outdoor observations recorded in the Table. All of these were made at times when the ordinary dry and wet-bulb

Date, and character of weather.	Air Temperature.		Cooling power as recorded by		
	Dry bulb.	Wet bulb.	Dry kata.	Wet kata.	Difference.
Jan. 9—Strong N. wind	38°	35°	56	91	35
Nov. 17—Strong S.E. wind: sunny after frost	38°	35°	27	55	28
Nov. 2—Mist: almost calm	42°	42°	13	33	20

determinations were nearly the same, but both the wet and dry kata observations showed a very marked cooling effect in the strong wind, and a much smaller one on the calm day. The extent of evaporation, as recorded by the difference between the wet and dry kata readings, was nearly twice as great in the strong north wind as on the calm day.

Similar observations can easily be made indoors by taking kata readings with and without the draught caused by an electric fan, whilst smaller effects are usually observed in workshops where the ventilation is controlled by windows and doors. For instance, the data adduced[1] show that, as judged by kata readings, the ventilation of shops (1) and (2) was good, whilst that of shops (3) and (4) was bad.

[1] Cf. Final Report of Health of Munition Workers Committee, p. 85.

Character of workshop.	Temperatures.		Cooling power.			Conclusions concerning ventilation.
	Wet bulb.	Dry bulb.	Wet kata.	Dry kata.	Differ-ence.	
(1) Brass foundry ...	60°	72°	24	7.3	16.7	Good
(2) Cartridge annealing and cleaning	54.5	60.0	24	9.0	15.0	Good
(3) Ditto	64.5	80.5	17.5	3.0	14.5	Bad
(4) Machine shop ...	61	72	15	4.6	10.4	Bad

In investigating the conditions of the ventilation in a workshop, it is necessary to take numbers of kata readings at various points and determine by experiment the effects of opening and shutting windows and doors, and turning on or off the radiators. Hence the use of the instrument and the interpretation of the results require a good deal of experience, but it is easy for everyone to understand Dr. Hill's main conclusions concerning the stimulating effect of moving air, and the depressant effect of stagnant air. When introducing his system of moving air, it is better to adopt rather gentle methods at first, for, as Dr. Shadwell points out,[1] workpeople generally prefer a stuffy atmosphere and make a practice of closing windows and blocking up ventilators. Subsequently the velocity of the air currents can be somewhat increased, but it is wise to observe moderation at all times.

In dangerous and unhealthy industries, where dust and fumes are produced which are injurious to the workers, the Factory Acts require that local or exhaust ventilation be introduced. Such ventilation should consist of a duct along which a flow of air is maintained in a definite direction, and suitable openings in the duct through which the dangerous substances are withdrawn. Also there should be suitable openings for the admission of air into the workroom. The air current is usually produced by pressure fans or exhaust fans.[2]

THE OPTIMUM TEMPERATURE.—No hard and fast rule can be laid down as to the most suitable temperature for worshops and factories. We saw in a previous chapter that the accidents at a fuse factory reached their minimum at a temperature of 65°— 69°F., but this is distinctly too high for the maximum efficiency of operatives engaged in fairly active work. It may suit their comfort, but it is not sufficiently stimulating. Undoubtedly the temperature ought to be varied in the different shops, according

[1] " Industrial Efficiency," p. 323.
[2] Cf. Home Office Report on Ventilation in Factories and Workshops, 1920.

to the character of the work done, and one American firm worked out the following scale of temperatures, which were placarded throughout the works, and were maintained, so far as possible, by a " temperature boss " who was chosen in each shop to keep an eye on the thermometer.[1]

Offices, drafting rooms and rooms where workmen are seated at their task, 67°—69° : rooms where men are moderately active and able to move about, 65°—67° : foundries, smithshops and carpenters' shops, where active work is the rule, 55°—65° : storage rooms where men are not regularly employed, 40°—50°. These temperatures are somewhat high, unless there are fairly good currents of moving air.

The average temperatures recorded at a number of factories ' where complaints are infrequent ' are stated to be, for factories where sedentary work is performed, 58° to 66° : for those with light labour at machines, 50° to 61° : for those with heavy labour at machines, 46° to 51°, and for those with heavy manual labour, 44° to 48°.[2] Supposing it is difficult or inconvenient to vary the temperature of different shops in a factory according to the character of the work done, it is often possible to attain the same end, viz., the comfort of the workers, by varying the degree of ventilation. The worker, owing to his physical exertions, produces more bodily heat than when he is at rest, and in order that his temperature may not rise unduly, it is necessary that he should lose more heat by the ordinary processes of radiation, convection and evaporation. He himself usually augments these processes by discarding some of his clothing, but such measures are often insufficient of themselves, and his body temperature rises sufficiently to produce visible sweating. An increased heat loss from evaporation is thereby induced. Hill has shown,[3] however, that by increasing the velocity of air currents so as to

Trade.	Total heat output during work.	Probable cooling power (dry kata) required to prevent sweating.
Tailor	77 + 35 = 112	5.4
Bookbinder	77 + 65 = 142	6.9
Shoemaker	77 + 72 = 149	7.2
Carpenter	77 + 111 = 188	9.2
Metal worker	77 + 113 = 190	9.2
Painter	77 + 124 = 201	9.8
Stonemason	77 + 240 = 317	15.4
Man sawing wood ...	77 + 302 = 379	18.5

[1] Tarbell. " New Ideals in Business," 1916, p. 12.
[2] " The Organiser," August, 1919, p. 196.
[3] Op. cit., p. 54.

get increased kata-thermometer readings, it is possible to keep the body temperature nearly steady. The Table shows the average heat outputs (in calories per hour) of men engaged in various trades,[1] and the probable cooling power (as registered by the dry kata) required to prevent visible sweating. The men, when sitting at rest and doing no work, gave out 77 calories of heat per hour, so that the most vigorous worker, the man sawing wood, increased his energy output five-fold.

The test of clothing affords a simple method of sorting out workers according to the strenuousness of their occupation. I found that the men employed at iron and steel works, where they were usually working under roofs but without the protection of side walls, could be separated up into three groups : (a) those who worked with their coats on ; (b) those who worked with their coats off ; (c) those who worked with coats and waistcoats off, and shirts open at the neck. This classification corresponded well with the character of the work done, and the circumstances (such as exposure to furnaces and hot metal) under which it was performed. The observations were made at a large number of works during the winter months, and no doubt a different scale would be necessary in the summer months.

Seasonal Variation of Output

In some industries, and especially in the heavier occupations, there is a distinct seasonal variation in the output. For instance, Fig. 37 shows the average output of the millmen at five tinplate factories. Output data were obtained every week for periods

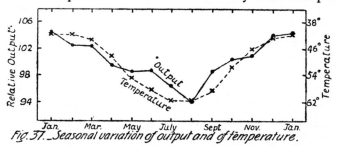

Fig. 37.—Seasonal variation of output and of temperature.

of $1\frac{1}{2}$ to 7 years, and the relative values were averaged for the four or five weeks included in each month.[2] The output varied from a maximum of 104.4 in January to a minimum of 94.0 in August, and it will be seen that the changes correspond roughly with the average temperature changes. These temperatures

---

[1] Calculated by Lusk from observations of Becker and Hämäläinen. Skand. Arch. f. Physiol., Vol. 31, p. 198, 1914.

[2] Report No. 1 of Industrial Fatigue Research Board, 1919.

were taken at Swansea, the centre of the tinplate factories investigated, for the seven years over which the output observations extended.

A large number of observations on the chief processes in the iron and steel trade were made in various industrial districts in England, Scotland and Wales,[1] and it was found that in almost every case there was a greater or less amount of seasonal variation in output. It was not usually so regular as that observed in the tinplate millmen, so the results recorded in the Table have been grouped according as they fell in the four coldest months of the year, viz., December to March, the four hottest months, viz., June to September, or the four intermediate spring and autumn months, when the temperature was intermediate. Of the ten sets of data recorded, seven show a maximum output in the winter months, and two in the spring and autumn. Only at one works was the output (from the rolling mills) as great in the summer as in the winter. The seasonal change varied considerably in different processes, and in different works. This was undoubtedly due, to a large extent, to the call made upon the physical energies of the men. The more strenuous the work, and the less favourable the conditions under which it was performed, the more did the output tend to fall off in hot weather. For instance, the melters engaged in producing steel by the open hearth process at works C showed 11 per cent. less output in the summer than in the winter, probably because their

SEASONAL CHANGES OF OUTPUT

Occupation.	Relative output during		
	Winter (Dec.-March).	Spring and Autumn.	Summer (June-Sept.).
Men charging blast furnace ...	105.0	**106.5**	88.5
Open hearth steel melters at works C	**107.7**	102.0	96.2
Ditto ditto D	**85.7**	85.1	84.8
Ditto ditto F	**102.5**	100.5	97.2
Ditto ditto J	102.5	**104.6**	102.8
Rolling mill men at works III. ...	**107.0**	106.5	107.0
Ditto ditto V. ...	**124.0**	118.0	111.0
Ditto ditto VI. ...	**105.2**	98.4	96.5
Men puddling wrought iron ...	**104.7**	102.2	96.0
Tinplate millmen ...	**103.3**	99.9	96.9
Mean temperature at Greenwich...	40.0°	48.5°	60.2°

[1] Report No. 5 of Industrial Fatigue Research Board, 1920.

shops were narrow and had a low-pitched roof. In consequence, the ventilation was very poor in comparison with that found at the other steel works. These other works either showed practically no seasonal variation, or less than half as much as at works C.

The considerable seasonal variation observed in blast-furnace output (for this varied directly with the rate of charging) was due partly to a physical phenomenon, viz., the greater waste of heat in the summer resultant on the larger quantity of moisture contained in the air blast, but almost the whole of the seasonal changes observed in the other processes must be ascribed to the effects of temperature, humidity and ventilation on the physical energies of the men. The dependence of output on ventilation was investigated at the tinplate factories. Owing to the high temperatures at which the millmen have to work, it is the custom, in many factories, to supply artificial ventilation. At factory A, the best ventilated factory observed by me, large fans or paddles, about 6 ft. by 2 ft., were revolving in a vertical plane immediately above the heads of the men, and they caused an excellent draught. At factories B and C an air current was driven from outside into pipes opening over the heads of the men, and though it cooled the upper parts of their bodies, it was inadequate to cool the lower parts, which were specially exposed to the heat from the red-hot metal sheets manipulated. At two other factories, and at one of the two millhouses in factory C, there was no artificial ventilation whatever, though the natural ventilation at factory D was better than at factory E. In correspondence with these differences of ventilation, it will be seen from Fig. 38 that the seasonal variation of output at factory A was comparatively slight, whilst it became more and more marked in other factories as the ventilation became less. A comparison of output in July and August with that in December and January gave the following results.

INFLUENCE OF VENTILATION ON SEASONAL VARIATION OF OUTPUT

Factory.	State of artificial ventilation.	Relative output in		Per cent. reduction in summer.
		Dec. and Jan.	July and Aug.	
A	Good	100.5	97.5	3.0
B	Moderately good ...	102.5	97.0	6.4
C	Moderate (or none) ...	105.5	94.5	10.4
D	None (but good natural)	104.5	93.0	11.0
E	None (but poor natural)	108.0	93.5	13.4

P

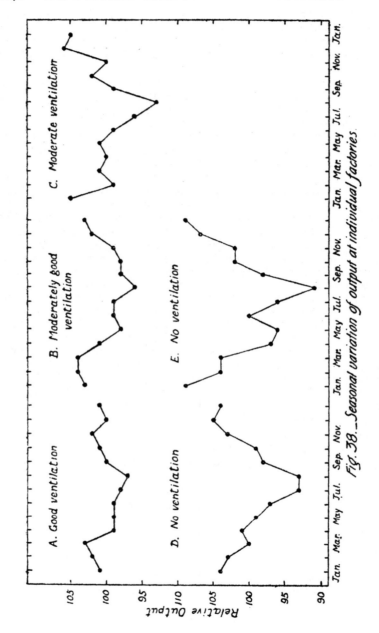

Fig. 38.—Seasonal variation of output at individual factories.

It should be stated that the ' relative output ' holds only for each individual factory, and it is not possible to compare outputs at different factories in absolute terms. The dependence of output on humidity was investigated at a tinplate factory, where the output during such weeks as the mean temperature was at 60°F. or more, or at 55° to 59.9°, was compared with the average humidity during the week, and the average wet-bulb temperature. The mean observations, which relate to 129 weeks, are recorded in the Table, and they show a small but distinct effect of humidity on output.

EFFECT OF HUMIDITY ON OUTPUT

Per cent. saturation with moisture.	Mean temperature of 60° or more.			Mean temperature of 55° to 59.9°.			Mean output at 55° or more.
	Number of observations.	Mean output.	Mean wet bulb temperature.	Number of observations.	Mean output.	Mean wet bulb temperature.	
Under 70	6	97.0	56.0°	10	98.9	51.3°	98.0
70 to 74	16	97.2	57.1	21	98.2	52.4	97.7
75 to 79	23	97.4	58.1	14	96.8	53.3	97.1
80 to 84	11	93.9	59.6	15	99.1	54.2	96.5
85 or more	6	94.2	60.0	7	97.7	55.1	95.9

SEATING ACCOMMODATION

Many employers still think it unecessary and undesirable to provide any seats for their workers, and they maintain that seats encourage laziness. It is possible that they may do so in the time-worker who is bent on doing the minimum amount of work compatible with the retention of his job, but for the keen and conscientious worker they afford a most valuable method of reducing fatigue, and increasing efficiency. As has already been pointed out in an earlier chapter, every industrial worker starts his day's labour with a certain supply of energy, and the more of it he expends in useless and unnecessary directions, the less there is available for useful work. Hence the greater the saving of energy effected by a man sitting instead of standing during his rest periods, or during his work periods, if he can work equally well when seated, the greater should be his efficiency.

The Factory Acts do not require seats to be provided for workers, but the Home Secretary has power to make an order requiring an employer to make reasonable provision for " the supply and use of seats in workrooms." An order was made[1]

[1] Cf. Final Report of Health of Munition Workers Committee, p. 95.

for the provision of seats for women engaged in turning shells, and in 1916 a condition was inserted in an order governing the employment of women at night on wool-combing that " the employer shall provide suitable seats for the use of women and girls at times when their work is not in need of attention." It is to be hoped that in course of time similar orders will be made applying to day workers in wool-combing and other occupations and industries, just as they now apply to shop assistants under the Shops Act.

Seating accommodation for use during resting periods can take the form of light folding seats, fastened to walls or partitions, which can be folded back when not in use, or swing seats screwed to the leg of a table, or other support, and swung under the table when not in use.[1] Gilbreth[2] is prepared to go much further, and to provide really comfortable seats such as arm chairs, reclining chairs and couches. He quotes a case in which they were introduced, to the amusement of the men, but it was found, nevertheless, that after a few days of actual use the men were able to handle their work in greater quantities and with less fatigue.

Gilbreth has devoted much attention to the provision of specially devised chairs for use during work periods.[3] One chair is suitable for doing work, hitherto considered sedentary, in a sitting or a standing posture, whilst another chair permits the same choice in the worker engaged on work (e.g., heavy filing) hitherto considered possible only when standing. A third chair is provided with springs, so as to eliminate the vibration of floors that carry much high-speed machinery. The operative is provided with a foot-rest, which stands on felt so as to kill the vibration. Gilbreth maintains that sedentary workers, since they spend about half of their waking hours at the factory, ought to be measured for their working chairs, and have chairs of their own properly adapted to their height, and the character of the work they are engaged on. Alternatively adjustable chairs should be provided.

Rest from work is generally much more effectual if taken in quiet ' rest ' rooms instead of in the workshops, as the noise inseparable from most industrial work is an undoubted source of fatigue and nerve strain. Most of the workers get more or less used to the noise, and it does not appear to affect them, but it is probable that if two groups of workers engaged on the same operation could be compared, one of them working in a noisy shop and the other in a quiet one, the output of the former group

---

[1] Cf. Final Report of Health of Munition Workers Committee, p. 95.
[2] " Fatigue Study," 1917, p. 43.
[3] *Op. cit.*, p. 104.

would prove to be less, whilst the fatigue at the end of the day's work would be greater. The fatiguing effect of noise is chiefly due to its influence on the faculty of attention. Noise distracts attention, and therefore necessitates a more intense mental application to the task in hand in order to overcome the distraction. Müsterberg[1] quotes a case of a woman at a printing shop who was occupied with work which demanded her complete attention. When she was placed in a quiet corner of the shop she increased her work 25 per cent. above that done when she was seated at her task near a passage where trucking was done.

At many munition factories, where the hours of work were long and night shifts were usual, rest rooms were established for women to retire to if they got overwrought by their work, and they proved a great boon. With short working hours and no night work there is less need for them, though in nerve-racking occupations such as that of telephone operators they are very desirable.

Washing Facilities

The provision of washing accommodation is not compulsory under the Factory Act, except for workers engaged on processes in which poisonous materials such as lead are manipulated. Nevertheless it will be generally admitted that employers ought to provide it in all cases, as the workers often get very grimy over their work, and they sometimes have to work at a high temperature which induces heavy perspiration. The best system is for men engaged on heavy or dirty work to keep their working clothes at the factory, and change into them on arrival. At the end of their day's work they can change back into their clean clothes, after having a wash and a bath. This system of changing is frequent in Germany and some other countries, but is very exceptional in Great Britain. Dr. Shadwell[2] maintains that English workmen prefer to be dirty all the week, and regard dirt as the honourable badge of toil, though on Saturday evenings and Sundays no one is cleaner, and few are better dressed. He says that he has frequently seen rows of washing basins which were never used, or were used for anything but washing, and he instances the case of the British Westinghouse Company, who provided extensive lavatories with some 2,000 basins for the use of their 3,000 or 4,000 employees. Yet he himself, when he paid a visit, observed only a solitary workman using the lavatories when the day's work was done.

[1] " Psychology and Industrial Efficiency," 1913, p. 210.
[2] " Industrial Efficiency," p. 328.

Contrary evidence is adduced by the Health of Munition Workers Committee.[1] A representative Trade Unionist stated that ' Material improvements in the arrangements for washing are desirable. It would be a great help if a worker could have the opportunity for really washing up and putting himself in a condition to go out with his family without having to return home first.' Again, an employer informed the Committee that " Spray baths are provided for the foundrymen . . . Seven minutes out of working hours are allowed each man in the foundry to wash thoroughly before stopping time. Though the foundrymen are not in any way specially selected they use the spray baths greatly, especially in summer." Still again, the Committee state that douche baths have been installed with success in many factories.

Doubtless the provision of washing facilities varies greatly in different industries. In my own experience, they were often provided in munition factories, but I have never seen them in iron and steel works, though I have visited over 30 works altogether, many of them among the biggest in the country. It is true that if they were provided to-morrow, it would be a long time before many of the men got into the way of using them. Habits long ingrained are not easily eradicated, but this is no argument against the provision being made.

If the workmen are to be allowed to change their clothes at the factories, it follows that changing rooms and numbered lockers must be provided. In some factories the lockers are made of metal mesh, so as to offer free ventilation, and in wet weather the rooms in which they are fixed are heated so as to dry the clothes placed in them.

The importance of adequate sanitary accommodation needs no exposition. By the Factory Act every factory and workshop must be provided with sufficient and suitable accommodation in the way of sanitary conveniences, and the Factory inspectors labour strenuously to see that the act is carried out thoroughly.

INDUSTRIAL CANTEENS

The physical efficiency and health of the workers can only be maintained if they get an adequate supply of nutritious food, and there can be no doubt that in the past many industrial workers suffered from malnutrition. This held especially for badly paid women workers, who often could not afford to spend sufficient on their food, and who likewise were apt to spend injudiciously on unsatisfying food such as tea and pastry, instead of a more substantial and digestible dietary. The splendid achievements of most munition workers during the war, and

[1] Final Report, p. 90.

especially of the women, has frequently been attributed in large part to the better food they could afford to buy, because of their good wages.

It is open to most employers to assist in the adequate feeding of their employees by providing dining rooms in the factory, or near by. The simplest accommodation provided generally consists of a room in which the workers can eat the food brought by themselves. A great improvement is the provision of hot water, and the means of heating up the food by means of a warming cupboard. Best of all is the provision of cheap hot and cold meals at a well-appointed canteen. In order to ensure quick service at meal times, it is usually found best to prepare a number of portions of food beforehand, and store them in hot closets close to a serving counter, from which they are taken by the workers to adjoining tables. The food provided should be varied, fresh, and good, well cooked and obtainable at a low cost. No attempt should be made to run the canteen at a profit. In many instances there is a steady loss, and the real test of success is found in the improved health and efficiency of the workers.

During the latter part of the war the industrial canteens in munition factories came under the guidance of the Central Control Board, which endeavoured to establish canteens on as wide a scale as possible. In 1917 some 800,000 of the munition workers were at establishments where canteens were provided, and in 1918 the number had increased to 990,000.[1] The Health of Munition Workers Committee[2] collected opinions from all parts of the country as to the benefit of these canteens, and they were impressed by the substantial advantages they conferred, both on employers and employees. There was "a marked improvement in the health, nutrition and physical condition of the workers, a reduction in fatigue and sickness, less absence and broken time, less tendency to alcoholism, and an increased efficiency and output."

Moreover, such of the workers as had formerly gone home for meals now benefitted by getting increased opportunity for rest and recreation, whilst those who had been accustomed to eat the food they had brought with them in the workshops got a salutary change of venue, and the shops got a better mid-day ventilation.

The relation between food and health was strikingly manifested by the results obtained when a canteen was established in a Bristol factory, in 1908. It was observed that the sickness rate among the workers using the dining-room fell gradually, until

[1] Fourth Report of Central Control Board (Liquor Traffic), 1918, p. 11. [Cd. 9055.]

[2] Final Report, p. 58.

eventually it stood at half its former height. American telephone companies discovered a marked connection between unsatisfactory food and the number of bad calls and wrong numbers.[1]

Some indication of the influence of nutrition on efficiency is afforded by studying the hourly variations in the occurrence of faintness cases at factories. Faintness is usually due to exhaustion provoked by insufficient food, too long an interval since the last meal, or by more strenuous physical labour than the worker is suited for. At the fuse factory mentioned in previous chapters I tabulated the faintness cases treated every hour at the surgery, and the results obtained between February, 1916, and December, 1917, are recorded in the Table.[2] The men's cases were too few to be reliable, but the women's cases, which were three or four times more numerous than the men's, show a rapid increase in frequency during the course of the morning spell, till in the last full hour of work they were two-and-a-half times more numerous than in the first hour. Presumably this was owing to insufficient breakfast being eaten before work, for in

FAINTNESS CASES PER HOUR

Day Shift.			Night Shift.		
Time interval.	Men.	Women.	Time interval.	Men.	Women.
7.0 to 7.30 ...	12	22	6.30 to 7.0 ...	12	19
7.30 to 8.30 ...	13	48	7.0 to 8.0 ...	12	41
8.30 to 9.30 ...	7	63	8.0 to 9.0 ...	16	74
9.30 to 10.30 ...	15	103	9.0 to 10.0 ...	6	60
10.30 to 11.30 ...	4	119	10.0 to 10.30 ...	10	76
11.30 to 12.0 ...	6	72			
			11.30 to 11.45 ...	0	24
1.0 to 1.30 ...	0	33	11.45 to 12.45 ...	6	53
1.30 to 2.30 ...	10	62	12.45 to 1.45 ...	7	62
2.30 to 3.30 ...	15	73	1.45 to 2.45 ...	13	52
3.30 to 4.30 ...	10	60	2.45 to 3.0 ...	4	56
4.30 to 5.30 ...	12	30			
5.30 to 6.0 ...	2	22	3.30 to 3.45 ...	4	16
			3.45 to 4.30 ...	5	32
			4.30 to 5.15 ...	12	32
			5.15 to 6.0 ...	5	15
			6.0 to 6.30 ...	0	10
Cases per 10.000 workers per week.	5.7	19.6		9.5	29.0

[1] Bulletin No. 15 of Advisory Council of Science and Industry (Australia), 1919, p. 76.
[2] Memo. No. 21 of Health of Munition Workers Committee, p. 31.

the afternoon spell of work, after a substantial mid-day meal had been taken, the cases were only two-thirds as frequent as in the morning. The women on night shift showed no rapid increase in frequency during their first spell, as they would in all cases have had a good meal shortly before work. However, the night shift conditions, taken as a whole, appeared to upset nutrition considerably in comparison with day-shift conditions, for the figures in the bottom line of the Table, which represent the number of cases per 10,000 workers per week, show that the proportion of faintness cases treated by night was half as great again as those treated by day, both in the men and the women.

A discussion of factory conditions does not, with a few exceptions, bear directly on the question of efficiency in relation to the consumption of alcoholic liquors, for in most industries the workers are prohibited from bringing such liquors into the factories. Almost all of the canteens established under the auspices of the Control Board were ' dry ' canteens, and they exerted a powerful incentive to temperance, for the workers would not usually trouble to go outside the factory in their dinner hour to get a drink. If they wanted one at all, they would postpone it till their day's work was done, and their working efficiency could no longer be influenced, unless the effects lasted till the following morning. The Health of Munition Workers Committee specially comment on the influence of industrial canteens in increasing sobriety, reducing ' industrial drinking,' and serving as a counter-attraction to the public-house. They conclude by hoping that these and the other substantial gains above mentioned may be maintained in the future, and that the industrial canteen will be a permanent and essential factor of the modern factory.

CHAPTER XIII

PRACTICAL CONCLUSIONS

CONTENTS

Introduction—General Principles—The Collection of General Statistical Information—The Collection of Information relating to Specific Occupations—Applications of the Experimental Method.

INTRODUCTION

It will be realised, from a study of the preceding chapters, that though many of the problems relating to industrial fatigue offer no great obstacles to the investigator, yet the identification of harmful fatigue is usually an exceedingly difficult matter. Up to a certain point fatigue is a natural physiological condition, which is inevitably incurred as the result of industrial work, and it does good rather than harm to the worker. Beyond this point it becomes pathological and acts injuriously upon him, but the pathological condition arises so gradually out of the physiological, and the evil effects produced at first may be so slight, that it is quite impossible to put a finger on the line of demarcation. Often one can judge only by the cumulative effects of the over-fatigue, which may take weeks, months, or even years, to reveal themselves beyond question, and then it may be too late to effect a remedy. Hence the employer of labour who wishes to avoid all industrial conditions which injure the health of his employees, and the investigator who wishes to advise on the means of attaining this end, often have to act, or suggest action, on general principles. They may not be able to adduce specific reasons which can be substantiated by a direct appeal to the industry or occupation under consideration. For technical reasons it may be almost impossible at any time to secure the evidence desired, or it may take years to accumulate it. But this is no reason for postponing action. Let the conditions suggested by a study of other industries be adopted. Some of them can be followed boldly and without question, whilst others, about which less certainty exists, should be pursued cautiously, in gradual stages. Let the effects of such changed conditions be carefully studied, not for a few weeks only but for many months, till definite conclusions can be drawn. That is to say, every substantial change · in industrial conditions ought to be regarded as an experiment, the effects of which should be carefully ascertained, not only because of their immediate interest to the employer who has made them, but because they concern everyone who is in any way connected with the industry in question, and to a less extent those connected with other industries. The secret of progress in the science of Industrial Fatigue is the adoption of the *experimental method,* and the rate of progress depends very largely on the interest and co-operation of employers.

GENERAL PRINCIPLES

On what general principles ought the conscientious employer to proceed, in order to eliminate conditions of work which induce injurious or unnecessary fatigue in his employees? An answer to some aspects of the question is given in preceding chapters of this book. Firstly, he must adopt healthy factory conditions— adequate lighting, heating and ventilation of his workshops, washing facilities, cloak rooms, an ambulance room, and if possible, a well found canteen. There should be no delay in the adoption of most of these conditions, though the establishment of a canteen, which often means a considerable outlay, may not be immediately feasible.

The weekly hours of work in most industries are now fixed on a reasonable scale by arrangement between employers and employees, though some of the smaller industries, which are not backed by powerful Trade Unions, still lag behind the general movement in favour of shorter working hours. However, the arrangement of work spells, meal breaks and rest periods usually depends on the employers, and the selection of the most suitable scheme is a matter of great importance. The principles to be borne in mind have been discussed in previous chapters, but to get the best possible system it is very desirable to test the results of the scheme adopted by the experimental method, and modify it, if necessary, in the light of the information obtained.

The adoption of a Saturday half-holiday is now recognised in almost all industries. So are the usual public holidays, but these are not sufficient. They may well be prolonged by an extra day or two, whilst a full week's holiday in the summer is a reasonable concession, likely to result in improved health and efficiency of the workers.

THE COLLECTION OF GENERAL STATISTICAL INFORMATION

In addition to regulating the conditions of factory life on general principles, it is very important that the employers should take further action on specific grounds, specially appropriate to their own industry, and to their own individual factories. They can only do this satisfactorily if they themselves collect information relating to their employees in a systematic manner, and analyse it. In many industries it is the custom to keep records relating to output and hours of work, though often they are not in a convenient and easily accessible form, but I have found that in some of our largest and most important industries it is quite exceptional for lost time data to be kept, or any register of accidents, other than those officially notifiable. Yet it is evident that all accident data are important if there be a desire to reduce accident frequency by the adoption of safety methods. The accident data ought to be sorted out into different categories, and classified according to the sex of the worker, and the time of their occurrence. Also, if large groups of workers are engaged on the same occupation, it is probable that useful information would be obtained by classifying separately the accidents incurred in such occupation.

The effect of occupation and other conditions on the health of the workers can only be ascertained if systematic records are kept of the time lost from sickness. Information as to the total time lost is much less valuable for this purpose, though it is better than nothing. Now that so many large factories, and especially those employing women and young persons, are introducing welfare workers, the sickness of the individual employees can be verified and investigated in detail.

The output of all piece workers in each occupation ought to be tabulated and classified from time to time if it be suspected that any intentional restriction of output is being practiced, for we saw in a previous chapter that output records afford definite information on the point. It would often be worth while to ascertain the output of the time workers for the same reason, but such a procedure is impossible in many cases, and it is liable to arouse the resentment of the workers. Still, it may be the only means of demonstrating the existence of the evil.

THE COLLECTION OF INFORMATION RELATING TO SPECIFIC OCCUPATIONS

In addition to the collection of general information relating to the whole body of workers, detailed information should be obtained, whenever possible, concerning such occupations as are thought to be specially fatiguing to the workers. For instance, the most strenuous occupation known to me in the steel trade is that of the steel melters employed on the open hearth process, hence I collected as much statistical information as I could about it.[1] As has been mentioned in a previous chapter, these steel

[1] Report No. 5 of Industrial Fatigue Research Board, 1920.

melters have, from time to time, to undertake the excessively severe and exhausting work of fettling, *i.e.*, of mending the bottom of the white-hot furnace, as soon as possible after the tapping of the steel, and the fatigue of their calling depends very largely on the time required for fettling. I found very great variations in the average time required at different steel works, the extreme variations for furnaces of similar size being from 27 minutes to 203 minutes. One naturally wondered why, in the manufacture of the same product, the furnaces at some works took so much longer to mend than those at others, and some of the conditions influencing the fettling time were investigated, but the question of improvement is mostly one for the technical staff at the individual steel works. In this instance it was the business of the fatigue investigator to point to the existence of the evil rather than to suggest a remedy.

In some cases the analysis of information relating to an occupation at once suggests a remedy, even though the investigator may have no exact technical knowledge of the processes involved. An instance in point was recorded in the last chapter, when it was shown that the output of the millmen in tinplate factories had more, or less, seasonal variation according to the extent of the artificial ventilation. The results obtained suggested that the installation of thoroughly efficient ventilation in an unventilated factory would raise the hourly output of the men more than if the working hours were reduced from eight a shift to six a shift.

APPLICATIONS OF THE EXPERIMENTAL METHOD

The best known application of the experimental method to the elimination of unnecessary fatigue has purposely received no reference in previous chapters, as the subject is such a large one that it needs independent treatment. I refer to the branch of scientific management known as time and motion study. Such study implies detailed observations on individual workers, and detailed corrections of the movements they make during the course of their work. Hence it is experimental in all its stages, until the best movements and methods have finally been decided upon. Then the experimental method usually ceases, and the worker is confined by rigid regulations. He is forced into a mould and tends to become a machine rather than a human being of whims and fancies. It is obvious, however, that there is no necessity to adopt a cast iron rigidity of method as the result of time and motion study, or of any other system. It is, in fact, a mistake to aim at rigidity. The continuance of experiment in one direction or another ought always to be maintained.

Another branch of the experimental method has likewise been omitted from discussion. I refer to vocational selection, the discovery of particular kind of work for which a man is best fitted, or the discovery of the best man for some particular occupation. Such selection implies the carrying out of observations and experiments on every industrial worker before he or she is assigned to an occupation. The tests usually employed are *laboratory* tests, which are found by experience to afford a fair criterion of the capabilities of the individual in workshop practice. For instance, his physical strength may be tested by means of dynamometers, his quickness of eye or of brain by suitable psycho-physiological tests. Sometimes, however, tests directly based on workshop practice have been employed. The most elaborate test of this kind was undertaken during the war, when women were tried at a number of different occupations and industries hitherto considered the preserve of men. At some of them they were a great success. At others, chiefly owing to lack of physical strength, they were a comparative failure. In the light of the results obtained by this huge experiment,[1] it is possible to say definitely in many cases whether women ought, or ought not, to continue working in an occupation now there is no longer a shortage of male labour.

The employment of laboratory methods for the scientific investigation of industrial fatigue has hitherto not been attended with striking success, but there is good reason for thinking that more valuable results will be obtained in course of time, when the methods hitherto adopted have been improved and better methods are evolved.

We see, therefore, that real progress in the investigation of industrial fatigue is dependent at every stage on the adoption of the experimental method, and a great step forward will be achieved when those concerned in industrial problems, the employees as well as the employers, can be induced to realise the importance of experiment. To this end, every boy ought, during his school days, to devote a portion of his time to the study, and especially to the practical study, of some branch of natural science such as chemistry or physics. He will thereby acquire a scientific habit of mind which will be invaluable to him in after life.

[1] Cf. Report of War Cabinet Committee on Women in Industry, 1919. [Cmd. 135 and 167.]

INDEX

PAGE

Output, hourly, not always a good index of fatigue 21

Output, hourly, of various types of machine and hand work ... 24

Output, hourly, of blast-furnace men 25

Output, hourly, during night shift 95

Output, hourly, during one-break system 101

Output, hourly, in drillers ... 123

Output, hourly, in fuse body turners 123

Output, hourly, and accidents 183, 190, 192-195, 199

Output, weekly, showing effect of fatigue 56

Output, weekly, and end-spurt 57

Output, weekly, and practice-efficiency 58

Over-fatigue, due to overtime 53, 55

Over-fatigue, due to long hours of work 56

Over-fatigue, due to incentives 136, 138

Over-fatigue, causing neurasthenia 169

Over-fatigue, causing accidents 184, 186

Over-fatigue, cumulative effects of 250

Overhead charges 85, 138

Overstrain, in industry, see "Over-fatigue."

Overtime, evils of 52

Overtime, methods of imposing 52

Overtime upsets equilibrium between output and hours ... 53

Overtime causes over-fatigue ... 53

Overtime reduces output ... 54, 55

Overtime in various industries 76, 141

Owen, R., on 10½-hour day ... 59

P

Pauses, rest 103-110
See Rest pauses.

Pay, rate of, in relation to output 139

Pay, in relation to lost time 149-152

Physique, in relation to industry 162-164

Piece-rates, differential 111, 137, 138

Piece-rates, straight 138

Piecework causes overstrain ... 170

Piece-workers and time-workers 117, 132, 135, 137, 149, 153, 154, 155

Pieraccini, G., on errors in type-setters 8

Pig-iron carriers, rest pauses in 111

Posture, effect of, on output ... 113

PAGE

Potters, mortality of 172

Power load as an index of output 19

Practical methods of investigating fatigue 250-254

Practice-efficiency, definition of 13

Practice-efficiency in hourly output of women on stamping presses 14

Practice-efficiency in hourly output of chocolate coverers... 14

Practice-efficiency of blast-furnace men 26

Practice-efficiency of women turning fuse bodies 20

Practice-efficiency, loss of, at week-ends 28, 58

Practice-efficiency in daily output 28-31

Practice-efficiency, effect of, on accidents 186

Prevention of accidents ... 210-226

Probable error 7

Probability curves 120, 123

Production, law of maximum, with minimum effort 26, 52, 53, 58, 109, 110, 112, 115

Production, Rate of, see Output.

Profit-sharing 139

Psychical influences, effect of, on output 5

Psychical influences, effect of, on accidents... 189, 193, 196, 210

Psychology of monotonous work 83

Psychology of compulsion ... 98

Public Health Bulletin of U.S.A., No. 106, on hourly output 12, 24

Public Health Bulletin of U.S.A., No. 106, on rest periods 106

Public Health Bulletin of U.S.A., No. 106, on stereotyped output 131

Public Health Bulletin of U.S.A., No. 106, on accidents 194

Puddlers, output of 75

Puddlers, sickness of 175

Puddlers, mortality of 177

Puddlers, seasonal variation in output of 240

R

Rae, J., on eight-hour day ... 59

Rate-cutting 139

Reaction time, of bicycle ball inspectors 112

Redmayne, R., on coal mining 62

Registrar-General, records of 170-172

Reid, R., on mortality of potters 172